THE DEVELOPMENT OF SHAKESPEARE'S IMAGERY

The Development of
SHAKESPEARE'S IMAGERY

by

WOLFGANG H. CLEMEN

Professor of English in the University of Munich

with a preface by

J. DOVER WILSON

METHUEN & CO. LTD., LONDON
36 Essex Street, Strand, London, W.C.2

First published June 21st 1951
Reprinted once
Reprinted 1959

1.3
CATALOGUE NO. 5346/U

PRINTED AND BOUND IN GREAT BRITAIN BY
BUTLER AND TANNER LTD, FROME AND LONDON

PREFACE

IT is an honour to be asked to write a brief preface to this book, and a happiness to see the proofs of it lying before me, since they ensure that a critic whom I have long admired and learnt from will now at last be accessible to English readers unfamiliar with the German language and especially to students in our universities, who, amid the babble of tongues about Shakespeare, need to be "put through" to all the sane voices on the air.

Twenty years ago Caroline Spurgeon began reading papers in London which first set some of us thinking about imagery in Shakespeare, and in 1935 she published her completed results in *Shakespeare's Imagery and what it tells us*. At the same time, as it happened, I had independently been driven to investigate a corner of the subject for the preparation of an edition of *Hamlet*, in which the dramatic effects of imagery and its twin, the quibble, were too obvious to be overlooked. Miss Spurgeon had much to say that was interesting, but little to help one with this aspect of the matter. I felt, too, that her statistical method, correct and indeed essential in a bibliographical or other scientific inquiry, was ill-suited, if not at times definitely misleading, when applied to a work of art, useful to some extent as her collections might be as demonstrating what images frequently occurred in any given play. Still less was I persuaded by her attempt to deduce Shakespeare's personal propensities from these collections : I even remained unconvinced that he detested dogs! Anyone who writes constantly knows how a metaphor, perhaps first picked up from another writer (as many of Shakespeare's were), and entirely unconnected with his own interests, may grow upon him and become a habit of mind. And then, two or three years later *Shakespeare's Bilder*, of which the following book is a revised and augmented English version, came to my hands and satisfied the appetite that Miss Spurgeon had aroused. I owe my knowledge of it to an enthusiastic letter from Sir Arnold Wilson, who was killed flying over

France in November 1940, so that I was never able to thank him properly or to compare notes with him on the book we both regarded as an impressive contribution to the understanding of Shakespeare's art.

Professor Clemen speaks respectfully of Miss Spurgeon's work, which is indeed in its own field never likely to be superseded, and his *Shakespeare's Bilder* was published a year later than her *Shakespeare's Imagery*. Yet he had clearly been long working upon lines quite independent of hers, and a brief statement of their different aims and methods is perhaps the readiest way of indicating the special qualities of his book. Whereas her method is statistical, his is organic; her aim is to throw light upon the mind of Shakespeare the man, his to elucidate the art of Shakespeare the poet-dramatist. Thus while she is mainly concerned with the images of the canon as a whole, classified according to their content with a view to discovering the writer's views, interests and tastes; he concentrates upon the form and significance of particular images or groups of images in their context of the passages, speech or play in which they occur. The play above all; for to him "the fundamental fact" is that

the image is rooted in the totality of the play. It has grown in the air of the play; how does it share its atmosphere or contribute to its tenor? To what degree is the total effect of the play enhanced and coloured by images?

Such are the problems discussed in the pages that follow: technical problems, not biographical, except in so far as they wonderfully illuminate the development of Shakespeare's art.

It is in *Hamlet* that the two critics draw closest together and where, if anywhere, the later book is indebted to the earlier. Yet one could not find a better illustration of their difference in outlook and approach than here. Pointing out the dominant part played in *Hamlet* by images of disease and corruption, Professor Spurgeon relates this first to the state of Denmark, to the mental condition of its Prince, and by inference to the mood of the dramatist. Shakespeare, she concludes, sees "the problem of *Hamlet*

not as the problem of an individual at all, but as something greater
and even more mysterious, as a condition for which the individual
himself is apparently not responsible any more than the sick man is
to blame for the infection which strikes and devours him, but which
nevertheless, in its course and development, impartially and relent-
lessly, annihilates him and others, innocent and guilty alike. That is
the tragedy *Hamlet*, as it is perhaps the chief tragic mystery of life." [1]

Behind this pronouncement looms an image of the philosophic Shakespeare, brooding upon life at the threshold of
the Tragic Period which Dowden labelled "The Depths"
in 1875. In other words, it expresses the emotional reaction
of the nineteenth-century school of Shakespearian criticism.
Turn to the chapter on *Hamlet* below and you will find
much that is highly suggestive about particular aesthetic
matters, including the light which the hero's choice of
images throws upon his character, but nothing at all about
"the problem of *Hamlet*". As for the images of corruption,
which Professor Clemen agrees contribute greatly to the
general atmosphere of the play, these are related not to the
character of *Hamlet*, still less to the mood of his creator,
but to the dramaturgy which gave the play its artistic
unity, springing as they do from two fundamental "facts"
of the plot: the filthy incestuous crime of Gertrude which
infects the mind of her son, and the "leperous distilment"
by which Claudius had infected the body of his sleeping
brother,

    Most lazar-like, with vile and loathsome crust.

But I keep the reader too long with this "bush" of
mine, dallying at the door of the tavern, when he might be
tasting the good wine within. Indeed, a septuagenarian,
who has survived and suffered like the rest of his generation
from two internecine struggles with Germany, finds some
encouragement for the future of a much troubled world in
the fact that this lovely, sensitive and penetrating study of
England's greatest poet should have come from the mind
of a German scholar. It is cheering too to know that he
is still a young man, and the book only the first fruits of
what he has still to give us.

J. DOVER WILSON

[1] *Shakespeare's Imagery*, p. 319.

FOREWORD

THE material of the present book is in general based on my earlier study written in German, *Shakespeares Bilder. Ihre Entwicklung und Ihre Funktionen im dramatischen Werk*, Bonn 1936. The text of this former book has, however, been considerably altered, revised and augmented; some new chapters have been added, others are not contained in this version. Since 1936 much has been written on the subject of Shakespeare's imagery so that several aspects of the imagery touched upon in this book will be found more fully discussed in other studies and articles. But it appears that no book has as yet been published on the development of Shakespeare's imagery treating its various features from the point of view of the growth of the dramatist's art. Thus, in spite of the flood of new books on Shakespeare, the publication of this study seemed justified, especially since my earlier German work was out of print shortly after its publication.

I wish to express my sincere and deep gratitude first and foremost to Professor Una Ellis-Fermor for untiring help and valuable advice, and also to Professor John Dover Wilson for his active interest and encouragement at the start of the project. I also owe warm thanks to Mr. J. P. Dickson, Dr. J. W. P. Bourke and Mrs. Margaret D. Senft who helped me in the final wording of the English text. Further thanks are due to Dr. Lotte Schmetz for permission to quote from her as yet unpublished excellent thesis, *Sprache und Charakter bei Shakespeare* (Munich University, 1949) and to Martha Ziegler and Elizabeth Meierl for typing the manuscript and checking the quotations. The text used is that of the Globe Edition.

In a book of this kind the author's indebtedness to the wide field of Shakespearian scholarship is beyond acknowledgement and cannot even be indicated by footnotes. I therefore offer my sincere thanks to all those critics who helped me to understand and read Shakespeare.

WOLFGANG H. CLEMEN

MUNICH, *January* 1951

CONTENTS

PART III
THE IMAGERY IN THE "ROMANCES"

PART IV
SUMMARY AND CONCLUSION

INTRODUCTION

ANYONE who will take the trouble to compare the imagery in *Antony and Cleopatra* with the imagery in *Henry VI* or in the *Two Gentlemen of Verona* cannot but be greatly impressed by the vast difference between them. They lie so far apart that a connection, a transition between these two styles seems scarcely possible. But if one delves deeper into Shakespeare's dramas, and if one examines each of the plays in turn, from the earlier works to the late tragedies, it will become apparent that in the former, this art is prepared for, step by step. Here we stand before an amazing and unique development of an element of poetic expression, an evolution so striking and of such compass as is difficult to find in any other poet. It is the aim of this book to describe this in its separate phases and forms and to show its connection with Shakespeare's general development.

Anyone who has occupied himself with Shakespeare at all has at least some conception of the general development of his art. If, however, we are to study this evolution more in detail and if we are to become fully conscious of what we at first feel in a vague and general way, we shall be constrained to return again and again to the individual, concrete fact; we must fix our gaze upon separate courses of development in order to grasp the more comprehensive and the more general. Thus, for example, similar scenes and situations in the various plays must be compared with one another; we must investigate how Shakespeare manages his plot, how he characterizes his men and women, and how his description of nature, his technique of exposition, his method of preparing for a crisis, and his manner of resolving a conflict undergo changes and attain to perfection. Only from such individual investigations can we gain a definite picture of what one may term the general development of Shakespeare's art. By investigating the special development of a very important element of Shakespeare's style, this book would seek to help towards a more distinct conception of the history of Shakespeare's art in its entirety.

It must be remembered, to be sure, that every investigation of an individual development carries with it the danger of overlooking the connection of this element with the play as an organic whole. Only too easily do we forget that the distinction which we make between different elements of dramatic art is at bottom an artificial one. Delineation of character, plot, atmosphere and dramatic structure of a play do not, in fact, exist as independent spheres, distinct one from the other. Only one thing really exists: the play as a whole, as a totality. Everything else is simply an aspect which *we* detach from the whole in order to facilitate our investigation and make it feasible. Herein lies the final difficulty which is responsible for the problematical character of all literary investigation concerned with poetic development. It is only by means of the individual study of such isolated aspects that the total development can become tangible and clear to us. But it is just this method of isolating and cutting out that may easily destroy the living organism of the work of poetry.

Hence it must be our aim to reduce to the minimum errors due to isolating the "imagery" from the other elements of the dramatic work. This study seeks to show how manifold and various are the conditions and qualifications determining the form and nature of each image, and how many factors are to be considered in order to grasp fully the real character of the imagery of a play. It is very tempting to examine a passage from Shakespeare by itself, and it often gives us great aesthetic pleasure. But it is a method suitable only in a few definite cases. In most cases it is deceptive, because we examine the given passage from a viewpoint which does not coincide with Shakespeare's own intention. When Shakespeare wrote this passage, he wrote it for a certain particular situation, for a particular moment of his play. The special circumstances involved in this situation he kept before his mind's eye, and of them he thought while composing the passage. Sometimes, he sought by means of the imagery to lend enhanced expression to the feeling of the character concerned; at other times, it might have been his intent to give the audience a hint towards understanding what was still to come, or perhaps to provide a counterpoint to one of the central themes of the play. Before we can claim to appreciate and appraise rightly an image or a sequence of images, we must first know what particular purpose this image serves where it occurs.

An isolated image, an image viewed outside of its context, is only half the image. Every image, every metaphor gains full life and significance only from its context. In Shakespeare, an image often points beyond the scene in which it stands to preceding or following acts; it almost always has reference to the whole of the play. It appears as a cell in the organism of the play, linked with it in many ways.

It is the aim of this book to investigate these relations and connections, in order to arrive at a truly organic method of understanding the images. There are certain important questions which naturally follow from this angle of approach.

We must first of all consider the immediate context in which the image stands. How is the image, the metaphor related to the train of thought? How does it fit into the syntax of the text? Are there criteria by which we may distinguish between degrees of connection?

The further question arises, whether certain forms of dramatic speech, the monologue or the dialogue, have an influence upon the nature of the image.

As a dramatic situation, a specific motive or induce-ment, stands behind every image, the following questions arise: What motives are especially productive of images, out of what situations do most images grow? What is the relationship of the images to their occasion?

Each image is used by an individual character. Is the use of imagery different for each character, can any relation be discerned between the nature of Shakespeare's men and women and the way they use imagery? Are characters to be found in Shakespeare which are especially marked by speaking in images?

All these relationships point, each in its own way, to

the fundamental fact that the image is rooted in the totality of the play. It has grown in the air of the play; how does it share its atmosphere or contribute to its tenor? To what degree is the total effect of the play enhanced and coloured by images? For the distribution of the images in the whole play is often very striking, and leads to an investigation of the relationships between dramatic structure and the use of imagery.

Thus imagery necessarily suggests to us the fundamental problems lying beneath the complex construction of a play. Swinburne has already pointed out "That the inner and the outer qualities of a poet's work are of their very nature indivisible" . . . and emphasized that "criticism which busies itself only with the outer husk or technical shell of a great artist's work taking no account of the spirit or the thought which informs it, cannot have even so much value as this. . . ."[1] One should go even a step further and say that it is not possible to interpret stylistic peculiarities before being perfectly clear about this "thought which informs the artist's work". Style is a word of many meanings, and hence is subject to the most varied interpretation. In the past few years there has been no dearth of attempts to raise the concept of style to a higher plane and to interpret it in a way that illuminates its real significance.[2] Shakespeare's style has not long ago been happily defined "as the product of the characters, the passions, the situations, which in fact are the living, driving forces behind and determining the style".[3] This book, too, attempts to view the imagery in this way and to discover the forces determining it.

The answer to all these questions will only be found when the problem is considered as one of evolution. The power to associate the imagery with the very fabric of the play, at first a mere potentiality, develops and extends, step by step, with Shakespeare's development. In Shake-

[1] Swinburne, *A Study of Shakespeare*, 1902, pp. 7, 8.
[2] Cf. Middleton Murry, *The Problem of Style*, London, 1925; Owen Barfield, *Poetic Diction*, London, 1928; Henry W. Wells, *Poetic Imagery*, New York, 1924; Stephen J. Brown, *The World of Imagery*, London, 1927; C. Day Lewis, *The Poetic Image*, London, 1947; Rosemond Tuve, *Elizabethan and Metaphysical Imagery*, University of Chicago Press, 1948.
[3] Oliver Elton, *Style in Shakespeare*, British Academy Lecture, 1936.

speare's early plays we miss many of the functions of which
the images in later plays are capable. Only little by little
did Shakespeare discover the possibilities which imagery
offers to the dramatist. In his hands metaphors gradually
develop into more and more effective instruments: at first
fulfilling only a few simple functions, they later often serve
several aims at one and the same time and play a decisive
part in the characterization of the figures in the play and in
expressing the dramatic theme. The image eventually
becomes the favourite mode of expression of the later
Shakespeare. This fact, well known to the majority of
Shakespeare's readers, deserves, however, investigation and
explanation. Why does Shakespeare, especially in the
greatest plays, repeatedly replace the direct statement by a
metaphorical phrase? Why does the later Shakespeare say
the deepest and wisest things through an image instead of
in "plain language"? It is a superficial and unsatisfying
explanation to declare that metaphorical language is "more
poetical". We must seek better answers.

As a rule, too little attention is paid to the fact that
images in a play require quite another mode of investigation
than, say, images in a lyric poem.[1] We are able to comprehend a lyric poem—like a painting or a statue—almost at
one single glance, "immediately"; a drama, on the other
hand, we can understand only through a series of impressions, "successively". This holds equally true of the essential
nature of the epic poem or of the novel, but in the case of
the drama, the sequence of time, the process of the successive
exposition, plays a far more important rôle.[2] For the action
of the drama unfolds itself in one evening, visibly and
audibly, before the eyes and ears of the audience; its effect
depends largely upon how far the audience can be brought
under the spell of this sequence of events in time, how far

[1] A clear recognition and appreciation of the particular functions of imagery in drama
is to be found in Una Ellis-Fermor's book on *The Frontiers of Drama*, London, 1945 (Chapter
V, "The Functions of Imagery in Drama").

[2] J. Dover Wilson says of the Elizabethan play, "Above all it was action in motion, a
work of art which, unlike that of architecture, sculpture, painting, or lyrical poetry, was not
to be apprehended in all its parts at one and the same moment, but conveyed the intentions
of its creator through a series of impressions, each fleeting as the phases of a musical symphony,
each deriving tone and colour from all that had gone before and bestowing tone and colour
on all that came after, and each therefore contributing to the cumulative effect which was
only felt when the play was over" (*What Happens in Hamlet*, 1935, p. 230).

2

it experiences with the characters the course of the dramatic happenings, and lives in it during the actual performance. The dramatist himself shapes everything in his play according to this immanent law of the succession of time. His art, as Dover Wilson once put it, is one of "progressive revelation".

In every epic poem and in every novel, we find sections which can be taken by themselves, which lose none of their significance even when we do not know their connection with the temporal course of the events. The novelist can allow himself digressions, broad descriptive passages and historical or sociological explanations; he often brings in something that has no significance for what is to come and likewise much that did not necessarily result from what preceded. Time, the progress of things and events, often seems to stand still in the novel and the epic poem; a protracted lingering occurs at some point without our being able to detect any advance. In the drama, which is subject to entirely different laws, this would be utterly impossible. The texture of the drama is of a much closer web, and the necessity of an inner continuity, of a mutual cooperation and connection of all parts, is greater in the drama than in the epic poem or the novel. This becomes clearer if we look at a play of a great dramatist (dramatists of lesser rank naturally often fail to fulfil these conditions) and examine the often apparently insignificant details which he introduces. Almost every single detail is used later on, reappears suddenly at an important point. Individual touches which seemed insignificant when they were introduced for the first time, acquire real meaning with the progress of events. In a truly great drama nothing is left disconnected, everything is carried on. The dramatist is continuously spinning threads which run through the whole play and which he himself delivers into our hand in order that, by their aid, we may understand what follows, and accompany it with greater tension and keener participation. It is one of the artistic achievements of the great dramatist to prepare in the mind of the audience a whole net of expectations, intuitions and conjectures so that each new act, each new scene, is approached with a definite predisposition. This unobtrusive preparation of our mind for what is to come is one of the most important preliminary conditions necessary for a powerful dramatic effect. For the climax of the drama does not come suddenly; we ourselves have gone the whole way and have followed the separate threads which led up to the climax.

It has been necessary to emphasize this peculiar feature of dramatic art because certain conclusions that are important for the examination of the images in a play result from it. Just as every detail has its proper place in that dramatic structure, and is only to be understood when this has been examined, so, too, each image, each metaphor, forms a link in the complicated chain of the drama. This progress of dramatic action must, therefore, be understood in order to appreciate the function of the image.

Since Aristotle men have thought and discussed again and again the nature of metaphor; what forms of thought find expression in it, what types of metaphorical expression there are and what kinds of application. Even in recent years this subject, which cannot be further pursued here, has been dealt with from widely differing angles.[1] We must refrain from applying any one of these definitions or one of the conventional systems of classification to Shakespeare's images. Such classification is alien to the vital, organic quality of Shakespeare's language. A separate treatment of comparison, simile, personification, metaphor and metonymy, would only be illuminating if there were a definite and regularly recurring relationship between these formal types and the imagery—e.g. if from the fact that an image appears in the guise of comparison, specific and similar conclusions could be drawn as to the nature and the function of the image. But that is not the case; the same formal type has manifold possibilities of application, and it is solely the context in which the image stands that can offer any information about what a particular formal type may signify "just here".

It is an odd fact that our critical endeavours are generally

[1] Cf. Middleton Murry, *The Problem of Style*, London, 1925; "Metaphor" in *Countries of the Mind*, 2nd series (1931); Hermann Pongs, *Das Bild in der Dichtung*, Marburg, 1927; Stephen J. Brown, *The World of Imagery*, London, 1927; C. Day Lewis, *The Poetic Image*, London, 1947.

satisfied when we have succeeded in classifying and cata-
loguing something. We believe that our perceptive faculties
have reached their goal when we have divided and sub-
divided phenomena of poetry and history into a system of
pigeon-holes and have pasted a label on to everything. That
is a curious error. Often enough such a rigid schematic
system of classification destroys a living feeling both for
the unity and for the many-hued iridescent richness of the
poetical work. This is especially true of Shakespeare's
style, which is of an incomparable variety and elasticity.
The principal source of error in the statistical method of
approach is that a set of statistics gives us the illusion that
all the phenomena encompassed by it are equal among
themselves. In reality, however, this is only seldom the
case. If, for example, we state that in a certain play there
are three sea-images as opposed to eight garden-metaphors,
the statistical statement itself is still of very little help and
may indeed be misleading. The three sea-images may be
comprehensive, they may stand at important points and
may have a far greater significance for the drama than the
eight metaphors from the garden. The statistical method
can never tell us anything about the relevancy, the degree
of significance of the individual image; under the same
heading it lists unimportant, mere "padding"-images
together with images of the greatest dramatic import. Is it
not true that everywhere great poetic art seems to begin
just where statistics end—where no measuring of things is
any longer possible and numbers no longer have anything
to tell us? Neither the statistical method nor the systematic
classification of all the images is suited for the plan and the
purpose of this study. In order not to lose sight of the general
line of development it has proved necessary to make
selections and to offer typical illustrations instead of detailed
lists. With regard to the plays to be treated, it has also been
necessary to make a selection. The point of view varies with
the different plays; it is naturally impossible to investigate
in all the dramas all of the questions outlined above. In each
case one aspect which appears especially clearly in the
drama under consideration, will be discussed—the rest will
be merely touched upon.

The examination of Shakespeare's imagery under the aspect of development and of the factors determining it is, of course, by no means the only approach to this extensive theme. Shakespeare's images in their total effect may also bear witness to the wealth of the things he knew, loved and hated. In the human world of the dramas, these images form, as it were, a second world. What is not conjured up and evoked by them—animals and plants, heavenly bodies and elements, callings and trades, arts and sciences, innumerable details of the Elizabethan world even down to the humble utensils of everyday life! The main task which Professor Caroline Spurgeon set herself in her book, *Shakespeare's Imagery*, was to exhibit this world in all its comprehensiveness and to use it as a means of discovering Shakespeare's personality, his "senses, tastes, interests" and, of course, his views. To attain such a goal the systematic classification of all the images is naturally indispensable; it was carried out by Professor Spurgeon for the first time with the greatest accuracy. The second part of her book deals with "The Function of the Imagery as Background and Undertone in Shakespeare's Art". Every student of Shakespeare's dramatic art can learn a great deal from these chapters. The present study is much indebted to Professor Spurgeon's pioneer work in this field that had found little attention before her book was published.[1] The main difference, however, between Professor Spurgeon's method and that of the present study lies in the fact that she is primarily interested in the *content* of the images.[2] But a study which aims at describing the development of the language of imagery and its functions must of necessity investigate the form of the images and their relation to the context. This accounts for a fundamental difference of approach and point of view, notwithstanding the fact that, in many respects, points of contact will be seen to exist. Professor Spurgeon's book will be discussed in greater detail in the next chapter.

[1] Msgr. F. C. Kolbe's book, *Shakespeare's Way*, London, 1930, seems to be the only book previous to Miss Spurgeon's study to examine Shakespeare's imagery in detail.
[2] Cf. Spurgeon, *Shakespeare's Imagery*, p. 8.

IMAGERY IN THE HISTORY OF SHAKESPEARE CRITICISM

THAT Shakespeare's imagery has had to wait long for the attention and consideration it deserves is no matter of mere chance, but the result of a gradual process, in the course of which men have slowly learned to understand Shakespeare's work in all its different aspects.

The generation of poets which followed almost immediately after Shakespeare, the "Metaphysical Poets", still possessed a fine appreciation of the lavish employment of images in dramatic poetry. Perhaps these poets carried the possibilities of metaphor too far in their sophisticated conceits; their use of imagery had a strong intellectual quality which, on the whole, is rarer in Shakespeare and less typical of him.[1] What was for Shakespeare the expression of a powerful and passionate feeling, often became in their hands a clever and subtle play of the mind. Consequently, a natural reaction followed in the more rationally disposed late seventeenth and eighteenth century. The lavish use of imagery common to almost all Elizabethans was repudiated, and the qualities demanded of style were clarity, precision and restraint. This naturally led to a great restriction of the possibilities of metaphorical language.

Dryden appreciated and greatly admired Shakespeare, but Shakespeare's use of imagery appealed to him so little that it was precisely this side of Shakespeare's art that he accounted one of the "failings" of the poet:

. . . yet I cannot deny that he has his failings; but they are not so much in the passions themselves as in his manner of expression: he often obscures his meaning by his words, and sometimes makes it unintelligible. . . . 'Tis not that I would explode the use of Metaphors from passion, for Longinus thinks 'em necessary to raise

---

[1] For a full and competent discussion of the difference between Elizabethan and Metaphysical Imagery, confined, however, to non-dramatic poetry, see Rosemond Tuve, *Elizabethan and Metaphysical Imagery*, Chicago, 1947. Some excellent observations on the same subject may be found in F. P. Wilson, *Elizabethan and Jacobean*, Oxford, 1945.

it; but to use 'em at every word, to say nothing without a Metaphor, a Simile, an Image, or description, is I doubt to smell a little too strongly of the Buskin (Preface to *Troilus and Cressida*, 1679).

Dryden's version of *Troilus and Cressida* is in itself an example of how "the metaphorical incrustation is chipped off" in order to make the style more acceptable to an English audience in the 1670's and 1680's.[1] In Dryden's view Shakespeare's style is "so pestered with figurative expressions, that it is as affected as it is obscure". This, however, did not prevent him from admiring Shakespeare's wealth of imagery as such. What he says about this holds good even to-day, but Dryden did not mean it in respect to Shakespeare's style:

He was the man who of all modern, and perhaps ancient poets, had the largest and most comprehensive soul. All the images of nature were still present to him, and he drew them not laboriously but luckily; when he describes anything, you more than see it, you feel it too (*Essay of Dramatic Poesy*).

Dryden's opinion is characteristic of the estimation of Shakespeare in that classical period of English poetry: his greatness and power, his portrayal of character, are admired, but a certain anxiety prevails lest Shakespeare's style should become a model. For this style appeared to be too bombastic, too irregular and, often enough, too obscure. But even during Dryden's lifetime, voices were raised to declare Shakespeare guiltless of this excessive employment of imagery. Thus Charles Gildon in his essay against Rymer, probably Shakespeare's most bitter critic at the time, takes up the position that Shakespeare's manner of expression and his style are not to be condemned as bombastic.[2] In the preface of Rowe's edition of Shakespeare we read:

His images are indeed every where so lively, that the Thing he would represent stands full before you, and you possess every Part of it. I will venture to point out one more, which is, I think, as strong and as uncommon as any thing I ever saw, 'tis an image of Patience.

---

[1] See James Sutherland, *A Preface to Eighteenth-Century Poetry*, Oxford, 1948, p. 15.
[2] *Some Reflections on Mr. Rymer's Short View of Tragedy*, 1694.

Rowe then proceeds to quote the famous passage, "she never told her love", from *Twelfth Night* (II. iv. 114), and goes on to say:

What an image is here given! and what a task would it have been for the Masters of Greece and Rome to have expressed the Passions design'd by this Sketch of Statuary?

Pope, too, praised Shakespeare's imagery:

. . . all his metaphors appropriated and remarkably drawn from the true nature and inherent qualities of each subject (Preface to the edition of 1725).

But this enthusiasm for Shakespeare's imagery is not the rule in the rationalistically inclined eighteenth century. Dr. Johnson, whose criticism of Shakespeare displays an astonishing acumen and understanding, also takes a somewhat negative attitude towards Shakespeare's style. "The stile of Shakespeare was in itself ungrammatical, perplexed and obscure." . . . "In narration he affects disproportionate pomp of diction. . . . He is not long soft and pathetic without some idle conceit." Thus we read in the preface of 1765.

In the commentaries and emendations of Shakespeare's editors in the eighteenth century, we find the most interesting examples of this failure in appreciation. For it is just the metaphorical passages which had to suffer most of the misunderstandings, emendations and alterations. In many cases the metaphorical language of a passage was replaced by rational, plain language, in others it was simply stated that such an image was impossible. The metaphorical passages of the tragedies in particular had to submit to a great number of false emendations in the eighteenth century. Pope terms one of the most important images in *Othello* (Like to the Pontic sea . . . (III. iii. 453)) an "unnecessary excursion", Dr. Johnson says of another image (where it is a question of the coupling of heterogeneous elements, common in Shakespeare) that the words are "improperly joined" (*Othello*, IV. ii. 59), and calls an image from *Macbeth* (II. iii. 118) "forced and unnatural metaphors". Steevens altered many images which appeared too bold to him; he suggested that *sea* should be replaced by *assay* in that well-known Hamlet passage "to take arms against a sea of troubles" (III. i. 59), whereby the rational-conceptional sense gains, but the imaginative and pictorial quality loses; he would like to change "Glamis hath murder'd sleep" (*Macbeth*, II. ii. 42) into "Glamis hath murder'd a sleeper", with the result that the peculiar forcefulness of just this identification is lost.

One of the first writers, still in the eighteenth century, to grasp the mystery of Shakespeare's imagery was the little-known Walter Whiter.[1] In the year 1794 there appeared a book with the verbose title: "*A Specimen of a Commentary on Shakespeare*. Containing I. Notes on *As You Like It*. II. An attempt to explain and illustrate various passages, on a new principle of criticism, derived from Mr. Locke's doctrine of the association of ideas." The title points to the fact that Whiter, under the influence of Locke's doctrine, inquired into the process of formation of imagery through association. In truth, Whiter's investigation anticipates an observation which was to be made for the first time again only in the twentieth century by Msgr. F. C. Kolbe, Mr. E. E. Kellet, Mr. Middleton Murry and Miss Spurgeon: namely, that images may be related to one another by association;[2] there exists a subterranean continuation of the same idea, as it were, which may then produce a sequence of imagery long after the original image has been forgotten. The second part of Whiter's book is thus the first special treatise which was called forth by Shakespeare's imagery.

A natural outcome of the attitude of the Romantic Movement to poetry is that it resulted in a wholly new appreciation of Shakespeare. The creative imagination of the poet enjoyed a new understanding, and a new poetic language was brought forth, in which imagery was to play a much greater part than hitherto. The best remarks on Shakespeare's imagery were probably made by Coleridge; it was he who once said: "O the instinctive propriety of Shakespeare in the choice of words!" His lectures on Shakespeare contain excellent observations on Shakespeare's metaphors. The other critics and essayists of the

[1] Cf. the leading article in *The Times Literary Supplement*, September 5, 1936.

[2] The psychology of association as exemplified in Shakespeare's imagery has been recently dealt with more fully by Edward A. Armstrong in *Shakespeare's Imagination*, London, 1946.

Romantic period are in comparison unimportant in this respect. In his essay "On Dryden and Pope", Hazlitt devotes a section to Shakespeare's imagination, and on this occasion also speaks of his imagery; in his "Specimens of Dramatic Poetry", Charles Lamb compares the use of images by Beaumont and Fletcher with Shakespeare's technique, a fine individual observation.

Among the poets, John Keats was most influenced by Shakespeare's diction and imagery.[1] His pocket editions of the Shakespearian dramas,[2] edited by Caroline F. E. Spurgeon, show us how Keats again and again underlined images and metaphorical phrases; it is often possible to trace the source of an immediate inspiration taken over into his own poetic work. But in the great admirers of Shakespeare among the German poets, like A. W. Schlegel or Ludwig Tieck we seek in vain for a single remark on Shakespeare's imagery.

Among their contemporaries, it was Goethe who best recognized the importance and nature of Shakespearian imagery. "Shakespeare's work is rich in strange tropes", so begins one of his prose aphorisms. And in his essay on Shakespeare, "Shakespeare und kein Ende", he summarizes the fact that Shakespeare's language draws upon all the spheres of life in the words, "Shakespeare's works are one huge and lively country-fair". The only one, however, who saw the dramatic relevance of Shakespeare's imagery seems to have been the philosopher Hegel. In the first part of his "Aesthetic" he analyses the function of image and comparison in dramatic poetry, illustrating his remarks by examples taken from Shakespeare.[3]

But it was long before Shakespeare's style and language began to be seriously studied and the value of the imagery for the interpretation of the individual dramas was recognized. With the exception of Edward Dowden and A. C. Bradley, Shakespeare critics up to the beginning of the present century say practically nothing about Shakespeare's

[1] Cf. John Middleton Murry, *Keats and Shakespeare*, Oxford, 1925.
[2] *Keats' Shakespeare*, edited by C. F. Spurgeon, Oxford, 1929.
[3] Hegel, *Aesthetik*, *I*, p. 521 seq. See Emil Wolff, "Hegel und Shakespeare"; *Vom Geist der Dichtung*, *Gedächtnisschrift für Robert Petsch*, Hamburg, 1949 (see particularly pp. 167–172).

metaphors and images. In fact, one of the presidents of the German Shakespeare Society listed Shakespeare's employment of imagery among his "faults and defects".[1] It was certainly necessary to come to a clear understanding of the significance of style and diction in poetry before attempting to consider Shakespeare's imagery in relation to his dramas. This was undertaken in the last two decades by several illuminating works, some of which also touch upon the subject of the Shakespearian metaphor.[2]

Caroline F. Spurgeon deserves the credit of having classified and investigated the whole treasury of Shakespeare's images in a systematic manner for the first time.[3] And here, for the first time, is shown for almost all the plays, how in the imagery of a drama *leitmotive* appear which are closely related to the play's theme and atmosphere. In the first part of her book, Miss Spurgeon introduces the reader to the subject matter of the images with the aim of approaching Shakespeare's personality in this way. She evaluates the images as documentations of Shakespeare's senses, tastes and interests, and also as witnesses to his personal equipment, his bodily and mental qualities. Miss Spurgeon holds that the fact that Shakespeare preferred certain groups and classes of images reveals his own sympathies and dislikes. His imagery is thus taken to be a transcript of his own personal world, a mirror of his own individual outlook on things. The conception underlying the following study differs from this view. It seems evident that Shakespeare's choice of an image or simile at a given moment in the play is determined far more by the dramatic issues arising out of that moment than by his individual sympathies. We admit that Shakespeare preferred certain motifs and fields of imagery and that these preferences may

[1] Ulrici, "Ueber Shakespeares Fehler und Mängel" (*Shakespeare Jahrbuch*, 1898).
[2] Apart from the works quoted in the first chapter, cf. W. P. Ker, *Form and Style in Poetry*, London, 1928; George Rylands, *Words and Poetry*, London, 1926; Elizabeth Holmes, *Aspects of Elizabethan Imagery*, Oxford, 1929. For a full account of recent studies on the subject of Shakespeare's imagery up to 1937 see Una Ellis-Fermor, *Some Recent Research in Shakespeare's Imagery*, Shakespeare Association, 1937 (Oxford University Press); Edward A. Armstrong, *Shakespeare's Imagination*, London, 1946; Rosemond Tuve, *Elizabethan and Metaphysical Imagery*, Chicago, 1947; Moody E. Prior, *The Language of Tragedy*, New York, 1947; Sister Miriam Joseph, *Shakespeare's Use of the Arts of Language*, New York, 1947.
[3] *Shakespeare's Imagery and What it Tells Us*, Cambridge, 1936. In the following pages this work is referred to either as *Shakespeare's Imagery* or "Miss Spurgeon's book".

occasionally give hints as to his personal sympathies. But it may be repeatedly observed that both the range and the motifs of imagery in a drama are constantly modified by factors not inherent in the poet's personality. Is it not precisely the sign of a great dramatist that he possesses a character more comprehensive, more capable of transformation and metamorphosis than the ordinary man's, a character which renders irrelevant the question of what he may have liked best in his everyday life?

A new and important avenue of approach to Shakespeare's imagery was opened by G. Wilson Knight who, in a series of stimulating books[1] set out to treat the imagery as belonging to a "pattern below the level of plot and character" (in Mr. T. S. Eliot's phrase[2]), examining it less in its temporal aspect within the drama but independently of the time sequence of the play. Wilson Knight's emphasis on the imagery as an integral part of the spatial content of the play has led to a clearer recognition of the subtle correspondences existing between the different strains and motifs of imagery and has yielded illuminating insight into the relationship of the imagery to the mood, the theme and the specific experience underlying the play. It has also led to regard the imagery as expressive of a certain symbolism which, in Mr. Knight's view, can disclose to us the meaning of the play better than anything else. This symbolical interpretation of Shakespeare's imagery gained more and more ground in Mr. Knight's later books and was followed up by other critics who, in compliance with an important new trend in poetic criticism, applied this method even more exclusively than Mr. Knight had done. It is obvious, however, that an interpretation of Shakespeare based solely on this approach is apt to lose sight of the "dramatic reality" of his plays and to neglect such important aspects as dramatic technique, plot, stage conditions, etc.[3]

---

[1] *The Wheel of Fire*, Oxford, 1930; *The Imperial Theme*, Oxford, 1931; *The Shakespearian Tempest*, Oxford, 1932; *The Crown of Life*, Oxford, 1947.

[2] Preface to *The Wheel of Fire*.

[3] For a discussion of the dangers inherent in an interpretation of Shakespeare that is based too exclusively on the imagery, see O. J. Campbell, "Shakespeare and the New Critics" in *Joseph Quincy Adams Memorial Studies*, Washington, 1948. Cf., too, E. E. Stoll, "Symbolism in Shakespeare" in *MLR XLIII*, 1947. William T. Hastings, "The New Critics of Shakespeare", *The Shakespeare Quarterly*, I, 3, 1950.

For the student of Shakespeare, there should not therefore arise the alternative of investigating *either* the temporal course of the action or the imaginative "timeless background", nor the necessity of assuming such a line of demarcation as the point of departure for a study of the Shakespearian drama. It will be one of the future tasks of Shakespeare criticism to bring these diverging avenues of approach together again.

Part I

THE DEVELOPMENT OF IMAGERY IN THE PLAYS OF SHAKESPEARE'S EARLY AND MIDDLE PERIOD

TITUS ANDRONICUS

IN which sense and to what extent Shakespeare may be called the author of *Titus Andronicus* is still a disputed question.[1] But even if we assume that Shakespeare wrote only part of it, there is no other play by which we can so well form a notion of Shakespeare's "beginning", of the platform from which he started.

When we have read *Titus* or have seen it on the stage we are under the impression that we have witnessed prodigious events and prodigious speeches without having any clear notion of their necessity or their logical motivation. The frightful deeds of horror, the terrific outbursts of passion take us by surprise with their suddenness, but they fail to convince us. This happens not only because real motivation is lacking, but also because the nature and character of the persons from whom these gigantic effects derive do not yet appear to us as truly great. We apprehend in *Titus* only the great effects, the consequences of the nature of the characters, but not their source and essential foundation in the personalities. This means, if transferred to the words and the style of *Titus*, that many expressions and speeches remain for us little more than an empty gesture. The words are not yet necessarily individual to the character by whom they are uttered. Some other could as well have spoken them. And there are many passages in *Titus* which neither serve the characterization nor further the course of events, the action of the play. The pleasure derived from impassioned forms of expression, from bombastic and high-flown speech and lurid effects leads again and again to a deviation from the inner organic structure of the drama.

[1] A survey of the more important theories concerning the problem of authorship together with a new and challenging presentation of the case is to be found in the introduction to Professor John Dover Wilson's *Titus Andronicus* in the "New Shakespeare". Important arguments in favour of Shakespeare's authorship based on his use of classical sources are brought forward in a noteworthy article by Emil Wolff, "Shakespeare und die Antike", *Die Antike XX*.

Hence it is characteristic of *Titus* that the desire for effective expression is greater than what is to be expressed; the dramatist's own conception of those colossal deeds and people was not plastic and realistic enough to mould the means of expression. If we are at all to credit Shakespeare with *Titus*, it was not his own experience and conviction but rather the desire to surpass Kyd and Marlowe by grand effects and frightful deeds which is at the root of the play.

In the nature and use of the imagery this inner disproportion becomes apparent through the predominance of the unrestrained desire for expression over any real necessity for it. The images "run wild", they are not yet organically related to the framework of the play, just as all the other means of expression are but little disciplined in *Titus*. The failure in organic connection between the images and their context can be recognized by a stylistic feature. In *Titus* the comparison *added on* by means of "like" or "as" prevails. The particles "as" and "like" not only make the image stand out from the text and isolate it in a certain way; they also show that the object to be compared and the comparison are felt as being something different and separate, that image and object are not yet viewed as an identity, but that the act of comparing intervenes. It would be false to exaggerate the importance of such a fact, because in Shakespeare's late plays we also find many comparisons introduced with "like" or "as". Nevertheless the frequency of such comparisons with "as" and "like" in *Titus Andronicus* is noteworthy, and this loose form of connection corresponds entirely to the real nature of these images. If we take, for example, passages such as these:

> . . . then fresh tears
> Stood on her cheeks, as doth the honey-dew
> Upon a gather'd lily almost wither'd.   (III. i. 111)

> . . . that kiss is comfortless
> As frozen water to a starved snake.   (III. i. 251)

we see that these images are simply added on to the main sentence afterwards, dove-tailed into the context, appended to what has already been said as flourish and decoration. They occurred to Shakespeare as an afterthought, as

"illustration", as "example", but they were not there from
the very beginning as simultaneous poetic conception of
object and image. One could leave out these images without
the text's losing any of its comprehensibility and clarity.
Indeed there are also longer passages in *Titus* which may
be cut out from the text without our feeling the omission
—either in thought or construction:

> Now climbeth Tamora Olympus' top,
> Safe out of fortune's shot; and sits aloft,
> Secure of thunder's crack or lightning flash;
> Advanced above pale envy's threatening reach.
> As when the golden sun salutes the morn,
> And, having gilt the ocean with his beams,
> Gallops the zodiac in his glistering coach,
> And overlooks the highest-peering hills;
> So Tamora:
> Upon her wit doth earthly honour wait,
> And virtue stoops and trembles at her frown.   (ii. i. 1)

The sun-simile lines 5–8 could be left out without the loss
of anything important and even without our noticing it.
This simile is inorganic because it is heaped as a second
image upon the image already contained in lines 1–4 and
because it puts too long an interruption between line 4
and line 10.

Here we might speak of a tendency to make the images
independent. Shakespeare writes a sentence suggesting
an image to him. He then proceeds to enlarge upon this
image and to elaborate it for its own sake—and in the meantime almost forgets the starting-point. The comparison in
this case is an independent enclosure. It belongs to the
order of the epic-descriptive similes such as often appear in
Spenser's *Faerie Queene*, for example. Hence, Shakespeare
may be said to employ here a type of image which does not
generically belong to the drama and in consequence appears
here as an extraneous addition. Although it is a characteristic
of the epic style to expand upon every detail and to interrupt
the action time and again by broad descriptions and elaborated digressions, the drama cannot afford such a lingering
manner and such an easy, calm, delineation of the circumstances. The more Shakespeare became a dramatic artist,

the fewer do such descriptive similes become. In *Henry VI* we still occasionally meet with such similes; if they—rarely enough—occur in later plays they have a dramatic motivation, are portentous or characterizing and can thus maintain their right to existence. But these early similes are the very opposite of "dramatic imagery". As early as *Richard III*, there are no more such loosely inserted similes which could be removed from the context without difficulty.

This lack of internal and external connection between the images and the framework of the text or the train of thought is itself only one aspect of the principle of addition which characterizes the whole style of *Titus*. If we take any one of the longer speeches and investigate whether the image concerned has been prepared for by other stylistic means, whether it grows organically out of what has gone before or is the climax of a passage, we must answer all these questions in the negative: one line is tacked on to the other and the images are added on just as much without preparation as the thoughts. This principle of addition finds its metrical counterpart in the general absence of *enjambement* resulting in a pause after every line, and the necessity for every new line to start off afresh:

> The birds chant melody on every bush,
> The snake lies rolled in the cheerful sun,
> The green leaves quiver with the cooling wind.
>
> (ii. iii. 12)

Moreover, this manner of adding on, of letting the separate motifs stand side by side in isolation from each other, may be also observed in the structure of the thought of the speeches. In every speech we can neatly divide the separate thoughts and themes. In each case a subject is brought up, carried through to its end, and with no transition the new theme commences. The art of transition, of inner connection, is lacking in the structure of the whole drama just as much as in the style and in the imagery. Suddenly the characters make their most important decisions, their attitude changes from one extreme to the other in a twinkling (cf. Titus' behaviour in i. ii.; iii. i., etc.). Shakespeare is not yet quite aware of the fact that great deeds must bud and ripen in the "womb of time", that conflict and collision develop gradually and in a manifold, complicated dependency upon all the other happenings. Instead of preparing us for *one* great event, for *one* climax and leading us through all the stages of development up to this peak, Shakespeare overwhelms us from the first act on with "climaxes", with a multiplicity of fearful events and high-sounding words.[1]

What thus holds true of the action on a larger scale can now be observed on a smaller scale in the style of the whole drama. The language adds and accumulates and would seek to replace clarity and definiteness by multiplicity. The heaping up of images is a token of the fact that the pleasure taken in building up comparisons is greater than the need for unequivocal metaphorical characterization. As an example of such piling up of imagery we quote a passage from the second act:

> MART. Upon his bloody finger he doth wear
> A precious ring, that lightens all the hole,
> Which, like a taper in some monument,
> Doth shine upon the dead man's earthy cheeks,
> And shows the ragged entrails of the pit:
> So pale did shine the moon on Pyramus
> When he by night lay bathed in maiden blood.
> O brother, help me with thy fainting hand—
> (ii. iii. 226)

The learned comparison with Pyramus is a second image for Bassianus' ring, which has already been compared with the taper. It is a learned addition, quite uncalled for, which could just as well have been omitted. In our discussion of *Henry VI* we shall have occasion to deal with the characteristic habit of the younger Shakespeare of coupling several images with one another by means of *or*. This can already be demonstrated by some examples from *Titus*.

The passage just quoted leads to another question. For what is the occasion for this image? Martius has just fallen into a deep pit, upon the corpse of Bassianus concealed therein. In this gruesome situation, almost ready to faint,

---

[1] For accumulation of effects and motifs as a characteristic feature of Elizabethan tragedy see L. L. Schücking, *Shakespeare und der Tragödienstil seiner Zeit*, Bern, 1947.

as he himself admits, Martius produces these learned and circumstantial comparisons for Bassanius' ring.

The best example of such absurd contrast between occasion and image is offered by the speech of forty-seven lines which Marcus makes upon finding the cruelly mutilated Lavinia in the wood (ii. iv. 17). It is not only the idea that a human being at sight of such atrocities can burst forth into a long speech full of images and comparisons which appears so unsuitable and inorganic; but it is rather the unconcerned nature of these images, as it were, their almost wanton playfulness which reveals the incongruity. The stream of blood gushing from the mouth of the unfortunate Lavinia is compared by Marcus "to a bubbling fountain stirr'd with wind", her cheeks "look red as Titan's face", and of her lily hands he says in retrospect that they "tremble like aspen-leaves upon a lute, and make the silken strings delight to kiss them".[1] The speech is, moreover, adorned with a number of studied mythological references (Tereus and Philomela, Cerberus).

In this connection the use of mythology in *Titus* is very instructive. In the later plays Shakespeare employs mythology in order to lend an event or a person a particular and individual colour (the parallel mythological situation often being vividly represented to us).[2] In *Titus*, on the other hand, the use of mythological comparisons is still wholly due to the desire of displaying *knowledge*. When it is said of Saturnine's virtues that they "reflect on Rome as Titan's rays on earth" or of Tamora that she outshines the Roman women "like the stately Phoebe 'mongst her nymphs" (i. ii.), these are stereotyped images, at best—in the case of more abstruse mythological comparisons—learned quotations with which Shakespeare seeks to prove that he is as much a master of mythology as Greene.

It is this ambition to display his own command of the

---

[1] In the Introduction to his edition of *Titus Andronicus* Professor John Dover Wilson interprets this and similar instances of "tawdry rant" or "bleating pathos" as having been *deliberately* written, Shakespeare "knowing it for what it was". We would thus have to take many of the fustian speeches as a caricature of a style that Shakespeare despised and therefore handled in a mocking vein.

[2] This is the case, for example, in the second part of *Henry IV* when Northumberland is reminded, by the appearance of the messenger, of that messenger of misfortune who brought Priam the news of the burning of Troy (*B Henry IV*, i. i. 70).

fashionable stylistic devices of the time which leads Shakespeare so often to the involved conceits we already meet in
Titus. To-day the conceit may appear to us as ·a form in
which the spontaneous image has become frozen into a
mathematical figure. In the early Shakespeare we often
find passages in which the simple image is expanded into
an elaborate conceit. Whereas the simple image, the
metaphor, can lend a greater passionateness to the speech,
the effect of the conceit which is developed out of it is
often quite the contrary. The rational, circumstantial
manner in which the conceit splits up a whole situation
is apt to rob the speech of its passionate movement,
making it appear as cold and artificial. When Titus
cries out:

> Let my tears stanch the earth's dry appetite; (III. i. 14)

this seems still natural. In the lines following, however, a
long conceit is spun out of that line. In this way the
spontaneity of this outburst of feeling is subsequently
lamed by the artificial working out of the image (cf. also
III. i. 45). To be sure, these are judgements according to
modern standards of taste, for the Elizabethans themselves
took pleasure in the skilful invention and clever intricacy
of their conceits. Shakespeare, nevertheless, with his sense
of proportion in all things, turned away more and more
from the unnatural character of the conceits;[1] and although
he still uses conceits in the tragedies he no longer employs
them in that artificial manner.

It is perfectly natural that in a play strongly influenced
by Marlowe in its action and its conception of man, the
imagery as well, often reflects that influence.[2] Lines like
these bear witness:

> Or with our sighs we'll breathe the welkin dim,
> And stain the sun with fog, as sometime clouds
> When they do hug him in their melting bosoms.
> (III. i. 212)

---

[1] Oliver Elton in his "Annual Shakespeare Lecture, 1936", *Style in Shakespeare,* discusses
Shakespeare's growing "distaste for artifice in speech". Cf. also Miss G. D. Willcock, *Shakespeare as Critic of Language,* Shakespeare Association, 1937.

[2] A. Verity's study, *The Influence of Marlowe on Shakespeare's Earlier Style,* Strassburg,
1886, fails to go into the question of the influence of Marlowe's imagery.

Shakespeare could learn from Marlowe not only how to use images for comparing or illuminating concrete things or specific characteristics but also how to employ the image as a means for expressing great aspirations, wishes and passions of men. Of all the Elizabethans before Shakespeare, Marlowe is the dramatist who remains the least conventional in his imagery. By making imagery the personal form of expression of the characters speaking, Marlowe lent the images a wholly new function. The common forms of expression could not suffice for the tremendous ambitions of Tamburlaine. Only the world of imagery offered the requisite gigantic proportions. In the realm of reality Tamburlaine could still conquer the earth, but not heaven. And for this still greater desire Tamburlaine creates in his images a realm beyond reality, reaching for the stars and the elements as if they were playthings, traversing (in his imagination) the immeasurable vastness of the firmament with ease. In Marlowe's *Tamburlaine* the images accordingly have an important "dramatic" function. Tamburlaine's greatness as it already appears from his deeds and his bearing is enhanced and raised by them to an even more incredible height of fancy; they characterize Tamburlaine by repeating again and again on another level the colossal nature of his aspirations and his individuality. At the same time, by the repeated employment of such images, by their common theme, Marlowe creates an impression of gigantic dimensions and of passions which colour the whole play and correspond to the titanic nature of Tamburlaine.

It is necessary to recall this peculiarity of Marlowe's imagery in order to understand what Shakespeare adopted from him and what he did not adopt. When the characters of the early histories express their great desires, their threats, their emotions and their passions through imagery, we have here a function closely related to the rôle of the images in Marlowe. But we soon perceive wherein Shakespeare differs from Marlowe. Marlowe employs almost exclusively those gigantic images in which the cosmic forces and the elements rage in whirling movement. But he also uses such images when there is no question of the greatest things and the greatest passions (which alone could justify such excess). Shakespeare, on the other hand, grades and selects, and in *Henry VI* and *Richard III* we can already trace how his sense of proportion and fitness gradually prevails. The Marlowe images disappear more and more; and this not only because Shakespeare gathers his images more from the concrete observation of nature, from the objects of daily life,[1] but also because he begins to follow the special observance which Hamlet enjoins upon the first player when he bids him "to suit the action to the word, the word to the action;" (III. ii. 19).

But in *Titus* there is little trace of this "special observance and discretion". We may add one further observation. In no play of Shakespeare's are there so many rhetorical questions as in *Titus*. The frequency of this stylistic device throws light upon the attitude of the characters to one another. For the rhetorical question is a question which expects no answer and awaits no answer, a question which is put for its own sake. The dialogue in *Titus* often only pretends to be dialogue; in reality the characters are not yet talking with *each other*, but are delivering pompous orations to the audience. The revelling in rhetorical questions to be observed in *Titus* is a token of the padding of the language with mere rhetorical decoration, with empty gesture and pomp. Many images, too, often appear in the form of rhetorical questions. For example:

> What fool hath added water to the sea,
> Or brought a faggot to bright-burning Troy? (III. i. 68–69)

> When heaven doth weep, doth not the earth o'erflow?
> (III. i. 222)

However, rhetorical style is not restricted to the early works of Shakespeare[2]; it frequently reappears even in the late tragedies, but there it has become the adequate form of expression of the character and is in harmony with the inner and outer situation.

[1] Cf. the comparison of Marlowe's imagery with Shakespeare's imagery in Miss Spurgeon's book, p. 15.

[2] For illuminating remarks on Shakespeare's attitude towards rhetoric and his "rhetorical" use of imagery in *Titus*, see the admirable article by W. F. Schirmer, "Shakespeare und die Rhetorik" in *Kleine Schriften*, Tübingen, 1950.

THE EARLY COMEDIES

COMPARED with *Titus Andronicus*, the images in *Love's Labour's Lost*, Shakespeare's first comedy, are of a more organic nature because the poet has here represented a world in which a manner of comparison such as we have become familiar with in *Titus* is really quite at home. Although it appeared improbable in *Titus* that Martius should produce mythological comparisons out of his situation in the pit with the murdered Bassianus, the same comparisons no longer appear so unnatural when they are uttered by a courtier, who is thereby following the etiquette of his court. In the court of Navarre, Shakespeare has created an atmosphere which positively demands this sort of flowery ornamental speech. But this world is still not yet Shakespeare's own world; like the blood-thirsty and murderous world of horror in *Titus*, it has been adopted from predecessors and literary models. In *Love's Labour's Lost* there is much of the furbelowed, witty and playful atmosphere of *Euphues*, much of the Arcadian love of clever inventiveness and sentimentality. The parallels in style found in *Euphues*, the *Arcadia* and *Love's Labour's Lost* all point to this; the people are all related to one another, hence they speak in similar figures of speech and similar comparisons. In many respects Shakespeare is still following a fashion in *Love's Labour's Lost*. And just as every fashion has its day, so this fashion was restricted to a brief generation, and already after half a century it had become quite incomprehensible and unbearable. Hence the difficulty which we have in trying to understand many of those fashionable witticisms and puns. In *Love's Labour's Lost* the humour is still expended to a large degree in such fleeting allusions of the day; in the comedies of the "middle period", on the other hand, it embraces far more of the common human interests, the eternally comical situations and incongruities which are independent of a narrow limitation or a particular constellation in time.[1] This transition is especially clearly shown by the imagery.

But although *Love's Labour's Lost* is a true embodiment of this fancy world, it signifies at the same time a turning aside from it. While Shakespeare presents this whole atmosphere with the stylistic means natural to it, he is already growing conscious of its very unnaturalness. And this criticism makes itself felt in some passages in the form of a fine satire. Biron's often quoted "Taffeta phrases, silken terms precise . . ." (v. ii. 406) is not the only example of this; the part which Holofernes and Sir Nathaniel play also confirms it; these two exaggerate the quest for the learned simile, the abstruse terminology, and thus distort this faculty for cleverness into the ridiculous. Shakespeare treats this fashion with a delicate irony and lets it kill itself; and thus he overcame it.

In *Love's Labour's Lost* the figurative expression often takes its rise from the pun. Whole scenes in this play live on the punning. The twisting, bending and substituting of the words in *Love's Labour's Lost* is not something occasional; on the contrary, it forms a main part of the conversation—it is practised for its own sake. That warns us not to lay aside the pun as a bothersome eccentricity but to inquire into its nature. In the pun there is reflected the pleasure the Elizabethans took in the wealth and ambiguity of their own language. From the critical writings in praise of their own tongue we know how convinced the Elizabethans were of having discovered their language anew. This exhausting of the linguistic possibilities can take the most varied forms. It can be truly creative and may lead to a new poetic diction—as is the case with Spenser. It can make its appearance in attempts to cultivate and embellish the style, as with Lyly and Sidney. But it can also appear as merely a game, a courtly diversion, as in the play on words. Here the interest in the language is seen to be pleasure in the mere phenomenon, desire to show one's own cleverness in splitting and substituting words and finding "a most singular and choice epithet", as Nathaniel once says

[1] This is well pointed out by E. K. Chambers (*Shakespeare, A Survey*, chapter on *Love's Labour's Lost*).

(*L.L.L.* v. i.). However, this modish and often foolish amusement of the courtiers and fools in Shakespeare's early comedies contains something that can be viewed as an important factor in the development of Shakespeare's art of expression. Shakespeare first takes a "technical" interest in the words; his knowledge of the ambiguity and interchangeableness of words is given free rein in this form of amusement. In the play on words Shakespeare acquired a greater versatility in finding words and turning a phrase; and these are faculties without which that very complex imagery of the mature dramas could never have arisen.

The extensive and prolonged playing with words and images with which we meet in the early comedies is further of great significance for the dialogue. The pun was of real importance in the development of the quick and witty dialogue by means of which the stiffness of the encounters of characters on the stage was overcome. In the pre-Shakespearian drama, Marlowe's included, the dialogue is clumsy and weak. The characters deliver what is virtually often a monologue; their speeches are not yet in relationship with one another and the characters do not really listen to one another. But the play on words is like a game of ball demanding lively partners, quick replies and lightning-like readiness of wit. The words are tossed hither and thither like balls, and anyone who does not follow and play up to the other is eliminated. But at the same time an image passing from hand to hand in such a game, like a musical theme going through different variations and inversions, binds the dialogue closer together. The artistic device of linking closer together, by means of the similarity or the continuity of the image-themes, the dialogue which otherwise easily falls asunder will often meet us in Shakespeare's later works; at this point it still appears in a wholly superficial "technical" form.

But the pun, too, has developed. In *Love's Labour's Lost* it still appears as a sociable diversion in which everyone engages. In these battles of wit, these masterful tricks of language and sudden twistings of words the mental alertness and agility of the Elizabethans is reflected. In *Two*

Gentlemen of Verona it is still carried on by Speed and Launce, the two servants, but is no longer there in the speeches of Valentine and Proteus. Thus the self-sufficiency of the pun vanishes and it becomes more and more a means of characterization. In the comedies of the "middle period" it develops into a fine instrument for the deliberately ambiguous interpretation of a situation, and with the fools it becomes a very ingenious means of making doubly significant remarks to the audience over the heads of their fellow-players. In *Hamlet*, in *Lear* and in other great tragedies the puns frequently are important clues and connecting links in the structure of the dramatic action. The ambiguous image which plays such a large part in the tragedies grows out of the play on words. With deep irony Shakespeare often lets the ambiguity of the world shine through the ambiguity of the metaphor.

In the reply which Armado gives to Moth, "Sweet smoke of rhetoric", there is a reference to rhetoric which has exerted its influence even down to those triflings. Rhetoric—employed in a wider sense—is the best explanation for the use of imagery in Shakespeare's early plays. The text-books on rhetoric, several of which existed in Shakespeare's day, contain directives how to decorate and embellish the style.[1] But this embellishment does not derive from an inner demand for adequate expression; the comparisons and images do not form an organic connection between content and mode of expression. The chief thing is rather the technical pleasure in the artistic creation of such stylistic embellishments; these ornaments are produced for their own sake.

Thus when Shakespeare employs the images in his early plays like brocade embroidery, like decorative finishings and artistically executed arabesques, he belongs to a tradition which runs from antiquity down to the Renaissance, being of particular importance and wide application in the sixteenth century.[2] When we say that the young Shakespeare employs images as superfluous adornment and that

---

[1] Cf. T. W. Baldwin, *William Shakespeare's Small Latine and Less Greeke*, 1944.

[2] The importance of sixteenth-century rhetoric and poetics for Elizabethan imagery is convincingly shown by Rosemond Tuve in *Elizabethan and Metaphysical Imagery*, Chicago, 1947. Cf. also Sister Miriam Joseph, *Shakespeare's Use of the Arts of Language*, New York, 1947.

the mature Shakespeare—in contrast—employs them as a direct form of expression, as the vehicle of his thoughts, this implies not merely a personal development from a youthful beginning to mature mastery, but rather the reflection of the transition which has taken place in the historical course of poetry itself. That the image should become the "unique expression of a writer's individual vision", as Mr. Middleton Murry once put it, may only be said of the more modern poetry.

The "rhetorical" attitude of the early Shakespeare in the treatment of the imagery becomes apparent in various ways. The conceit is once again the most typical form. Let us take, for example, this passage from the conversation between Boyet and the Princess:

> BOYET.   Therefore change favours; and, when they repair,
>   Blow like sweet roses in this summer air.
> PRINCESS. How blow? how blow? speak to be understood.
> BOYET.   Fair ladies mask'd are roses in their bud;
>   Dismask'd, their damask sweet commixture shown,
>   Are angels vailing clouds, or roses blown.
> PRINCESS. Avaunt, perplexity!   (v. ii. 292)

Boyet expresses himself in such a complicated manner that the Princess does not understand him. Thereupon Boyet develops the conceit, which does not contain the key to his "Blow like sweet roses" until the very last line, after the wholly unnecessary digression "are angels vailing clouds". This passage illustrates the exaggerated nature of this studied elaboration: a *roundabout road* to the subjects is sought; they are purposely "transcribed" in a complicated way.

When, however, the Duke in *Twelfth Night* says in a conversation with Viola:

> For women are as roses, whose fair flower
> Being once display'd, doth fall that very hour.
>   (*Twelfth Night*, ii. iv. 39)

he employs a figurative expression, because the comparison with the rose can better express his thought than an abstract word. These lines do not contain a single superfluous word.

The image in *Love's Labour's Lost* is quite different; the rose is not a clarifying symbol but rather a decorative convention concealing what is really meant, minimizing instead of emphasizing.

Exaggeration is characteristic of many of the conceits of the early plays. In *Two Gentlemen* it is said of Proteus' mistress:

> She shall be dignified with this high honour—
> To bear my lady's train, lest the base earth
> Should from her vesture chance to steal a kiss
> And, of so great a favour growing proud,
> Disdain to root the summer-swelling flower
> And make rough winter everlastingly. (II. iv. 158)

This conceit, too, is carried out for its own sake and for the sake of an exaggerated inventiveness. But what points to Shakespeare's early period is not the fact that nature has here been violated, and that it is somewhat extravagantly demanded of her that she take consideration of a woman. For Shakespeare has also used this motif at a later time. When, for example, after the happy landing of Desdemona in Cyprus it is said by Cassio of the wild rocks and foaming seas:

> Traitors ensteep'd to clog the guiltless keel,—
> As having sense of beauty, do omit
> Their mortal natures letting go safely by
> The divine Desdemona. (*Othello*, II. i. 70)

we have here, too, a violation of nature and a motif like that of *Two Gentlemen*. But the difference is that the image from *Othello* results organically from the joyous excitement over the rescue of Desdemona in the storm just experienced; the rescue appeared to the hard-pressed seafarers in a miraculous light, and Cassio rivets this impression with an image. But this organic relationship is still wholly lacking in the image from *Two Gentlemen* in which the two friends outbid each other with praises of their mistresses. And out of such mutual rhetorical rivalry grows the conceit.

Love is the chief theme of the early comedies, but the

characters of these early plays scarcely express their own amorous *feelings* in the form of imagery; it is rather their *opinion*, their *theory* of love that they are discussing. Hence it may be said that it is the conventional "parlance of love" that produces the abundance of images here, not the individual men and women who are in love. It is enlightening to note that "love" (not the love of a definite person, but "love", the general theory) is defined in a rather large number of images.[1] In these plays love is a social game which may be learnt and studied like a theory. In the later comedies these images of "love" become scarcer and less theoretical; less is said *about* love because it is now personally experienced. But in *Love's Labour's Lost* Biron is still lecturing for sixty-three lines on the various peculiarities of love; for him it is an art, the attributes of which can be enumerated (cf. *L.L.L.* iv. iii. 337; v. ii. 770). *Two Gentlemen*, in comparison, no longer shows the rigid principle of schematic enumeration; but here, too, love is still a subject for conversation, leading to many a pretty image. The best example for this is the scene in which Julia and Lucetta talk about love (ii. vii. 19). Julia will not have it that the fire of love should be quenched or qualified. She seeks to prove this to her waiting-woman with the image of the free-flowing current which "being stopp'd, impatiently doth rage". But now this image pleases her so much that she goes on to dilate upon it in the following lines for its own sake.

The dependency upon tradition is naturally also displayed in the content of the images. Many motifs of the sonneteers, who are forever talking of sun, moon, roses, dewy pearls, jewels, gold and silver, are employed in a conventional manner. In the Elizabethan sonnets these motifs fulfil the function of decoration and intersperse the thought of the poem with glittering mosaics. One of the most important reasons for the abundance of the images in Elizabethan poetry is the passion for adornment. Hence it is significant that in the early comedies, the most frequent images are precisely those which have objects of adornment

---

[1] This, of course, is also in keeping with the rhetorical precepts. Cf. Sister Miriam Joseph, *op. cit.*, p. 108.

as their content, namely, gold, silver, pearls and jewels.
Thus Valentine revels in such motifs when he describes his
mistress:

> . . . why, man, she is mine own,
> And I as rich in having such a jewel
> As twenty seas, if all their sand were pearl,
> The water nectar and the rocks pure gold.
>
> (II. iv. 168)

Even tears are called "A sea of melting pearl which some
call tears" (*Two Gent.* III. i. 224), and this is said of the
King in *Love's Labour's Lost*:

> Methought all his senses were lock'd in his eye,
> As jewels in crystal for some prince to buy; (II. i. 242)

His heart is "like an agate" (II. i. 236). The combination
of gold and pearls occurs three times in *The Taming of the
Shrew*, but a predilection for gold, silver and crystal can be
detected also in the other early plays.

The most traditional motifs and epithets occur, however,
in descriptions of the beloved one: she is "fair sun" (*Com.
Err.* III. ii. 56; *L.L.L.* IV. iii. 69), "celestial sun" (*Two
Gent.* II. vi. 10), "twinkling star" (*Two Gent.* II. vi. 9),
"gracious moon" (*L.L.L.* IV. iii. 230), the "roses in her
cheeks" and the "lily-tincture of her face" are spoken of
(*Two Gent.* IV. iv. 160), and she looks as fresh "as morning
roses newly wash'd with dew" (*Taming*, II. i. 174). The
best example of this kind of imagery is the sonnet which
the King in *Love's Labour's Lost* reads aloud:

> So sweet a kiss the golden sun gives not
> To those fresh morning drops upon the rose,
> As thy eye-beams, when their fresh rays have smote
> The night of dew that on my cheeks down flows:
>
> (IV. iii. 27)

But beside such sentimental "images of adornment" there
are many comparisons in the comedies which mark the
exact contrary: keen wit and frank realism. It is indeed in
this contrast that the peculiar tension of the comedies finds
expression. The prose especially is rich in images whose

4

scope is not limited to the conventional flowers and jewels, but includes practical things of everyday life, social classes and trades.[1] These realistic and often drastic comparisons are particularly impressive when Shakespeare uses them to characterize people. For example, Moth says to Armado, ". . . with your arms crossed on your thin-belly doublet, like a rabbit on a spit" (*L.L.L.* iii. i. 19). Again, Speed, in an amusing series of comparisons, describes to Valentine the behaviour of the enamoured, " . . . to weep, like a young wench that had buried her grandam; to fast, like one that takes diet; to watch, like one that fears robbing; to speak puling, like a beggar at Hallowmas" (*Two Gent.* ii. i. 23). In both these instances is already heralded that art which is to appear in the famous Falstaff passages and in the unforgettable fools' dialogues of the comedies of the "middle period": the art of grasping the essential gestures of men at a glance and of sketching them by means of humorous comparisons, as a caricaturist can do with a few strokes of the pen.

Let us summarize: characteristic of the imagery in the early comedies is the pleasure taken in the phenomenon itself, in its technical, rhetorical aspect, as it were. Images are uttered for their own sake and heaped upon each other; the privileged position of conceit and simile points to this. There is a tendency to make the images independent. For this reason much appears superfluous to us, affects us like padding, like appended arabesques or embroidered decoration. As has been very correctly said, in these early plays the poet in Shakespeare often outweighs the dramatist.[2] For the dramatist must reject the image introduced as an ornament for its own sake because it hinders the course of action. The chief aim of the dramatist must be concentration and rapid movement; the youthful Shakespeare scatters, spreads out and digresses. Thus the structure of the early plays has, as it were, leaky and open seams into which creep many a device and much that is not to the point.

The images in the early comedies elaborate, veil and

---

[1] Cf. the enumeration in Miss Spurgeon's book, p. 266 sqq.

[2] Cf. George Rylands, "Shakespeare the Poet" in *A Companion to Shakespeare Studies*, Cambridge, 1934; Granville-Barker, "for a while the dramatist had a hard time with the lyric poet" (*Prefaces to Shakespeare*, I, p. 8).

adorn, but they do not yet elucidate. Their purely decorative function is often prominent.

The images in the early plays are organic only in so far as they are an element of style in the flowery speech uttered by the courtiers. But we cannot speak of a true organic relationship of the images to the individual characters who employ them, nor to the whole of the play.

5

HENRY VI

THIS lack of organic relation of the imagery to the play, the characters, and the situation as well as its decorative rather than expressive purpose is also to be found in Shakespeare's early histories, especially in *Henry VI*. The content and style of the histories demand, naturally, a very different type of imagery, but this fundamental tendency to use imagery as an "embroidery" upon the text remains virtually the same as in the comedies.

The principle underlying this particular use of imagery determines Shakespeare's whole style in the early plays. If, for instance, a general theme like friendship, love, time, or youth is touched upon, Shakespeare does not leave it as it is, but expands it into a little digression, transforms it into a conceit or into a well-defined maxim. The simple statement is thus frequently turned into a pointed epigram, the plain utterance into a proverb. The result is, of course, that the originally individual and spontaneous utterance, by being shaped into a rather formal, impersonal saying, loses its very individuality. Thus characterization by individual speech is barred. To-day, we are prone to deprecate this habit of style which seems to prevent differentiated dramatic language. Digressions and amplifications intrude themselves on every possible occasion, so that the texture of style in Shakespeare's early plays is often loosely knit.

It is, however, not the inexperience of the beginner that causes Shakespeare to infuse into his plays many elements which, in fact, are of no dramatic import and indeed often counteract any dramatic effect. It is, as has already been suggested, a definite ideal of style, a rhetorical style, which Shakespeare aims at. "Amplification" was the most important feature of poetics in the Middle Ages; the tendency to amplify, adorn and expand accounts for most of the devices and figures found in "rhetorical" poetry of the

Middle Ages and the Renaissance. Indeed, "amplification" is, too, a main feature of Shakespeare's early style. In Shakespeare's early plays the rhetorical style discloses itself not only in artificial and formal patterning, in the frequent use of symmetry, parallelism, antiphony, but also in the taste for digressions and in the endeavour to weave into the tissue of the play at every opportunity some sort of decorative device.[1]

All this explains, too, why most of the images in *Henry VI* are not organically related to their context. They often seem superfluous, mere "padding". There is good evidence for this in the fact that to one image or comparison a second, expressing the same thing, is added, linked with the first by the particle *or*. One image would have been quite sufficient, but this accumulation of images shows that the pleasure of finding nice comparisons is still the chief motive.[2]

One type of imagery, frequent in *Henry VI*, is particularly characteristic:

> And such high vaunts of his nobility,
> Did instigate the bedlam brain-sick duchess
> By wicked means to frame our sovereign's fall.
> Smooth runs the water where the brook is deep;
> And in his simple show he harbours treason.
> The fox barks not when he would steal the lamb.
> No, no, my sovereign; Gloucester is a man
> Unsounded yet and full of deep deceit.
>
> (*B Henry VI*, III. i. 50)

These two proverb-like images are rather loosely inserted into Suffolk's speech. Suffolk, in introducing these commonplace remarks wants to strengthen his argument and to adorn his speech. These images are rhetorical devices which Shakespeare introduces into speeches of this kind in order to make them more persuasive, more emphatic. In *Henry VI*, whenever the lords meet in solemn and pompous assembly, we find these argumentative and formal speeches[3] in which

---

[1] Classified lists of Shakespeare's rhetorical patterns are given in *Shakespeare's Use of the Arts of Language* by Sister Miriam Joseph, *op. cit.*

[2] Examples: *B Henry VI*, III. i. 71; III. i. 228; III. ii. 331; *C Henry VI*, I. iv. 5; II. i. 15; II. i. 131; III. ii. 161.

[3] For this cf. M. B. Kennedy, *The Oration in Shakespeare*, Chapel Hill, 1942.

the lords or the king himself utter loud and grandiose protestations. And here we find, too, the same type of imagery. Thus there becomes apparent a relationship between a certain type of imagery and a certain type of situation. Such scenes are modelled on the same pattern, a pattern which determines the structure of the speeches and also the use of imagery.[1]

And so the question arises: In what soil does imagery flourish best? Is there, among the dramatic forms of speech (dialogue, monologue) one which more than the others nourishes imagery? If we peruse the early histories we find that it is above all the monologue that breeds imagery. The retarding quality of the monologue leaves more time for the elaboration of images than the usually quicker speed of the dialogue. The stream of action flows more slowly in the monologue, which is often like a pause in the course of the action. The reflective, often introspective mood prevailing in the monologue quite naturally chooses imagery as the most adequate form of expression.

Images occurring in Shakespeare's early monologues appear to be more direct, more "expressive" than the often superfluous and merely decorative imagery in other passages. If we consider, for instance, this passage from Gloucester's monologue in the third part of *Henry VI*:

> Like one that stands upon a promontory,
> And spies a far-off shore where he would tread,
> Wishing his foot were equal with his eye,
> And chides the sea that sunders him from thence,
> Saying, he'll lade it dry to have his way:
> So do I wish the crown, being so far off.
>
> (*C Henry VI*, III. ii. 135)

This image is called forth by Gloucester's overpowering desire to gain the crown. It is not casual or ornamental, for the central motive of the play is embodied in this image. Plain language was unable to give vent to this passionate wish of Gloucester's. Only the wide imaginative space of

---

[1] Examples: *B Henry VI*, III. i. 18; III. i. 153; III. i. 223; IV. i. 109; *C Henry VI*, I. iv. 41; I. iv. 145; II. i. 129; II. i. 12. For the recurrence in the Yorkist plays of "set speeches" founded on distinct types of Senecan declamation see the excellent study by Hardin Craig, "Shakespeare and the History play", *Joseph Quincy Adams Memorial Studies*, Washington, 1948.

the scenery of which Gloucester is dreaming could express
it. That passionate desire can give birth to imagery may
be seen on almost every page in Marlowe's *Tamburlaine*.
Marlowe created this type of imagery as a vehicle for the
expression of his hero's fantastic ambitions, which could
not be translated into plain language any more than into
action.

The following passage in which, again, the longing for
the crown is given utterance by York:

> I will stir up in England some black storm
> Shall blow ten thousand souls to heaven or hell;
> And this fell tempest shall not cease to rage
> Until the golden circuit on my head,
> Like to the glorious sun's transparent beams,
> Do calm the fury of this mad-bred flaw.
>
> (*B Henry VI*, iii. i. 349)

also recalls Marlowe's *Tamburlaine*. This image, however,
may be called still more "organic" than Gloucester's simile
touching upon the same theme. Gloucester used a comparison, York utters an imaginative wish in direct form.

Are there particular events which more than other
occasions call forth imagery? We find that in the presence
of death Shakespeare's characters always use metaphorical
language. The incomprehensible mystery of death, tran-
scending the compass of human understanding, demands
language different from the common and direct speech of
every day. Thus the younger Clifford, on finding his father
dead on the battlefield, bursts out:

> O, let the vile world end,
> And the premised flames of the last day
> Knit earth and heaven together!
>
> (*B Henry VI*, v. ii. 40)

This image is neither ornament nor rhetorical prolixity but
simply the most direct expression of the extremity of grief
Clifford is feeling at the sight of his dead father.

But this spontaneous and expressive sort of imagery
foreshadowed by the outburst of the young Clifford is not
yet characteristic of *Henry VI*. Even on the occasion of

death the language is often artificial.[1] Henry VI, with a
premonition of imminent death, elaborates a simile in
which he rather learnedly assigns mythological names to
himself, his son and to other persons involved in his tragic
end:[2]

> I, Daedalus; my poor boy, Icarus;
> Thy father, Minos, that denied our course;
> The sun that sear'd the wings of my sweet boy
> Thy brother Edward, and thyself the sea
> Whose envious gulf did swallow up his life.
>
> *(C Henry VI*, v. vi. 21)

This method of inventing a suitable simile for a certain
situation by means of which a detailed survey of the state
of affairs is given is typical of Shakespeare's early manner.
Its best example is the long speech of Queen Margaret
towards the close of *Henry VI*, where she compares her
distressing situation with a shipwreck. As in allegorical
poetry, the simile is first developed and then applied to the
situation of the moment:

> What though the mast be now blown overboard,
> The cable broke, the holding anchor lost,
> And half our sailors swallow'd in the flood?
> Yet lives our pilot still. . . . *(C Henry VI*, v. iv. 3)

After ten lines Queen Margaret's words become more
concrete and she likens the persons around her to the
details of the shipwreck.

> Say Warwick was our anchor; what of that?
> And Montague our topmast; what of him?
> Our slaughter'd friends the tackles; what of these?
> Why is not Oxford here another anchor?
>
> .   .   .   .   .
>
> And what is Edward but a ruthless sea?
> What Clarence but a quicksand of deceit?
> And Richard but a ragged fatal rock?
> All these the enemies to our poor bark.
>
> *(C Henry VI*, v. iv. 13)

---

[1] For *A Henry VI*, cf. II. v. 8; IV. vii. 18.

[2] Hardin Craig justly points out that such comparisons would certainly "not have been 'tasteless' to Shakespeare and his audience". "Shakespeare and the History Play", *Joseph Quincy Adams Memorial Studies*, Washington, 1948, p. 63.

It may well be said that this pseudo-allegorical interpretation of the situation by means of a detailed or extended
simile constitutes one of the formal devices which wandered
from medieval poetry into Elizabethan literature. The
fullness and explicitness with which such images are treated
in Shakespeare's early work result no doubt from the young
dramatist's eagerness to explain as fully as possible what is
going on, what is imminent, and what has just been happening. Later, Shakespeare's dramatic technique rids itself
entirely of these rather obtrusive expositions. In fact, at
every stage of the drama we know precisely what is happening, although it is not expressly told us. In a quite unobtrusive and subtle manner Shakespeare intersperses
occasional hints throwing light upon the historical, political
or personal issues involved in the situation. Unconsciously
we become informed about all the circumstances. But in
Shakespeare's early plays information is usually given all
at once, in one piece, and the imagery bears testimony to it.

Thus, besides detailed elaboration, obtrusiveness may
be counted among the characteristic features of Shakespeare's early imagery. Whenever imagery is used we cannot
but notice it, it strikes us as something exceptional—while
in later plays it often escapes our attention that images are
being employed at all. The images protrude themselves as
unexpected surprises. One example only: Suffolk, wooing
Margaret, says when she is about to depart:

> My hand would free her, but my heart says no.
> As plays the sun upon the glassy streams,
> Twinkling another counterfeited beam,
> So seems this gorgeous beauty to mine eyes.
> Fain would I woo her, yet I dare not speak:
> (*A Henry VI*, v. iii. 61)

This is in Shakespeare's earliest and most conventional
manner, somewhat playful and artificial. But in other
passages, too, the superimposed nature of imagery is
striking. This impression is confirmed by the fact that most
of the images (as in the last passage cited) are loosely linked
with their context by "as", "like", "even as", or "thus".

In later plays it becomes an important function of

imagery to create the atmosphere of nature. But in *Henry VI* this is seldom found. Take, for instance, this passage which is to create a background of nature for the murder of Suffolk that is to come:

> The gaudy, blabbing and remorseful day
> Is crept into the bosom of the sea;
> And now loud-howling wolves arouse the jades
> That drag the tragic melancholy night;
> Who, with their drowsy, slow and flagging wings,
> Clip dead men's graves and from their misty jaws
> Breathe foul contagious darkness in the air.
> Therefore bring forth the soldiers of our prize;
>
> (*B Henry VI*, iv. i. 1)

This little "introduction" is rather transparently put at the beginning of the scene.[1] Again, we find all that is said about nature in this scene in one compact piece, all at once. Whereas in Shakespeare's more mature plays (in fact, as early as *Romeo and Juliet*) the phrases that create a background of nature grow naturally and necessarily from the subject matter, this passage has no special relation to the speaker. The captain who utters these words is only the vehicle whereby Shakespeare introduces this nature-background. The words are put into his mouth, but any other character could just as well have spoken them. Later, Shakespeare would have woven this natural description unobtrusively into the texture of the scene (compare the first scene of *Hamlet*). Nature, in this scene, is unconnected with the characters and hence remains mere background, while in *Romeo and Juliet* and in all other tragedies the persons stand in a close relationship to nature and its elements.

Cf., too, *A Henry VI* ii. ii. 1.

6

RICHARD III

*R*ICHARD III is Shakespeare's first "heroic" drama. It is built around one figure. From one figure emanate the rays which spread in all directions through the play. This concentration of action-interest upon one single character demands a new technique of composition; the action of the play must be close-knit and compressed.

Richard III moves forward much more rapidly than *Henry VI*. The plot is more coherent and easier to survey than that of the earlier plays. There we had to deal with a concatenation of various events and with numerous disparate motives of action. But in *Richard III* the entire action of the play is dependent upon Richard alone. Even the action of the minor characters derives from him. And, finally, *Richard III* is the first play which gives expression to a powerful human passion.

Subject to this law of concentration and condensation, too, are the images in *Richard III*. The acceleration of movement in the entire play is perceptible in the images, which become briefer (there is no image exceeding four lines). There are no more lengthy conceits and digressions, no long general reflections spun out in detailed simile.

Both of the tests which were used for *Henry VI* demonstrate here, too, this tautening and concentrating of the stuff of the whole drama. We have not a single case of image-aggregation, and the similes introduced by "as" and "like" have largely disappeared.

A few examples may suffice to show how this structural change in the texture of the whole play affects the form of the images and their connection with the framework of the text. We contrast two scenes in which both Richard and Henry compare themselves with a ship:

HENRY VI. Thus stands my state, 'twixt Cade and York distress'd;
Like to a ship that, having 'scaped a tempest,
Is straightway calm'd and boarded with a pirate:
(*B Henry VI*, IV. ix. 30)

RICHARD III.   As I would rather hide me from my greatness,
  Being a bark to brook no mighty sea,
  Than in my greatness covet to be hid,
  And in the vapour of my glory smother'd.
            (*Richard III*, III. vii. 161)

Richard wholly identifies himself with the ship, while Henry, just as if he were an outside observer, views his state and then compares this with a ship. Richard no longer compares himself; he feels instinctively that the ship corresponds to himself; he *is* this ship while he speaks of it. We might say that the difference lies in the fact that Richard III uses metaphorical language, while Henry VI inserts a simile. Henry VI, moreover, constructs his simile circumstantially, while Richard III speaks much more briefly and directly. The two last lines of the passage quoted from *Richard III* show how the language of metaphor now has extended to cover even the abstract ("vapour of my glory").

In *Henry VI* it is possible to draw lines of demarcation everywhere; the transitions are wanting as well as the connective links. This is especially true of the imagery, which often appears as a foreign body in the text without preparation. In *Richard III* there is, however, the beginning of a change. Let us examine the passage in which the Queen-mother, making sore complaint against Richard, turns to the following image:

  My tongue should to thy ears not name my boys
  Till that my nails were anchor'd in thine eyes;
  And I, in such a desperate bay of death,
  Like a poor bark, of sails and tackling reft,
  Rush all to pieces on thy rocky bosom.   (IV. iv. 230)

This image has been prepared for already in the metaphor *anchor'd*, employed by Elizabeth. By association this metaphor calls forth the image of the ship, and as a result the notion hinted at in *anchor'd* now comes to full realization. Thus the train of thought here is not abruptly broken off; the metaphor *anchor'd* serves as a bridge leading to the image. Apart from this, the image stands at the end of a thirteen-line speech by Elizabeth, forming its culmination.

The emotion, growing stronger and stronger, eventually finds its most powerful expression in the image.

Often the image is preceded by an intensification of language called forth by other stylistic devices. Shakespeare employs many of the potentialities of language simultaneously, and so the image cooperates with other devices of style to give the utterances enhanced emphasis. Thus the great lament of Lady Anne in I. ii. at the bier of Henry VI ends with a magnificent image of execration. The whole speech contains eighteen lines—we quote the last eight here in order to show how the image is added to the other means of intensification as a climax:

> Thy deed, inhuman and unnatural,
> Provokes this deluge most unnatural.
> O God, which this blood madest, revenge his death!
> O earth, which this blood drink'st, revenge his death!
> Either heaven with lightning strike the murderer dead,
> Or earth, gape open wide and eat him quick,
> As thou dost swallow up this good king's blood,
> Which his hell-govern'd arm hath butchered!   (I. ii. 60)

The very first two lines show a parallelism (in the final words) which in the following pair of lines grows to a syntactical parallelism and verbal assonance. To the first two apostrophes, "O God, O earth", the final apostrophe is added, "O earth, gape open wide and eat him quick", as superlative and culmination.

Of course, all this is still in the formalistic and artificial manner, which has attained its height in this play. But all these rhetorical devices, such as antithesis, assonance, symmetry and parallelism are employed in *Richard III* in a more appropriate way than was earlier the case. The firm architecture of style and construction support the forcefulness and at the same time the symbolic significance of the scenes of lament and execration. The conventional stylistic figures, by being suited to the occasion, possess a new vitality. In the great laments these parallelisms and reiterations do not appear inappropriate or unnatural, because it corresponds to the nature of a lamentation to repeat the same thing over and over again. The common sorrow which the three women feel and share is lent emphasis and made most effective precisely by means of that symmetry of the sentences.

In this way the agglomeration of adjectives, nouns and metaphorical expressions—elsewhere merely a decorative device—serves to express even more emphatically the passionate spiritual excitement:

> I call'd thee then vain flourish of my fortune;
> I call'd thee then poor shadow, painted queen;
> The presentation of but what I was;
> The flattering index of a direful pageant;
> One heaved a-high, to be hurl'd down below;
> A mother only mock'd with two sweet babes;
> A dream of what thou wert, a breath, a bubble,
> A sign of dignity, a garish flag,
> To be the aim of every dangerous shot;   (iv. iv. 82)

Admittedly, this is a conventional pattern; it is still far from being the language of spontaneity. But we cannot fail to note how closely this rapid sequence of bold phrases corresponds to the pathos of the whole scene and to the desperate scorn of Queen Margaret, who seeks in her speech for even more appropriate symbols for Queen Elizabeth.

This passage already shows how, in *Richard III*, we have to deal no longer with mere individually elaborated images, but how the metaphorical element gradually pervades the language. The scene from which the last quotation was taken begins with the following lines:

> So, now prosperity begins to mellow
> And drop into the rotten mouth of death. (iv. iv. 1)

This could scarcely be put more briefly. Prosperity, ripening and then falling like a fruit (this is implied but not stated) into the rotten mouth of death, is a very bold image—in *Henry VI* wholly inconceivable. This passage marks the commencement of Shakespeare's peculiar art of expressing abstractions metaphorically; it also shows how Shakespeare, refining and extending his technique of foreboding and anticipation, no longer only relies on the use of omen and prophecy but resorts to new devices.

The omnipresence of the hero, Richard III, is a striking

feature of this drama. We have already said that the whole action depends upon him. But not only that—we feel his presence even when he is not upon the stage. Images are partly responsible for this. Again and again, the impression which Richard's nature makes upon the other characters and which lingers with them is reflected in their speeches, generally in the form of animal-imagery. The fundamental image for him is that of the repulsive dog, an image, of which we find traces as early as the last part of *Henry VI*.[1] In the great scene of lament in the fourth act Queen Margaret finds the most impressive formulation of this image:

> From forth the kennel of thy womb hath crept
> A hell-hound that doth hunt us all to death:
> That dog, that had his teeth before his eyes,
> To worry lambs and lap their gentle blood . . .
>
> (IV. iv. 47)

Richard III appears further as *poisonous toad*, as *foul hunch-back'd toad*, *bottled spider*, as *hedge-hog*, *elvish-mark'd*, *abortive*, *rooting hog*. To the avengers of the murdered princes Richard appears as a *boar*; thus Richmond describes him in the following image (derived from the source, the "Richardus Tertius" of Dr. Thomas Legge):

> The wretched, bloody, and usurping boar,
> That spoil'd your summer fields and fruitful vines,
> Swills your warm blood like wash, and makes his trough
> In your embowell'd bosoms, this foul swine (V. ii. 7)

We cannot exaggerate the imaginative value of these revolting animal-images. Without our becoming conscious of it, the repulsive figure of the hunch-backed Richard as we see it upon the stage is repeatedly transformed into animal bodies conforming to his nature, and thus his brutal, animal character is illuminated from this angle too. *Richard III* is Shakespeare's first play in which the chief character is delineated by symbolical images recurring as a *leitmotif* In *Henry VI* the animal-images,[2] which are occasionally

---

[1] See *C Henry VI*, v. vi. 53, 76.
[2] For a full treatment of animal-imagery in Shakespeare see Audrey Yoder, *Animal Analogy in Shakespeare's Character Portrayal*, New York, 1947.

employed for individual combatants, are not yet differentiated. Talbot as well as Clifford and Salisbury are all compared to lions. None of these characters is made to differ from the others by means of the images appertaining to him. When Shakespeare compares the warriors to bears, wolves, steers, eagles, etc., he is not thinking of the individuals; he is seeking to create the general atmosphere of battle and war. In *Richard III*, however, the imagery begins to serve individual characterization.

7

RICHARD II

WITH *Richard II* we are in a totally different atmosphere. Symmetry of structure, rigorous formalism and the specifically "rhetorical style" had reached their highest possible expression in *Richard III*. No further development was imaginable. Shakespeare does not, however, turn directly from this formal artificiality to a wholly spontaneous and flexible style. There are many gradations between these two extremes. In *Richard II*, too, there is still much artificiality and a great deal of purely declamatory style. But there is a new poetical element in *Richard II* which could not be traced in *Richard III*. There is, moreover, a further difference: *Richard III* is almost wholly in the same key; the same sort of loud, passionate eloquence is sustained throughout many scenes. In *Richard II* we find a greater variety of expression and a more subtle modulation. On the other hand (and in another sense), *Richard II* possesses a new unity of tone and feeling which we do not find in earlier plays, and which made Walter Pater compare it to a musical composition.[1]

The more lyrical and reflective note we perceive in *Richard II* may also be due to a change in Shakespeare's attitude towards his subject. Shakespeare seems to meditate on the significance of the actions, movements or events which he presents upon the stage. And this reflectiveness, this pensiveness, becomes apparent in the speeches of his chief actors. Some of them, too, are conceived of as being thoughtful and meditative persons, above all, of course, Richard II. The antagonism between Richard II and Bolingbroke would have been treated in the period of *Henry VI* as a mere enmity, as a contrast of power, as a fierce struggle of an enraged usurper against a weak, though lawful, king. In *Richard II*, what might have been

---

[1] *Appreciations*, 4th edition, p. 202. For this feature of the play cf. John Dover Wilson's Introduction to his edition of *Richard II*, Cambridge, 1939, pp. xiv., xv.

a mere outward contrast is conceived of as a fundamental opposition between two different principles. It was not Shakespeare's chief aim to show how the weak king must, in the end, yield to the greater power of the usurper; he rather wanted to make clear through his whole handling of the plot that a problem and a tragic issue are involved. Better perhaps than the other histories, the whole play reveals Shakespeare's attitude towards kingship, his profound interpretation of the "divine right of kings" and, as a corollary, of the "people's right to the good and just king". To both these principles he gives expression in his play; and the interaction of these two fundamental ideas imparts to each scene in the play a rich and subtle meaning.

It was necessary to touch upon these issues since the character and wealth of the imagery in *Richard II* result from this peculiar reflective mood pervading the play. For it is the nature of imagery to express and suggest something more than the bare details of the situation. Imagery is capable of adding a further meaning to the "immediate meaning"; it may reveal and underline the symbolic import of what is happening on the stage. By means of a certain kind of reflective imagery, the particular significance of a certain event may be expanded into a more general significance. In *Richard II* we find many scenes in which imagery has this function of enhancing and deepening the symbolic meaning of what occurs on the stage. This becomes especially apparent in the garden scene, where an intricate symbolism is developed relating gardening to statescraft, but it is also obvious in the famous abdication scene and in several minor scenes, such as Bolingbroke's departure from England (i. iii.), the prophecy of the dying Gaunt, etc.

The reflective and poetical vein is most apparent in the king himself. So far we have not been able to say that imagery originated in the peculiar disposition of any character in the play. In the early histories, imagery arose out of certain situations or it helped to emphasize some repeatedly occurring themes. Now, in *Richard II*, imagery becomes the characteristic manner of expression of the chief character. To talk in similes, to make use of metaphors,

is indeed a natural quality of the king's mind and temperament. *Richard II* is the first instance of Shakespeare's
habitual manner of endowing his heroes with unusual
imagination and the poetic gift.

It has often been pointed out that in *Richard II* Shakespeare has embodied the passive, contemplative side of
human nature. "It need hardly be said", writes Sir Edmund
Chambers, "that the antithesis between Richard and
Bolingbroke goes much further than politics; it rests upon
one of the ultimate distinctions amongst mankind, that of
the practical and artistic temperaments, the men of deeds
and the men of dreams and fancies."[1] But besides being a
poet and a dreamer, Richard is an actor; he has a keen sense
of theatrical effect; each new situation in which he finds
himself grows through him into a dramatic performance.
Richard II is king not only by birth, but also by the dignity
of his behaviour and stature. It is true, he lacks real states-
manship, justice and a profound regard for the nation's
welfare; but he, more than all other Shakespearian kings,
possesses a fine sense of the significance, the sacredness,
the grace, and the splendour of kingship. And if we say
that he is constantly acting, this does not mean that he is
feigning or is merely playing a rôle. He acts his own part
with all the tragic compulsion to suffer everything that this
rôle demands of him.

Poet,[2] actor, dreamer, passive spectator—all these
qualities unavoidably lead him to revel in imagery whenever
he speaks. Instead of deciding, he interprets the situation
by means of elaborate similes; instead of turning to action,
he prefers to reflect upon his own state. "He becomes an
interested spectator of his own ruin, dressing it out with
illuminating phrases and exquisite images. . . ."[3]

Only a few scenes in which this function of imagery is
manifest may be mentioned here. On his return from
Ireland the king lands on the shore of Wales, and salutes
his native soil with a splendid flow of eloquent speech in
which he compares this moment with the reunion of a

[1] *Shakespeare, A Survey*, London, 1935, p. 90.
[2] As was noted by H. Craig, one passage of Richard's is in the form of a sestet (edition of *Richard II* by Hardin Craig, Tudor Shakespeare).
[3] Sir Edmund Chambers, *Shakespeare, A Survey*, London, 1935, p. 91.

mother with her child. He exhorts the earth to protect its king against all enemies, and in developing this image he is carried away by his own imagination, and sees in his mind's eye spiders, toads and adders which join in hindering the king's enemies on their way:

> But let thy spiders, that suck up thy venom,
> And heavy-gaited toads lie in their way,
> Doing annoyance to the treacherous feet
> Which with usurping steps do trample thee:
> Yield stinging nettles to mine enemies;
> And when they from thy bosom pluck a flower,
> Guard it, I pray thee, with a lurking adder (III. ii. 14)

When his cousin calls him back to reality and reminds him of the growing power of the enemy, he disregards this warning and bursts out into a still more extravagant image, comparing his own return with the rising of the bright and radiating sun which disperses all dark adversaries. Indeed, he takes every opportunity to elaborate a magnificent image. To the simple question: "Why looks your grace so pale?" he answers:

> But now the blood of twenty thousand men
> Did triumph in my face, and they are fled;
> And till so much blood thither come again,
> Have I not reason to look pale and dead? (III. ii. 76)

Later in this same scene, instead of giving orders to the waiting lords, he utters a long meditation upon death and the transitoriness of all earthly things (III. ii. 144). This tendency of the king to give himself away to words instead of proceeding to action finds its counterpart in the emphasis laid throughout the play on the idea of speech, illustrated by the repeated and significant use of words such as *tongue*, *mouth*, *speech*, *word*.[1] The correlated use of these words not only underscores Richard's "propensity for verbalising" (Altick), but it also suggests another feature of the play, important in this connection, its preoccupation "with the unsubstantiality of human language" being most manifest in the king's own attitude towards words which serve him

---

[1] I owe this observation to Richard D. Altick's article "Symphonic Imagery in *Richard II*" (*PMLA LXII*, 1947, 2). Altick draws attention to Mark van Doren's *Shakespeare*, New York, 1939, who first stressed the importance of the word "tongue" in the play (pp. 85–87).

as a sort of substitute for reality, blinding his own sense for grim actuality.

It would be unjust, however, to say that all these magnificent speeches abounding in imagery are no more than abstract[1] and illusory speculations of a dreamer. For Richard possesses a fine insight into what could be called the inherent symbolism of a situation. Thus, when at last he finds himself in prison, he likens this prison to the world and this reflection reveals his own position to himself. All this is no longer decorative or rhetorical imagery; it is imagery which arises naturally out of the "image" lent by the situation itself. It thus constantly helps to make visible the hidden symbolic meaning contained in every dramatic situation of importance. This faculty of perceiving and visualizing the symbolism of certain situations by means of imagery is most manifest in the great abdication scene. Both Richard and Bolingbroke hold the crown with their hands before it is to be delivered to Bolingbroke, and Richard says:

> Here, cousin, seize the crown;
> Here, cousin;
> On this side my hand, and on that side yours.
> Now is this golden crown like a deep well
> That owes two buckets, filling one another,
> The emptier ever dancing in the air,
> The other down, unseen and full of water:
> That bucket down, and full of tears am I,
> Drinking my griefs, whilst you mount up on high.
>
> (IV. i. 181)

This simile, too, grows out of the scene on the stage. Richard has quite consciously created beforehand this symbolic situation by asking Bolingbroke to put his hands on the crown. So strong is his desire for significant imagery that even the outward action must serve this end. This image marks the climax of the scene, but at the same time it sums up the whole substance of the play: the tragedy of kingship which demands that the parting king must wane

---

[1] In this connection Dr. Schmetz has drawn attention to the fact that Richard's imagination seldom turns towards mere abstract terms. Abstract things become for him concrete, palpable and living. His preference for metaphor and direct identification instead of for comparisons, seems further to suggest that the imagery is prompted rather by intense emotion than by intellectual speculation (Dr. Schmetz, *op. cit.*).

in the same proportion as the new king waxes (the comparison with the two buckets).

For the Elizabethans who still believed in magic, the golden crown possessed a high symbolic value. They saw and understood the solemn act in which the sacred symbol was handed to the new king.

Thus imagery is here of important dramatic relevance. It would be quite impossible to consider this passage apart from its connection with the whole play. To appreciate it, we must not only understand Richard's peculiar character and the basic theme of the play; we must also bear in mind the symbolic significance of words as *crown*, *tears*, *griefs* occurring in this passage.[1]

Apart from the manner in which the king uses imagery, the subject matter upon which he most frequently draws in his imagery should be noted, as it also reveals his character. Two groups of images seem especially significant in this connection: those pertaining to grief and tears[2] (including the related metaphors of melting and dissolving, and the king's biblical and apocalyptic allusions).[3] Whereas the first group may reveal Richard's weakness and his self-pity, the second underscores the impression of the king as of a "royal martyr" which Shakespeare wished to convey. (This notion, as Professor John Dover Wilson has shown,[4] corresponding to what the later Middle Ages and Shakespeare's own times saw in Richard II.) These two image-threads reappear, too, in the words of other characters, illustrating the central theme of the play, but they seem to culminate in the king's own speeches.

The importance of imagery for the characterization of the chief persons in the drama became apparent as early as *Richard III.* But there it was a fairly simple device, for only animal-symbols were used, and these illuminated only *one* side of Richard's character. In *Richard II*, as we have

---

[1] For the interplay and meaning of these "leading metaphors" in *Richard II* see the article by R. D. Altick in *PMLA LXII.*

[2] Richard D. Altick says, "In no other history play is the idea of tears and weeping so insistently presented". Instances of Richard's use of tears: I. iv. 5; III. ii. 146; III. iii. 161, 164, IV. i. 188; IV. i. 207; V. i. 48; V. i. 86–89.

[3] Dr. Schmetz quotes the following instances: III. ii. 60–61; III. ii. 129–132; III. iii. 85–87; III. iii. 93–94; IV. i. 170; IV. i. 239–242; V. v. 14–17.

[4] Introduction to his edition of *Richard II*, Cambridge, 1939.

already seen, this function of imagery becomes more complex. By means of the very diverse images used both by Richard and by other characters, the king's nature and temperament are amply illustrated.

In full consciousness of his kingly dignity, the king frequently compares himself with the sun.[1] Upon his return from Ireland to England, he describes himself as the rising sun (III. ii. 50); in the next scene he calls himself "glistering Phaeton"; in the famous abdication scene, when a mirror is handed to him on his request, he asks: "Was this the face, that, like the sun, did make beholders wink?" (IV. i. 284). But the other characters, too, make use of this sun image. To Bolingbroke, Richard seems "the blushing discontented sun" (III. iii. 63), and when, at the end of the second act, the Welsh captain enumerates manifold forebodings, "These signs forerun the death or fall of kings", Salisbury adds: "Thy sun sets weeping in the West" (II. iv. 21). But, curiously enough, Richard himself feels in the end that he is no longer "the sun", he speaks of the sun of Bolingbroke, before which he, "a mockery king of snow", should like to melt (IV. i. 261). While these sun images underline the majestic splendour of the king, other images and proverbs denote his tragic guilt and doom. The dying Gaunt utters his warning:

> For violent fires soon burn out themselves;
> Small showers last long, but sudden storms are short;
>
> (II. i. 34)

and addressing the king himself, he compares him to a careless patient who has committed his "anointed body to the cure/Of those physicians who first wounded" him (II. i. 98). In the garden scene the king appears to the servants as a negligent and heedless gardener who has allowed the weeds to grow rank in the great garden of his country. This comparison is fully developed and the laws of the garden are in turn applied to that inconsiderate gardener:

[1] For the sun-imagery in *Richard II*, cf. Paul Reyher, "Le Symbole du Soleil dans la tragédie de *Richard II*" (*Revue de l'Enseignement des Langues Vivantes*, June, 1923); Spurgeon, *Shakespea e's Imagery*, pp. 233–238; John Dover Wilson, Introduction to *King Richard II*, Cambridge, 1939, pp. xii., xiii.

> He that hath suffer'd this disorder'd spring
> Hath now himself met with the fall of leaf:
> The weeds which his broad-spreading leaves did shelter,
> That seem'd in eating him to hold him up,
> Are pluck'd up root and all by Bolingbroke,   (III. iv. 48)

Richard's decline is given ample expression in the imagery used by the queen in the last act. "See my fair rose wither", she exclaims when Richard is being dragged to the Tower (v. i. 8), and subsequently she finds a series of fine comparisons which bring out the contrast between past splendour and present misery:

> Thou map of honour, thou King Richard's tomb,
> And not King Richard; thou most beauteous inn,
> Why should hard-favour'd grief be lodged in thee,
> When triumph is become an alehouse guest? (v. i. 12)

Again she develops the picture of the dying lion who defends himself with utmost tenacity until the end, and thus contrasts the cowardice of the king who is, or should be, in her phrase "a lion and a king of beasts" (v. i. 34). In the next scene a very illuminating comparison is used by York. He describes the people's behaviour on the occasion of Bolingbroke's and Richard's entrance into London, and tells of the enthusiasm of the Londoners for Bolingbroke, their new king. Asked by the Duchess about "poor Richard", he continues:

> As in a theatre, the eyes of men,
> After a well-graced actor leaves the stage,
> Are idly bent on him that enters next,
> Thinking his prattle to be tedious;
> Even so, or with much more contempt, men's eyes
> Did scowl on gentle Richard;   (v. ii. 23)

This comparison with an actor, indeed, reaches the core of Richard's nature; it is again taken up by Richard himself, who in his last monologue admits:

> Thus play I in one person many people,
> And none contented: (v. v. 31)

This last monologue perhaps best reveals the king's capacity "to think in images". Each image occurring to him kindles

his meditation anew and is sagaciously applied to his own
position and character:

> For now has time made me his numbering clock:
> My thoughts are minutes; and with sighs they jar
> Their watches on unto mine eyes, the outward watch,
> Where to my finger, like a dial's point,
> Is pointing still, in cleansing them from tears.   (v. v. 50)

Thus Richard's penetrating and reflective mind expresses
itself in this odd imagery, a last link in the long series of
characterizing images.

This rich and complex series of images[1] may well show
how Shakespeare characterizes his persons. He does not
pronounce a "judgement" that would touch only one side
of their nature. To every quality he gives its due justice,
to virtues as well as faults. And he does not express this
openly, but rather indirectly through hints and undertones
which, in fact, may best be conveyed by means of imagery.

There is, however, a further aspect of the use of imagery
in this play which entitles us to look upon *Richard II* as an
important stage in Shakespeare's development of imagery.
In a notable article on "Symphonic Imagery in *Richard II*",
Richard D. Altick has shown how the impression of
harmony and unity peculiar to this play is largely due to
Shakespeare's art of interrelating and interweaving the
various, frequently recurring image-threads into one
intricate texture and thought-web. The leading metaphors
and image-themes to be traced throughout this play[2] fall
into clearly distinguishable patterns which grow in meaning
and associative suggestiveness as the play advances. Thus,
not only are the separate scenes and acts bound more closely
together by these chains of iterative imagery; the speeches
of the different characters are also interrelated by this
means. We already find that at certain crucial points, in
particularly important passages or scenes, Shakespeare ties
together a greater number of image-strands, giving fuller

---

[1] For further examples of characterizing images see the valuable remarks on *Richard II*
in *The Voyage to Illyria* by Kenneth Muir and Sean O'Loughlin, London, 1937, pp. 97–99.
[2] Altick's summary gives the following key-words: *earth-ground-land*, *blood*, pallor, garden,
sun, tears, *tongue-speech-word*, *snake-venom*, physical injury and illness, *blot*, washing, sweet-
sour, generation, and jewel-crown (*PMLA LXII*, 1947, p. 359).

expression to the different motifs of the imagery which were previously prepared for by unobtrusive hints. As Mr. Altick says, we are thus, by a recognition of this peculiar technique of imagery, enabled to anticipate the future development of Shakespeare's art. The technique is already there in outline, the single images, however, when taken by themselves, still bear the marks of Shakespeare's earlier style.[1] For a student of the growth of Shakespeare's art, an examination of the function of the imagery in *Richard II* is therefore particularly illuminating.

[1] Richard D. Altick makes the interesting observation that the language of *Richard II* "suggests the existence of a vital relationship between two leading characteristics of Shakespeare's poetic style: the uncontrolled indulgence of verbal wit in the earlier plays and the use of great image themes in the plays of his maturity". He draws the conclusion: "In *Richard II* we see the crucial intermediate stage in the development, or perhaps more accurately the utilization of Shakespeare's singular associative gift . . ." (*PMLA LXII*, p. 364).

8

ROMEO AND JULIET

IN Shakespeare's work, conventional style and a freer, more spontaneous mode of expression are not opposite poles which may be definitely assigned to different periods. It is impossible to say that with a certain play, the conventional style comes to an end, and that from then on, a new style exclusively prevails. There are many transitions and interrelationships, and in some plays which stand at the turning-point between the young and the mature Shakespeare, the most traditional and conventional wording is to be found together with a direct and surprising new language which allows us to divine the Shakespeare of the great tragedies. *Romeo and Juliet* is the best example of this co-existence of two styles. H. Granville-Barker has shown how both in separate scenes and in the dramatic structure a new spontaneity often breaks through the conventional vestment, but is still not yet strong enough to pervade the whole of the play. The same thing may now be shown to hold for the imagery as well.

Many examples of the old conventional type can be selected. In the third act, Capulet finds Juliet in tears:

> How now! a conduit, girl? what, still in tears?
> Evermore showering? in one little body
> Thou counterfeit'st a bark, a sea, a wind;
> For still thy eyes, which I may call the sea,
> Do ebb and flow with tears; the bark thy body is,
> Sailing in this salt flood; the winds, thy sighs;
> Who, raging with thy tears, and they with them,
> Without a sudden calm, will overset
> Thy tempest-tossed body.   (III. v. 130)

This image still presents all the features of Shakespeare's early style—the vain pleasure taken in painting every detail of the little picture whose fastidious construction recalls the conceits of the early comedies. The situation, too, in which the father finds his daughter dissolved in tears, seems to us unsuitable for such an elaborate comparison. Of course, tears are often the occasion for an image. But, for example, when Richard III says to his mother, "The liquid drops of tears that you have shed shall come again, transform'd to orient pearl" (iv. iv. 321), the figurative phrase is meant to lend the whole chain of thought a greater force; Richard *intends* to express something by it. Capulet, on the other hand, pursues no aim with this image; the occasion is merely the excuse for the image. Expressions such as "thou counterfeit'st" or "which I may call the sea", as well as the agglomeration of words, betray the pleasure of invention. However, this artificiality and the very circumstantiality of this mode of expression is itself highly fitting for Juliet's verbose and conventional father, for his affability and vain self-admiration (cf. his simile with the "well-apparell'd April" at i. ii. 27). Thus this passage characterizes Capulet. A stylistic form belonging to Shakespeare's earliest period is here fitted into a place that suits it. This we may observe at many points in *Romeo and Juliet*. Brother Lorenzo is characterized in a similar way by his sententious and pedantic images, by the leisurely breadth of his flowery and often descriptive manner of speech.

On the whole it may be said, that the first scenes of *Romeo and Juliet* strike us as being more conventional in tone and diction than the later ones. The blank-verse, too, is handled more conventionally here than in the later parts of the play. It may very well be that this is intentional.[1] For the nearer the play advances towards its tragic culmination, the less powerful and significant becomes the conventional world from which the two lovers have freed themselves by accepting their fate. This transition of style has not, of course, been worked out consistently. The rhetoric and the declamatory style never quite vanish, and are certainly not meant to disappear entirely. Their persistence, however, may set off better those passages (more frequent in the last acts), in which we find a new simplicity and poignant directness of diction, as in Romeo's famous

---

[1] This surmise is also expressed by T. S. Eliot in a lecture given in Germany on "The Development of Shakespeare's Versification" published in German under the title "Shakespeares Verskunst", i. *Der Monat, II,* 20, 1950.

line, "Is it even so? Then I defy you, stars!" (v. i. 24).
This manner of placing significant moments and passages
into fuller relief, by contrasting them with very different
stylistic patterns has been most effectively used by Shakespeare throughout the whole play.[1] It is interesting to trace
this art of contrast in the use of imagery; it accounts not
only for many subtle dramatic effects, but also for several
juxtapositions which appear odd at first sight, but become
clear when judged from the context.

That the same characters speak in this play, now in a
very conventional, now in quite a new and different manner,
may best be seen with Romeo. It is he who (besides Juliet
and the nurse) is most often able to rise above the level of
flowery or witty, conventional phrase (as in the balcony
scene and in the garden scene). But, on the other hand,
he is just as much confined to this conventional mode as
all the others. If we look closer, however, we see that this
change in diction in Romeo is not the result of chance but
rather of a change in his mood.[2] Before Romeo has met
Juliet, he still finds pleasure in polished and witty dialogue
with Benvolio, speaks of "love" in the usual stereotyped
phrases, using in his speech, apart from metaphors, a great
variety of other figures which contribute to the artificiality
of his whole utterance at this stage of the play.[3]

> Love is a smoke raised with the fume of sighs;
> Being purged, a fire sparkling in lovers' eyes;
> Being vex'd, a sea nourish'd with lovers' tears: (i. i. 196)

and thus, in a similar dialogue which he—also in the first
act—holds with Mercutio, he cleverly and gracefully
catches up the image of Cupid's wings tossed to him by
Mercutio and proceeds to dwell upon it artfully (i. iv. 17).

[1] For this aspect cf. H. Granville-Barker, *Prefaces to Shakespeare*, 2nd series,
1930 (*Romeo and Juliet*).
[2] E. K. Chambers: "Romeo has been an amorist, posing before the mirror of his own self-
consciousness, with tears and sighs and early morning walks and an affectation of solitude
and the humorous night. He was for the numbers that Petrarch flowed in, has rhymed love
and dove, and nick-named Cupid with paradox and artful phrases . . ." (*Shakespeare, A
Survey*, p. 71).
[3] In an illuminating article on "Patterns of Style in *Romeo and Juliet*" (*Studia Neo-
philologica, XXI*), J. W. Draper traces the distribution of figures and their adaptation to
plot and character. Analysing the first scene he points out that the wealth of figures in Romeo's
language gives to his speech "a witty artificiality that suggests that his pangs of love are not
too deep " (p. 198).

He meets Juliet for the first time at the feast in the house of
Capulet (i. v.), and the image, with which their first conversation opens, is almost too well known to be quoted:

ROMEO. My lips, two blushing pilgrims, ready stand
        To smooth that rough touch with a tender kiss.

JULIET. Good pilgrim, you do wrong your hand too much,
        Which mannerly devotion shows in this;
        For saints have hands that pilgrims' hands do touch,
        And palm to palm is holy palmer's kiss.   (i. v. 97)

This passage, joined by its cross-rime, is a typical example
of the balanced, symmetrical and artificial style of the early
Shakespeare. In pretty and obedient fashion, this motif is
elaborated in seven lines by both parties. In these formal
surroundings the first meeting of the lovers must be formal,
too, and is accordingly reflected in a conventional language.

But this same Romeo speaks a new language in those
two scenes with Juliet, which stand out from the drama like
unforgettable peaks: the garden scene and the balcony
scene. Here two characters meet who no longer carry on
coquetry with elegant conceits on "love" but who are
passionately in love with one another and give direct
expression to their love. The fact that, in *Romeo and Juliet*,
Shakespeare shaped human love for the first time in *timeless* form gives this play an important position not only in
his own development, but also in the history of the
Elizabethan drama. This fundamental experience of deep
and passionate love is at the very base of the whole drama;
in these two scenes it finds its most genuine expression.
For these scenes bring the secret converse of the lovers,
freed from their conventional environment and from
distraction, but at one with the heart of nature. The warmth
and tenderness of these scenes raises the language to a
poetic height and richness unmatched in Shakespeare's
work and the imagery displays a complexity surpassing
everything hitherto found:

        O, speak again, bright angel! for thou art
        As glorious to this night, being o'er my head,
        As is a winged messenger of heaven

Unto the white-upturned wondering eyes
Of mortals that fall back to gaze on him
When he bestrides the lazy-pacing clouds
And sails upon the bosom of the air.   (ii. ii. 26)

Judged by its style, this is indeed still descriptive, meticulously handled imagery, rich in epithets. But the way this image is connected with the situation and the characters is new; it springs wholly from the situation and contains nothing extraneous, whereas up to this point, the images had been illustrated by comparisons from other spheres. Now the situation is itself of such a metaphorical nature, that it permits an organic growth of the image; Romeo stands below in the dark garden, above which slow-sailing clouds move in a star-strewn sky (all this is conjured up by his words!); Juliet appears above at the window. Romeo must lift his eyes, just as one must glance upward in order to perceive the heavenly bodies (the white-upturned eyes are his own eyes). When, in the first lines, the eyes of the beloved appear to Romeo as "two of the fairest stars in all the heaven", then this is no conventional phrase but is based on the reality of the moment, on the fact that he has raised his eyes to heaven and to Juliet at the same time. And when Juliet now appears to him—in the image quoted —as "winged messenger of heaven", this, too, results from the metaphorical character of the situation itself. So everything in this image has a double function: the clouds and the heavenly *messengers* may be reality, and at the same time they are symbols. The deeply organic nature of this image is to be seen also in the fact that it coincides as a poetic, enhancing element with Romeo's ecstatically uplifted mind. Its inspiration belongs to this moment and to no other; this symbolical moment gave Romeo's words the power to rise above the levels of expression hitherto achieved. In this image three functions merge, which we usually meet separately: it is the enhanced expression of Romeo's own nature, it characterizes Juliet (light, the most important symbol for her, occurs here), and it fills the night with clouds and stars, thus creating atmosphere.

In this scene, it must be admitted, there are still many themes of imagery which appear unoriginal, culled perhaps from the stock-motifs of Elizabethan poetry. Such are the two dainty bird-images which Juliet employs (159, 178), her asseveration "Else would I tear the cave where Echo lies" (162) and Romeo's

> . . . wert thou as far
> As that vast shore wash'd with the farthest sea (82)

Still the tenderness and intensity of the feeling which pulses through this whole scene, can occasionally permit so worn a comparison as that of love to the deepest ocean to appear in a wording whose simple straightforwardness[1] makes us wholly forget the conventionality of the image, such as Juliet's:

> My bounty is as boundless as the sea,
> My love as deep; the more I give to thee,
> The more I have, for both are infinite.   (133)

The transition we perceive in *Romeo and Juliet* cannot therefore adequately be described as a transition from "conventional" to "natural" speech. For Shakespeare does not simply abandon the language of conceit or the use of artificial and highly elaborated imagery. The change lies rather in the different impression these passages make on us.[2] For they strike us as being more natural, more spontaneous. And this is due to their being more closely adapted to the situation and to the moment. They convince us because we feel the intense emotion that is expressed by them, and we now believe the characters who utter such language.

If we ask how Shakespeare in *Romeo and Juliet* tried to individualize the characters by means of imagery, we are tempted to think first of the Nurse's language. The Nurse's language, however, though the most striking example of individualized speech in Shakespeare's work of this period, is characterized less by imagery than by certain features of style, syntax and rhythm. But the contrast between Mercutio's and Romeo's language is also a contrast

---

[1] In his chapter on *Romeo and Juliet* H. Granville-Barker gives several examples for the spontaneity of the language, which then slips back into rhetorical declamation and masterly verbosity, as, for example, Juliet's "O serpent heart, hid with a flowering face!" (III. ii. 73) or Romeo's eloquent and conventional lament of the dead before he takes his own life (v. iii. 83 sqq.).

[2] For this process cf. John Middleton Murry, *Shakespeare*, London, 1936, Chapter XII.

between their different use of imagery. The heightened lyricism of Romeo's idealizing language is set off by Mercutio's sparkling and realistic speech, which abounds in drastic comparisons, witty puns and vivid concrete pictures. In the sequence of the scenes, Shakespeare makes rich and effective use of this contrast, gay, turbulent and restless scenes being set against the more solemn and lyrical pathos of the scenes between the two lovers. The contrast in imagery, however, is developed gradually. In I. iv. Mercutio and Romeo still meet on the same level of clever word-play and conventional love-imagery. The famous Queen-Mab speech by Mercutio—though being more in the poetical than in the realistic vein[1]—shows that even in this highly imaginative passage Mercutio does not lose hold of firm reality, for a wealth of minutely observed concrete and palpable things taken from the everyday world appears in his images and comparisons. As to the difference between Romeo's and Juliet's imagery, Dr. Schmetz has drawn attention to Juliet's imagery being more tinged by the familiar objects of her life-sphere and her child-experience, whereas Romeo's imagery appears less concrete and more spiritualized.[2] This subtle differentiation shows that typical features of the character's background and mood slip into the imagery. As with other aspects of the imagery in *Romeo and Juliet*, however, this discrimination has not been consistently carried out. We find a

---

[1] L. L. Schücking emphasizes that the Queen-Mab Speech is "out of character" and little consistent with Mercutio's temperament (*Character Problems in Shakespeare's Plays*, London, 1922, p. 97). For a divergent opinion cf. J. I. M. Stewart, *Character and Motive in Shakespeare*, London, 1949, p. 60.

[2] Thus, for Juliet, night is "a sober-suited matron" which she asks:

Hood my unmann'd blood . . .
With thy black mantle.   (III. ii. 14)

Juliet speaks of "bud of love" (II. ii. 121) and "mansion of a love" (III. ii. 26) and compares her impatience to that of a child "that hath new robes/And may not wear them" (III. ii. 30). To show the more spiritual and less sensuous quality of Romeo's imagery, Dr. Schmetz, elaborating an observation first made by Gregor Sarrazin (*Aus Shakespeares Meisterwerkstatt, Stilgeschichtliche Studien*, Berlin, 1906) compares Juliet's

. . . when he shall die,
Take him and cut him out in little stars,
And he will make the face of heaven so fine
That all the world will be in love with night.   (III. ii. 21)

with Romeo's

. . . her eyes in heaven
Would through the airy region stream so bright
That birds would sing and think it were not night.   (II. ii. 20)

tentative beginning of Shakespeare's later technique of giving each character his own language and imagery, but we do not find this technique fully or consistently developed.

Nature, which plays so great a part in the garden scene and is referred to again and again by the imagery, accompanies the whole action of the play almost symbolically. A brief review may make clear the advance which *Romeo and Juliet* signifies in this respect. Only occasionally do the early comedies contain references to the time of day and atmosphere: there is, for instance, the first line of the fifth act of *Two Gentlemen*: "The sun begins to gild the western sky"; but in general, these comedies are without light and we are not conscious of the presence of nature. *Henry VI* has only two night scenes, which, however, are introduc d by fairly isolated images (namely, *B*, i. iv. and iv. i.). *Richard III* is the first play of Shakespeare's to contain a scene—but only one scene—in which the atmosphere is suggested by frequently interspersed references and images.[1] But such references to nature are not yet brought into harmony with the characters. Here lies the problem which faces the dramatist: all the words spoken by the characters must be the expression of themselves, must progressively reveal their nature and their mind to us. But the difficulty is now to bring in circumstances, atmosphere, historical and political explanations which are necessary for understanding and rounding off the whole, but which seem to bear relationship to no particular character. It is very illuminating to follow step by step how Shakespeare solves this problem. In the early plays, especially in the histories and in *Titus Andronicus*, Shakespeare obviously charges some figure or other in the opening scenes with the task of giving us an exhaustive description of the circumstances (the monologue is also often used for this purpose). This appears rather clumsy, and it is indeed an advance when this task is distributed among several characters. The same method, of course, now applies to the nature-images creating atmosphere. They are put into the mouths

[1] "The weary sun hath made a golden set", etc. (v. iii. 19); "In to our tent; the air is raw and cold" (v. iii. 46); "The silent hours steal on,/And flaky darkness breaks within the east" (v. iii. 86); "The early village-cock/Hath twice done salutation to the morn;" (v. iii. 210); "Who saw the sun to-day?" (v. iii. 277).

of certain characters as brief extra-dramatic digressions,
they preface the events like signs (cf. *B Henry VI*, iv. i. i).
In the development of imagery, the garden scene and the
balcony scene are of importance, because it is here for the
first time that "nature-imagery" derives from the characters
as their own expression of mood. Romeo and Juliet deliver
no excursive speeches, they utter merely their own being
and their love for one another, but their words reveal the
beauty of nature, the background to that wonderful night.
On the other hand, this fusing of the nature-images with
nature itself is perfect and complete only because Romeo
and Juliet themselves have a personal relationship to the
powers of night. A few lines from Juliet's monologue at the
opening of the second scene of the third act may serve as
example:

> Come, civil night,
> Thou sober-suited matron, all in black,
> And learn me how to lose a winning match,
> Play'd for a pair of stainless maidenhoods:
> Hood my unmann'd blood, bating in my cheeks,
> With thy black mantle; till strange love, grown bold,
> Think true love acted simple modesty.
> Come, night; come, Romeo; come, thou day in night;
> For thou wilt lie upon the wings of night
> Whiter than new snow on a raven's back.
> Come, gentle night, come, loving, black-brow'd night, . . .
> (iii. ii. 10)

Here the night is no longer something detached and
extraneous, it appears as Juliet's ally, which she longs for
and summons like a human being. The appeal to the night,
recurring in this monologue four times, like the theme of a
fugue, is intimately associated with the whole of Juliet's
speech. The apostrophe of a personified element of nature
is indeed a rhetorical artifice and a proven device, but how
has convention once again been quickened with throbbing
life and made to fit new aims! This great art of Shakespeare's
of blending outer nature with the inner spirit of his characters, finds clear expression in the parting scene of the
lovers (iii. v.). Here the dawning day becomes to them a
symbol of parting; but this interrelationship needs no

artful constructions in expression, because the situation is
so chosen that nature enters naturally and organically into
the lovers' dialogue.

In *Romeo and Juliet* Shakespeare employed a special
artifice by means of which the atmosphere of nature,
though itself a symbol, is introduced in an organic manner.
As Caroline Spurgeon was the first to show,[1] the two lovers
appear to each other as light against a dark background,
and all these light-images, in which sun, moon, the stars,
lightning, heaven, day and night figure, thus aid in spreading over the whole play an intensive atmosphere of free
nature. In the later tragedies we shall find in great perfection
this art of characterization through images, whereby a
particular atmosphere may be lent to the play.

That the "nature-imagery" grows so organically out
of the self-expression of the characters is true in this play
only of the speeches of Romeo and Juliet. The allusions
which Benvolio and Montague make to Romeo's melancholy
morning walks are still worded in the conventional manner:

> Madam, an hour before the worshipp'd sun
> Peer'd forth the golden window of the east,
>
> (I. i. 125)
>
> But all so soon as the all-cheering sun,
> Should in the furthest east begin to draw
> The shady curtains from Aurora's bed,   (I. i. 139)

And when brother Lorenzo commences his monologue
before his cell:

> The grey-eyed morn smiles on the frowning night,
> Chequering the eastern clouds with streaks of light,
> And flecked darkness like a drunkard reels
> From forth day's path and Titan's fiery wheels: (II. iii. 1)

This is still the old, somewhat declamatory method of
introducing the scene with isolated nature-images.

Thus *Romeo and Juliet* shows at several points how
Shakespeare produces a closer harmony between the
imagery and the characters, between the inner and outer

---

[1] *Shakespeare's Imagery*, p. 310 sqq. Professor Spurgeon shows how the *light-image*
pervades the whole play and how Shakespeare in his imagery continually represents the
sudden flaming and vanishing of this tragic love as "brilliance swiftly quenched".

situation and the theme of the play. But even here, we have
not yet what we should call "dramatic" imagery. With its
rich poetic decoration, its abundance of epithets, its
personifications, the imagery is still predominantly of a
descriptive character. Thus the long description of Queen
Mab appears as an extra-dramatic moment in the structure
of the play. Less interrupting, but also exemplifying the
tendency to elaborate, are the description of the effect
which the poison will have upon Juliet (iv. i. 99) and the
description of the apothecary and his dwelling by Romeo
(v. i. 38, 69). In *Romeo and Juliet* Shakespeare is still writing
in a style which leaves nothing unsaid. This tendency
towards complete representation, clarification, amplification
and description is nevertheless favourable to the development of a poetic diction of great wealth and colour in which
the metaphorical element can freely unfold. For, compared
to earlier plays, we find in *Romeo and Juliet* an increase of
metaphors used where formerly a conceit or an elaborate
comparison would have been inserted. These, it is true,
have not yet disappeared, but the growing predilection for
metaphors seems significant and suggests the way Shakespeare will go. Viewed from this angle, too, *Romeo and
Juliet* appears as a play of transition.

9

LANGUAGE AND IMAGERY IN
SHAKESPEARE'S MIDDLE PERIOD

IT is one of the aims of this study to show how the development of Shakespeare's imagery becomes peculiarly
manifest in the way the images adapt themselves more and
more organically to the structural form of the drama. As
the previous chapters sought to make clear, this development towards an organic association of the images with
the drama has several aspects. The relationship between
the imagery and the situation which gave rise to it could
become closer and more logical; or again, the imagery
could be made more nearly to fit the character of the person
employing it. Or the relationship of the imagery either to
the atmosphere of the play or to its theme, could be more
closely knit. The next chapter will point out how the
imagery becomes more organic because the images have
a share in the disclosure and the preparation of the dramatic
action. This chapter, however, will show how the images
become more intimately associated with the context; and
how the language of the drama becomes more and more
saturated with the metaphorical element; and, finally, how
the metaphorical element wins new fields of expression
in so far as, in the middle period of Shakespeare's work,
the abstract and the reflective element find increasing
expression in the imagery.

The assimilation of the images to the fabric of the text
(as early as *Richard III* we found the first traces of this
development), is connected with the formative process of
the images. In the early plays we found that in most cases
the images were "ready-made", and were inserted into the
text as complete units. In the middle period a new technique
is evolved, which has often been designated as the technique
of the associative rise of the image.[1] The images are formed

---

[1] Walter Whiter, a little-known critic of the eighteenth century, was the first to call
attention to this aspect of Shakespeare's imagery. Cf. the leading article in *The Times Literary
Supplement*, September 5, 1936. E. E. Kellett's book, *Suggestions*, Cambridge, 1923, contains

in the very act of composition; one word engenders another:

> Together with that pale, that white-faced shore,
> Whose foot spurns back the ocean's roaring tides
> *(King John,* II. i. 23)

Pale here gives rise to the notion of paleness of the face, which in turn is fully developed in *white-faced.* In this manner the coast is now represented by a human image and the notion of its foot, spurning the tides, is logically carried out.

> And shall our quick blood, spirited with wine,
> Seem frosty? O, for honour of our land,
> Let us not hang like roping icicles
> Upon our houses' thatch, whiles a more frosty people
> Sweat drops of gallant youth in our rich fields!
> *(Henry V,* III. v. 21)

Frosty was here the occasion for the associative image of the icicles.

> You are too shallow, Hastings, much too shallow,
> To sound the bottom of the after-times.
> *(B Henry IV,* IV. ii. 50)

Shallow, meaning here superficial in character, assumes a concrete significance in Shakespeare's mind and thus leads to the (unuttered) image of the ocean, whose bottom Hastings cannot sound.

The fact that we so often only gradually become conscious of what image is meant, indicates that Shakespeare no longer inserts the images "from outside", but that while writing, he begins to see something in a particular light and then creates an image out of it. At first this image is only suggested in metaphors; its realization follows later. A passage from *Henry IV* may serve as an example of this process:

> For the fifth Harry from curb'd license plucks
> The muzzle of restraint, and the wild dog
> Shall flesh his tooth on every innocent.
> *(B Henry IV,* IV. v. 131)

---

a very illuminating chapter on this subject, to which the following remarks are much indebted. The subject has been further developed by Edward A. Armstrong, *Shakespeare's Imagination, A Study of the Psychology of Association and Inspiration,* London, 1946.

With regard to *curb*, often employed by Shakespeare in a figurative sense, we are not yet in a position to say that Shakespeare had in mind the image of a dog. For *curb* means the curb-chain and *to curb* signifies *to master, to restrain*. But, taking this as a cue, Shakespeare was led to the *muzzle* and then to the *dog*. Here is a similar example from *King John*:

> . . . and England now is left
> To tug and scamble and to part by the teeth
> The unowed interest of proud-swelling state.
> Now for the bare-pick'd bone of majesty
> Doth dogged war bristle his angry crest
> And snarleth in the gentle eyes of peace:
>
> (*King John*, IV. iii. 145)

The second line consists mainly of verbs which can be used of dogs. The phrase *bare-pick'd bone of majesty* then comes nearer to the concrete notion of dogs. From the general idea of tugging and scrambling is developed the immediate image of dogs fighting over a bone, but the angrily snarling dog himself does not appear until the line before the last. In both passages, completely abstract ideas are joined by a common metaphorical figure. The "canine figure of speech", so to speak, is used of *England, majesty, war, restraint*, all wholly abstract matters. This process will receive more attention later on. Its consequence surely is that the image no longer appears as an interruption. For the train of thought is carried right along, only this time in another guise, coloured, as it were, by an image. In earlier plays, for example in *Henry VI*, a special image was inserted in such cases, with an explanatory, but naturally also interrupting effect. We are tempted to say that the images now steal into the speeches. Shakespeare has ceased to think of the images as something separable, they are continually at his disposal, are more easily associated with everything and follow each other more rapidly and smoothly. The mixed metaphor will now become more frequent; we shall find it very often in the tragedies. All this is, of course, connected with the increasing speed of Shakespeare's thinking and writing, as Charles Lamb, for example, notes, when he says of Shakespeare's style: "Shakespeare mingles

everything, he runs line into line, embarrasses sentences
and metaphors before one idea has burst its shell, another
is hatched and clamorous for disclosure" (*Specimens of
Dramatic Poets who Lived about the Time of Shakespeare*).

A few examples may serve as illustration. Morton, in
Henry IV, speaking of Percy Hotspur, relates:

> For from his metal was his party steel'd;
> Which once in him abated, all the rest
> Turn'd on themselves, like dull and heavy lead:
> And as the thing that's heavy in itself,
> Upon enforcement flies with greatest speed,
> So did our men, heavy in Hotspur's loss,
> Lend to this weight such lightness with their fear
> That arrows fled not swifter toward their aim
> Than did our soldiers,   (*B Henry IV*, 1. i. 116)

Here we have a sequence of quite different images connected,
nevertheless, by association. *Metal*, often used by Shakespeare to designate masculine courage and strength of
character, is here felt in its original significance and may
thus point to *steel'd*, upon which in turn the *lead* in the
third line is dependent. But before *lead* stands *heavy*, and
out of this *heavy lead* develops a further image which in its
turn now produces the image of the flying arrows through
the notion of flying (*flies*).

Many examples could be given to show how the images
now make their appearance more easily and naturally.
Thus, in the passage where Henry IV characterizes Prince
Harry, we find, within seventeen lines, no less than eleven
different images referring to the same theme.[1] Or Vernon's
description of the approach of the enemy; here we have a
sequence of nine images in thirteen lines.[2] These images
are generally not carried out, but are just hinted at.

The image which is merely suggested is a further
sign of the intensive penetration of the language by the
"imagery-consciousness". The whole image has sunk
beneath the surface,[3] as it were, and has left behind it only
one or two ideas connected with it. From Shakespeare's

[1] *B Henry IV*, IV. iv. 32.
[2] *A Henry IV*, IV. i. 98.
[3] Cf. chapter on "Hidden Images" in Armstrong's book *loc. cit.*

middle period on, we are frequently forced to ask "what image did Shakespeare here have in mind?" The following example from *Henry V* may serve as an illustration:

> And when the mind is quicken'd, out of doubt,
> The organs, though defunct and dead before,
> Break up their drowsy grave and newly move,
> With casted slough and fresh legerity.
>
> *(Henry V*, IV. i. 20)

Here the idea of the snake sloughing its skin forms the background. Often enough we have no concrete basis for the metaphor of a passage but merely verbs of action which are connected with an abstract content, as in the following:

> Whose want, and whose delay, is strew'd with sweets,
> Which they distil now in the curbed time,
> To make the coming hour o'erflow with joy
> And pleasure drown the brim.   *(All's Well*, II. iv. 45)

Distil here leads to the image of flowing, overflowing, and this is then carried out in *drown the brim*. In the case of "image-complexes"[1] which lie close to Shakespeare's heart, such as gardening and plant-lore, we often find that on each occasion, only individual figures of speech are selected from this field, without a special image being carried out each time. In the lines

> Provided that you weed your better judgements
> Of all opinion that grows rank in them.
>
> *(As You Like It*, II. vii. 45)

this image-complex of the garden becomes apparent in *weed* and *rank*, just as in the following passage from *Henry IV*:

> He cannot so precisely weed this land
> As his misdoubts present occasion:
> His foes are so enrooted with his friends
>
> *(B Henry IV*, IV. i. 205)

---

[1] The term "image-complex" is to indicate that Shakespeare, in his imagery, shows, as Miss Spurgeon has put it, a predilection for "certain classes of things, certain qualities in things and certain aspects of life" (*Shakespeare's Imagery*, p. 44). In the careful examination Miss Spurgeon has made of the subject matter of Shakespeare's images these fields of preference are clearly singled out.

There are innumerable examples of this type of imagery.[1]

In the early plays we find that metaphors which thus evoke a more comprehensive image are rare, and, if they occur, they mostly derive from such fields as gardening or the processes of blossoming, ripening, etc., which Shakespeare draws upon from the very beginning. In the "middle period", however, we often find unusual and uncommon metaphors, the range of Shakespeare's metaphorical language having been considerably widened. When Henry IV says of his predecessor, "He carded his state,/Mingled his royalty with capering fools," (*A Henry IV*, iii. ii. 62), the metaphor *card* is taken from the adulteration of liquors. In *As You Like It* we have "when you were gravelled for lack of matter" (iv. i. 74); *gravel* means the sand, *gravelled* suggests a ship which is stranded. In *Twelfth Night* we read: "That screws me from my true place in your favour," (v. i. 12). How such a figure of speech can intensify the expression of the thought! In the following example from *King John* we find a more complicated metaphor: "unthread the rude eye of rebellion" (v. iv. 11). Here the basic idea is the drawing out of the thread from the eye of a needle, which is as much as to say, "undo, turn back history".[2]

As already stated, in Shakespeare's middle period it is often abstractions which are expressed by the imagery. When Shakespeare in his earlier period expressed abstract issues in figurative language (he rarely does so in the first plays) he illustrated the abstract term by an extra comparison added on.[3] But he soon takes quite another course: he combines the abstract with metaphorical attributes without compunction. Thus a peculiar world is created, in which the concrete is continually mingled with the abstract. The abruptness of the transitions makes many passages difficult to understand, but, at the same time, a brief

[1] Many examples are given in Part I of Miss Spurgeon's book. Cf. also Miss Spurgeon's chapter "Association of Ideas", pp. 188–199.

[2] Further examples: "unmuzzle your wisdom" (*As You Like It*, i. ii. 74); "ungird thy strangeness" (*Twelfth Night*, iv. i. 16); "I was never so bethump'd with words" (*King John*, ii. i. 466).

[3] Cf. "Glory is like a circle in the water" (*A Henry VI*, i. ii. 133); "Civil dissension is a viperous worm" (*A Henry VI*, iii. i. 72).

passage may thus become more laden with meaning. In the Second Part of *Henry IV* we read:

> . . . my cloud of dignity
> Is held from falling with so weak a wind
> That it will quickly drop: my day is dim.
> (*B Henry IV*, IV. v. 99)

Cloud of dignity is the result of such a wedding of the abstract element with the concrete. At an earlier period we should have had: *my dignity like a cloud*, or, *my dignity, a cloud*. But such linkings are now frequent. Thus, for example, we find: *Tide of pomp, dust of old oblivion, muzzle of restraint*. What would have formerly needed several lines of exposition is here compressed into a few words. *So weak a wind*, too, suggests two things at the same time: first the expiring breath of the dying man, and then—in keeping with the concrete image—the real wind which keeps the cloud from falling down. Thus ambiguity has gradually become an important factor in the creation of the imagery. *My day is dim* is called forth by association by the first (half-concealed) image (of the rain-cloud) and may serve to show how laden with significance and how suggestive a brief line of Shakespeare's may be. Summing up, we observe as characteristic features of this passage the following: mingling of the concrete and the abstract, concentration of content, ambiguity, connection of the parts by association and suggestiveness.

10

THE DRAMATIC FUNCTION OF THE IMAGES
IN PLAYS OF THE MIDDLE PERIOD

WHEN Shakespeare employed imagery in his early histories and comedies, he used it, as we saw, either for decorative purposes, to intensify the expression of the emotions, or to present thoughts of a general nature in epigrammatic form. The significance of the imagery was often restricted to the situation of the moment in which it was used; only rarely did it point beyond this situation to the coming events of the drama. These images still lacked a clear relationship to their place in the dramatic structure. Hence we could quite disregard whether they occurred in the first or in the last act. The more Shakespeare becomes a conscious dramatic artist, the more he employs them for dramatic purposes. The images gradually lose their purely "poetic", often extraneous nature and become one of the dramatic elements.

The first attempts to foreshadow coming events through images are to be found in *Henry VI*. But here it is still a somewhat clumsy and obtrusive form; thus in the fifth act of the Third Part, when King Edward calls attention to the approaching calamity:

> But in the midst of this bright-shining day,
> I spy a black, suspicious, threatening cloud,
> That will encounter with our glorious sun,
> Ere he attain his easeful western bed:
> (*C Henry VI*, v. iii. 3)

Such an image[1] possesses dramatic significance, but its purpose is too obvious; it is not a natural product of the conversation, but is rather set before the scene like a danger-signal. *The Merchant of Venice* may serve as an example to show how Shakespeare's art in the dramatic employment of

---

[1] The image cited above belongs to the "tempest-imagery" which has been traced by G. Wilson Knight through the whole of Shakespeare's work. The tempest-images often have such a premonitory function. (G. Wilson Knight, *The Shakespearian Tempest*, Oxford, 1932.)

images is now ripening in the middle period of his development. The first lines of the play exemplify this. Salarino is
trying to give Antonio an explanation for the latter's
despondency:

> Your mind is tossing on the ocean;
> There, where your argosies with portly sail,
> Like signiors and rich burghers on the flood,
> Or, as it were, the pageants of the sea,
> Do overpeer the petty traffickers,
> That curt'sy to them, do them reverence,
> As they fly by them with their woven wings. (i. i. 9)

As an introduction to the whole play these images are of the
greatest importance: they immediately produce the atmosphere of sea, ships and well-to-do merchants in which the
play moves; with their reference to the dangers of trading
by sea, they strike the keynote of the play. Salarino's lines
suggest the central theme of the action, which is to keep the
audience breathless in the following acts:

> My wind cooling my broth
> Would blow me to an ague, when I thought
> What harm a wind too great at sea might do.
> I should not see the sandy hour-glass run,
> But I should think of shallows and of flats,
> And see my wealthy Andrew dock'd in sand
> Veiling her high-top lower than her ribs
> To kiss her burial.   (i. i. 22)

Here Shakespeare's art of dramatic irony becomes manifest:
Salarino—first thinking of his breath with which he cools
his soup—imagines what would probably happen if a
storm should strike the ships on the high seas. This is
spoken in passing, the picture is half-playfully executed,
almost for its own sake; in the conversation it is just casually
mentioned like a fantasy not to be taken seriously. For
indeed the very next verses would refute it: Antonio (and
it is he who is really concerned) declares that he is un-
worried, and the subject is quickly changed. But these
few seconds have sufficed for Shakespeare to attain his
aim; the audience has pricked up its ears; upon the imagination a very definite image has impressed itself for a brief

moment, and this will come to life again later on when reality demands it. Here we see Shakespeare's peculiar technique, which is to develop more and more in the great tragedies. By means of such delicate touches and hints, such vague and shadowy suggestions, often enough not understood at the moment, he succeeds in gradually preparing for something to come. It is precisely the fact that these intimations are not fully understood at the moment of their use which is important from the point of view of the dramatist: the audience has as yet no clear conception of the meaning, a residue of doubt remains, at once disturbing and a source of enhanced concentration.

When Antonio says after a few lines:

> I hold the world but as a world, Gratiano,
> A stage where every man must play a part,
> And mine a sad one.   (I. i. 77)

his words, too, have a premonitory effect. The word *sad* carries us back to the first line of the play (Antonio: *In sooth, I know not why I am so sad*). We, the audience, do not know the reason why Antonio is so sad, nor do his friends, and he admits himself that he does not understand the cause. Thus we spectators grow more and more sympathetic and interested, even curious, as regards Antonio. And when he now employs that significant and memorable image of the world as a stage, we take it in with a certain degree of tense expectation. Nothing has as yet occurred in this first scene, but Shakespeare has guided our imagination, our curiosity and our expectation into a definite path. Now the action can commence. Shakespeare's art consists in transporting the audience in the very first scene into the atmosphere and the problems of the play without, however, disclosing the outcome. Imagery offers the best means of such indirect and concealed statement needed for this art of foreshadowing coming events. Here is another example from the *Merchant* of this "dramatic function" of the images: At the beginning of the sixth scene of the second act Gratiano and Salarino are waiting in the street in front of Shylock's house for Lorenzo, who has bid them here. While waiting for his arrival, they pass the time in general conversation about the transitoriness of love which, once achieved, is less ardently sought a second time. To express this Gratiano employs a simile:

> All things that are,
> Are with more spirit chased than enjoy'd.
> How like a younker or a prodigal
> The scarfed bark puts from her native bay,
> Hugg'd and embraced by the strumpet wind!
> How like the prodigal doth she return,
> With over-weather'd ribs and ragged sails,
> Lean, rent and beggar'd by the strumpet wind!
>
> (II. vi. 14)

We know what real relation exists between this image of the ship proudly putting out to sea and returning as a wreck, and the action of the play; for Antonio's ships are on their way, and the following act will bring the news that first one ship, then others, finally all are stranded or have been wrecked. Thus Shakespeare consciously takes advantage of this almost inconsequential and casual conversation to slip in his images. We, the audience, may take this little street-conversation of the minor characters as merely a neat and pretty incident which is shown us before the play begins. But somehow or other that vivid image of the ship upon the high seas will make us pause a moment; we will remember Antonio's ships out there on the ocean, and thus we retain a slight premonition, a trace of anxiety, as to what will happen. The unhappy ending, the threatening doom which overshadows the early acts and which colours the words and images of the characters—all this is something truly Shakespearian. *Romeo and Juliet* contains far more examples of this foreshadowing of a tragic end at the very beginning of the play. Romeo's well known

> my mind misgives
> Some consequence yet hanging in the stars   (I. iv. 107)

is only one of these passages, and, as Professor Spurgeon has shown, the images of swift-flashing and as swiftly quenched light, the quick flash of gunpowder,[1] are symbolical hints of what is to come.

In *King John* we may perceive how these ill-boding, fateful powers, already sensed by the characters before the advent of the catastrophe, take shape and come to life through the imagery. As early as the third act such a suggestive and significant image is placed in the mouth of the Bastard:

> Some airy devil hovers in the sky
> And pours down mischief.   (III. ii. 2)

"withhold thy speed, dreadful occasion!" cries the King to the inevitable course of events, and he gives expression to his feeling of the power of the catastrophe overwhelming him by means of the image of the flood-tide:

> Bear with me, cousin; for I was amazed
> Under the tide: but now I breathe again
> Aloft the flood,   (IV. ii. 137)

The words of the Bastard at the end of the fourth act, however, are the most forceful expression of this premonitory sensation of a lurking impending doom:

> and vast confusion waits,
> As doth a raven on a sick-fall'n beast,
> The imminent decay of wrested pomp,
> Now happy he whose cloak and cincture can
> Hold out this tempest.   (IV. iii. 152)

In the dramatic structure of the play, too, these images of the Bastard have an organic function: before the final act, which will bring with it the worst turn of fortune, that character who possesses a deeper and more critical insight than all the rest is qualified to view the situation, apart from the dissension of the individuals concerned, as the tragic lot of the country itself. By the agency of these images pregnant with doom, the Bastard paves the way for the events of the next act. The image of "vast confusion"

---

[1] Spurgeon, *Shakespeare's Imagery*, p. 312. Important in this dramatic respect are Juliet's verses in which she calls the new bond of love

> too rash, too unadvised, too sudden,
> Too like the lightning, which doth cease to be
> Ere one can say "it lightens".   (II. ii. 118)

and also Brother Lorenzo's famous lines in the same act: "These violent delights have violent ends . . ." (II. vi. 9).

awaiting like a raven the imminent decay is of further significance, as it shows that Shakespeare now replaces the earlier premonitory imagery, mainly based on the traditional omens, by a new type in which abstract forces are called into being. Thus, we can trace in Shakespeare's work, step by step, how Romeo's "consequence yet hanging in the stars" takes on symbolic form. In the later tragedies it will produce more complex series of premonitory imagery awakening in our imagination the presentiment of coming catastrophe.

But in yet another respect *King John* shows how the reality of the later events is prepared for by the recurrence of certain words and images. Bloodshed is one of the main themes of the play, and the whole action leads up to the great battle in the fifth act as if under some compelling force. From the very beginning, by means of various figures and phrases, this conception of bloodshed, blood-atonement, and of the blood-thirsty, revengeful boiling of one's own blood is deliberately awakened. Thus what is later to become deed, already lies in the thoughts of men, and in the form of the imagery the future is made to pervade the present. In the first scene of the second act alone, for example, blood is mentioned seventeen times and generally in very characteristic phrases;[1] it wanders from the mouth of the one into the thoughts of the other, and every mention of it breeds another image. We shall see how the art of indirectly referring to coming events and of employing imagery with dramatic irony attains its height of perfection in the tragedies.

[1] The idea of blood-shedding, of blood-spouting, of blood-spilling, is frequent (II. i. 48, 256, 334); likewise the image of wading in blood (II. i. 42, 266); swords and hands are stained with blood (II. i. 45, 322; IV. ii. 252), even the sun appears covered with blood; this is a particularly important effect of such an image-complex: "The sun's o'ercast with blood: fair day, adieu!" (III. i. 326). We find characteristic expressions, such as: "Here have we war for war and blood for blood" (I. i. 19); "Blood hath bought blood and blows have answer'd blows" (II. i. 329). When King John and King Philip face each other in angry challenge, the Bastard enthusiastically cries out:

Ha, majesty! how high thy glory towers,
When the rich blood of kings is set on fire!   (II. i. 350)

and in the next act this feeling of blood set afire finds utterance in the words of the kings themselves when they call out to each other:

JOHN: France, I am burn'd up with inflaming wrath;
A rage whose heat hath this condition,
That nothing can allay, nothing but blood,
The blood, and dearest-valued blood, of France.

PHILIP: Thy rage shall burn thee up, and thou shalt turn
To ashes, ere our blood shall quench that fire: (III. i. 340)

Part II

THE DEVELOPMENT OF IMAGERY IN SHAKESPEARE'S GREAT TRAGEDIES

INTRODUCTORY

WE cannot speak of the development of Shakespeare's imagery without keeping before us the general development of his art and mind. For the changes and the advance perceptible in his use of imagery result from this more comprehensive evolution. Some aspects of this interrelationship are to be dealt with in these introductory remarks.

The tragedies display Shakespeare's dramatic technique at its best. This means that every element of style, in fact every single line, now becomes dramatically relevant. The same applies to the imagery, the images becoming an inherent part of the dramatic structure. They become effective instruments in the hand of the dramatist. We saw how they helped him to prepare the audience for coming events. But the imagery may also emphasize and accompany the dramatic action, repeating its themes; it often even resembles a second line of action running parallel to the real plot, and providing a "counterpoint" to the events on the stage.

The function of the images to forebode and anticipate, noticeable, as was shown, in such plays as *The Merchant of Venice* and *King John*, becomes more important and more subtle in the tragedies. The imagery unobtrusively reflects coming events, it turns the imagination of the audience in a certain direction and helps to prepare the atmosphere, so that the state of expectation and feeling necessary for the full realization of the dramatic effect is reached.

The fact that imagery plays such an important part in the tragedies, indicates a fundamental change in Shakespeare's manner of presentation. In the early plays, it was his aim to make everything as obvious and plain as possible. Hence the programmatic expositions, the explanatory monologues, which acquaint us with the intentions of the characters. This direct and outspoken style is replaced in the work of the mature Shakespeare by a more subtle and indirect method. Things are suggested, intimated, hinted at; they are seldom expressly stated. And for this manner of suggestive and veiled presentation imagery is most suitable.

Ambiguity[1] plays an important rôle in this connection, as is obvious where Shakespeare makes his characters say something, the significance of which they cannot possibly grasp at the time of utterance. For what they say may have two meanings. The one meaning which the speaker has in mind refers to the momentary situation, but the other meaning may point beyond this moment to other issues of the play. Imagery may serve this purpose better than plain language and may lend itself more easily to ambiguity. An image is altogether a more complex form of statement than plain diction. Consider this passage from *Julius Caesar*:

> O setting sun,
> As in thy red rays thou dost sink to-night,
> So in his red blood Cassius' day is set;
> The sun of Rome is set! Our day is gone;
> Clouds, dews, and dangers come; our deeds are done!
> (v. iii. 61)

The increasingly complex significance of the rest of the passage develops from the simple meaning of the first words of the sentence. The sun has doubly set, for the "sun of Rome" is both the sun of that day, and Cassius himself. But the words: "Our day is gone;" have a threefold meaning: first, "Our day" is the real day, which has just passed, then again it means Cassius (in the preceding line it was said that " Cassius' day is set"), and finally, it denotes the period of life which all the persons concerned have passed through. Something new is about to begin for all of them now. The past day may also refer to the approaching end of the play itself, because the play will be at an end after two more brief scenes.

Another passage, from *Coriolanus* this time, may further illustrate this ambiguity. Menenius says to the tribunes:

[1] For ambiguity in poetry and drama cf. William Empson, *Seven Types of Ambiguity*, London, 1930.

This tiger-footed rage, when it shall find
The harm of unscann'd swiftness, will too late
Tie leaden pounds to's heels. (*Coriolanus*, III. i. 312)

The tribunes to whom these words are said, apply "tiger-footed rage" as well as "unscann'd swiftness" to Coriolanus. But, on the other hand, in harmony with the underlying thought of the play, both these epithets apply to the tribunes and to their senseless agitation against Coriolanus, which is perceived and tempered "too late". By means of this ambiguity, then, Menenius, Coriolanus' friend, is able to speak with the tribunes as if he were on their side—whereas in fact he says precisely the opposite.

This double meaning of images is also of importance for the development of the dialogue in the tragedies. In interpreting the tragedies, we must continually ask whether one character has fully understood what the other said, or whether he or she understood it in a secondary or false sense. This is of great importance for the further course of the action. Shakespeare seems to employ quite consciously this mutual misunderstanding of the characters as an instrument of dramatic technique. In his early work, to be sure, we also find misunderstandings as a result of ambiguities; but there it appears only in the form of wit and punning. Whereas Shakespeare there employs the pun, the play upon words, merely as a form of witty entertainment, an opportunity for clever repartee, he develops it in his later work to a fine instrument of characterization and a means of double interpretation of a situation. By means of the multiplicity of meanings characteristic of the pun, Shakespeare is able to let his characters understand each other in different degrees. The characters may talk with each other and really believe that they understand each other. But the true (hidden) meaning of the one is not grasped by the other. The audience, however, may well understand it. Out of this situation significant tensions grow between what the audience already knows, and what the characters on the stage are saying. Thus a play on words may become the key to what is to follow. It is no longer mere arabesque and unessential decoration, but rather a necessary, if tiny, link in the chain of the dramatic structure—for much now depends upon the comprehension of this quibble or pun at this particular moment.

Naturally, it is impossible to generalize about the motifs and themes which find expression in the imagery of the great tragedies. There are, however, some recurring and especially characteristic features which may be considered.

In the early histories, the characters turned to images when they sought to lend expression to the magnitude and intensity of their emotions, desires and aims. Marlowe's *Tamburlaine* was the model for such a use of imagery; consequently, many of those images and comparisons were too hyperbolical, too exaggerated; they were seldom appropriate expression. But in the tragedies, that appropriateness which was lacking in the early histories, is achieved. The images no longer impress us as rhetorical and pompous; they are borne by great passion and correspond to the depth and immensity of human emotion. Thus we often meet with images which are built upon gigantic conceptions. Othello would not give up Desdemona:

> If heaven would make me such another world
> Of one entire and perfect chrysolite,
> I'ld not have sold her for it.
>
> *(Othello,* v. ii. 144)

Macbeth asks if the ocean would wash his blood-stained hand clean, and replies:

> No, this my hand will rather
> The multitudinous seas incarnadine,
> Making the green one red. *(Macbeth,* ii. ii. 61)

and Hamlet taunts Laertes:

> let them throw
> Millions of acres on us, till our ground,
> Singeing his pate against the burning zone,
> Make Ossa like a wart! *(Hamlet,* v. i. 304)

It is characteristic of this gigantic conception of life that Shakespeare's tragic heroes in their imagery repeatedly express the presumptuous desire for the destruction of the whole world:

ANTONY.   Let Rome in Tiber melt, and the wide arch
           Of the ranged empire fall!   (*A. and C.*, I. i. 33)

CLEOPATRA. O sun,
           Burn the great sphere thou movest in! darkling stand
           The varying shore o' the world.
                                  (*A. and C.*, IV. xv. 10)[1]

Almost all the heroes of Shakespeare's tragedies stand
in close relationship to the cosmos, the celestial bodies and
the elements.[2] This is a characteristic feature of the tragedies,
lacking in the histories. Not only do the cosmic forces
accompany the action of the tragedies; the characters feel
themselves to be closely related to them and to the elements.
When in the histories, the people turned their eyes to the
sun, taking its dull gleam for a foreboding of evil,[3] this
was in the tradition of omen. But in the tragedies, the
characters apostrophize the sun and stars directly.

              . . . Stars, hide your fires;
         Let not light see my black and deep desires:
                                   (*Macbeth*, I. iv. 50)

Macbeth cries before his murderous deed. "Moon and
stars!" we hear Antony say,[4] and Cleopatra: "O sun, burn
the great sphere . . ."[5] The heavens seem sympathetic
to what is occurring here on earth. To Hamlet, thinking
of his mother's hasty remarriage, "heaven's face doth
glow" (III. iv. 48); and Othello, convinced of Desdemona's
faithlessness, cries out: "Heaven stops the nose at it and the
moon winks" (IV. ii. 77). Macduff says, after the bad news
has come: "New sorrows strike heaven on the face that it
resounds".[6] Sorrow reaching even up to heaven and forcing

---

[1] Further instances:
    MACBETH: But let the frame of things disjoint, both the worlds suffer,
                                            (III. ii. 16)
    OTHELLO: Methinks it should be now a huge eclipse
            Of sun and moon, and that the affrighted globe
            Should yawn at alteration.   (v. ii. 99)
    LEAR: And thou, all-shaking thunder,
            Smite flat the thick rotundity o' the world!   (III. ii. 7)
[2] Cf. Max Deutschbein, *Die Kosmischen Mächte bei Shakespeare*, Dortmund, 1947.
[3] Cf. my article "Shakespeare und das Königtum" in *Shakespeare Jahrbuch*, 1932.
[4] *Antony and Cleopatra*, III. xiii. 95.
[5] *Antony and Cleopatra*, IV. xv. 10.
[6] *Macbeth*, IV. iii. 6.

entrance there is a motif frequently expressed in the imagery. Hamlet, referring to Laertes' lament, says:

> whose phrase of sorrow
> Conjures the wandering stars, and makes them stand
> Like wonder-wounded hearers?   (v. i. 278)

In *King Lear* Kent

> bellow'd out
> As he'ld burst heaven;   (v. iii. 212)

And Lear himself cries out at the end:

> Had I your tongues and eyes, I'ld use them so
> That heaven's vault should crack.   (v. iii. 258)

Moreover, in the dramatic structure of the individual tragedies the appeal to the elements makes its appearance at definite turning-points. Not until they begin to despair of men and earth do the tragic heroes turn to the heavens. When their firmest beliefs have been shaken, when they stand alone and forsaken, they renounce the earth and call upon the cosmic powers.

It is by means of the imagery that all the wealth of nature enters into the plays. Apart from *Midsummer Night's Dream* and *The Tempest*, the tragedies are the plays richest in nature-atmosphere. The world of animals and plants, the scenery itself are evoked by the imagery; they lend the play not only background and atmosphere, but also a vital connection with earthly existence, scarcely to be found in the work of any other dramatist. The word "atmosphere" is not, however, sufficient to denote the importance of the rôle of this varied nature-imagery. For nature, the animals and plants, are players, as it were; they are forces in the organism of the play and hence not dissociable. Goethe noted this "cooperation" of nature and the elements: "Even the inanimate world takes part; all the subordinate things have their rôle, the elements, the phenomena of the heavens, the earth and the sea, thunder and lightning" (*Shakespeare und kein Ende*).

Man and nature stand in a continuous relationship in the tragedies, and the imagery serves to emphasize this kinship. In many cases it would be inappropriate to say that the characters "use nature-imagery". For nature, like the cosmos, is often like a character on the stage to whom one appeals; it is then no longer a "tertium comparationis".

There was indeed a certain relationship between the characters and the world of nature in *Romeo and Juliet.* But to perceive the difference, let us compare Juliet's call to night, "Come, civil night, thou sober-suited matron" (III. ii. 10 sqq.) with Macbeth's appeal:

> Come, seeling night,
> Scarf up the tender eye of pitiful day;
> And with thy bloody and invisible hand
> Cancel and tear to pieces that great bond
> Which keeps me pale! Light thickens; and the crow
> Makes wing to the rooky wood:
> Good things of day begin to droop and drowse;
> Whiles night's black agents to their preys do rouse.
> (III. ii. 46)

In Juliet's monologue the night is still personified in traditional manner: *sober-suited matron*, *gentle*, *civil*. In contrast to this, Macbeth's *seeling night* is something entirely different. *Seeling* does not denote a quality of a person, as do the epithets *gentle* or *civil*. In the monologue from *Romeo and Juliet* the relationship of the person to the night is expressly stated, whereas in *Macbeth* it is merely suggested. In the lines which follow the actual apostrophe, Macbeth utters much of what he sees—but he leaves its significance unexplained. What Macbeth perceives in the world about him pertains to himself as well. The twilight—*light thickens*—is at the same time the twilight of his own soul. The *bloody hand* of the night recalls his own blood-stained hand; and from the word *invisible* we may gather the wish to make his own hand equally invisible. The good things of the outer world which "begin to droop and drowse" represent a like change in him, and, finally, *night's black agents*, turning to their prey, are equivalent to his own desires bent upon their victim.[1] Thus Macbeth in his description of nature reveals his own inner state of mind. Every feature of this picture is true of himself and his designs.

[1] Cf. William Empson, *Seven Types of Ambiguity*, London, 1930, p. 23.

A comparison of two other passages may show how differently Shakespeare now employs nature-imagery. The first passage is from the Second Part of *Henry VI*, the other is from *Othello*; the motif of both passages is the sea with its dangerous rocks, sparing man out of sympathy. In *Henry VI* the Queen relates to the King:

> The pretty-vaulting sea refused to drown me,
> Knowing that thou would'st have me drown'd on shore,
> With tears as salt as sea, through thy unkindness:
> The splitting rocks cower'd in the sinking sands
> And would not dash me with their ragged sides,
> Because thy flinty heart, more hard than they,
> Might in thy palace perish Margaret.
>
> *(B Henry VI*, iii. ii. 94)

In *Othello* Cassio tells the story of Desdemona's miraculous rescue after the stormy voyage:

> Tempests themselves, high seas and howling winds,
> The gutter'd rocks and congregated sands,—
> Traitors ensteep'd to clog the guiltless keel,—
> As having sense of beauty, do omit
> Their mortal natures, letting go safely by
> The divine Desdemona.   (ii. i. 68)

The diction in the passage from *Othello*, with its unusual and suggestive epithets and metaphors, is finer than in the lines from *Henry VI*. But the difference in the attitude towards nature is far more important. In the first case we have to deal with a "conceit" artfully constructed upon antithesis and parallelism. The sympathetic sea, the splitting rocks are very consciously inserted into the long speech of the Queen as a means of contrast. In *Othello*, however, the sea-imagery grows immediately out of the experience of the voyage. In the words of the other characters of this scene, too, we can feel the sea air. In the whole play the sea has an important rôle—as scene, background, and as Othello's own vital element.

Shakespeare's art of personification, of endowing abstract realities with the breath of life, undergoes a noteworthy development in the tragedies. The personifications, such as we often meet with in *King John*, for example,[1] are still patterned after the medieval type of personification. They derive from the allegorical world of the Middle Ages, from the time when all abstract qualities were thought of as human figures having certain attributes. In his later work, Shakespeare frees himself more and more from this tradition of the Middle Ages, although it was still living on in his own day in allegorical interludes and pageants. Those abstract images, behind which a visible human figure stands, become fewer and fewer. Shakespeare's manner of personifying becomes freer and bolder. He creates images of astonishing peculiarity and incomparable originality. At the same time the range of abstractions expressed by imagery becomes wider. These abstractions play an important part in the tragedies. Just as man now stands in closer connection with nature and the cosmos, so, too, he appears in relationship to certain forces determining and guiding his very existence. Be they called fate, doom, time or metaphysical powers, these occult forces have a hand in every tragedy; man appears to be surrounded by them. Their vivid reality often becomes perceptible in the imagery. Hence we must seriously consider the images which represent these abstract realities. It is not only that these images tell us what Shakespeare himself thought about certain subjects. Their appearance at a certain point in a play has a deep significance. Thus, for example, the frequent time-images in *Troilus and Cressida* reveal that in this play, Shakespeare wanted to show the changing and dissolving effect of the passing of time. Or again, in *Antony and Cleopatra*, the repeated appearance of fortune-images reflects the rôle fortune plays in determining the action.

In the tragedies—more than in all the other plays—the imagery expresses the mutual relationship of the forces at work in human nature. Ideas such as honour, judgement, conscience, will, blood, reason, etc., frequently appear in metaphorical guise. Whoever undertakes to investigate Shakespeare's conception of the human character will be amazed to find how many of the passages with the mutual relationship of spiritual and mental qualities as their

[1] Cf. Spurgeon, *Shakespeare's Imagery*, p. 246.

subject, appear in metaphorical language, or employ imagery.

This kind of imagery should warn us not to apply modern conceptions of human character to Shakespeare's plays; it gives us hints as to how Shakespeare conceived of mental processes and conflicting qualities of character.[1] For it is certainly not true that Shakespeare consciously "translated" into the language of imagery what he had to say about human qualities and dispositions (for the sake of a more poetic mode of expression, for example). On the contrary, imagery is an integral component of the thought; it discloses to us the particular aspect under which Shakespeare viewed these things. Imagery here is a form of imaging and conceiving things. "Metaphor becomes almost a mode of apprehension", says Mr. Middleton Murry.[2]

A passage from *Macbeth* may show us clearly in what new manner Shakespeare now visualizes abstractions and human characteristics.

Macbeth (speaking of Duncan):

> that his virtues
> Will plead like angels, trumpet-tongued, against
> The deep damnation of his taking-off;
> And pity, like a naked new-born babe,
> Striding the blast, or heaven's cherubim, horsed
> Upon the sightless couriers of the air,
> Shall blow the horrid deed in every eye,
> That tears shall drown the wind. I have no spur
> To prick the sides of my intent, but only
> Vaulting ambition, which o'erleaps itself
> And falls on the other.   (i. vii. 19)

This is very different from the gorgeousness of Spenser's allegories; it is bolder, mightier and more dynamic, and rather recalls the passionate sublimity of Milton. "Pity, like a naked new-born babe, striding the blast" may illustrate how far Shakespeare has moved from the conventional type of personification, and how his imagery tends towards the strange and unique. It is notable, too, that these abstractions are now placed in enormous space,

---

[1] For the background of Renaissance theory of humours cf. John W. Draper, *The Humors and Shakespeare's Characters*, Durham, N.C., 1945.
[2] *The Problem of Style*, 1923, p. 13.

transferred to a world of clouds and winds, of boundless distance. "That tears shall drown the wind" is hyperbolical, recalling Elizabeth's phrase in *Richard III*: "That I . . . may send forth plenteous tears to drown the world" (II. ii. 70). But whereas this phrase was a rhetorical exaggeration in the manner of Marlowe, "That tears shall drown the wind" grows organically from the whole comprehensive image which is based on gigantic dimensions. Furthermore, Macbeth's whole world is determined by these tremendous and strange powers which find expression in several such images. The last lines betray the intricacy and boldness of Shakespeare's fully developed art of metaphorical association technique. The image of the rider, touched upon in "heaven's cherubim, horsed upon the sightless couriers of the air" is picked up again in prick and spur, and is thus again used in another connection. Intent is conceived of as a horse, and vaulting ambition again as "rider". Thus an image, once set afire, as it were, seizes upon everything still to be said and creates bold and most extraordinary conceptions, like "vaulting ambition".[1]

This harmony between the given situation and the whole atmosphere of the play may also be traced in the imagery by which Shakespeare characterizes his men and women. A passage from *Julius Caesar* may serve as an example. In the third scene the conspirators meet in the streets of Rome at night during a terrific thunderstorm. By means of the imagery, the night and the thunderstorm are made very vivid, being also a suitable background for the dark conspiracy. The mood and situation naturally suggest the likening of Caesar to this fearful night.

> CASSIUS. Now could I, Casca, name to thee a man
> Most like this dreadful night,
> That thunders, lightens, opens graves, and roars
> As doth the lion in the Capitol,   (I. iii. 72)

The image fulfils two functions at one and the same time, it characterizes Caesar, and adds to the nocturnal

---

[1] Professor Spurgeon interprets this image as follows: "and finally, the vision of his 'intent', his aim, as a horse lacking sufficient spur to action, which melts into the picture of his ambition as a rider vaulting into the saddle with such energy that it 'o'erleaps itself', and falls on the further side" (*Shakespeare's Imagery*, p. 334).

thunderstorm atmosphere. That imagery thus serves a double purpose, is a characteristic of the tragedies.

This development does not necessarily imply that certain stylistic patterns of imagery which were characteristic of the early plays, now no longer appear. But if they are now used, they mean something different; they are purposely inserted to characterize the moment and the person concerned; they are employed at precisely this point with a dramatic intent. This may be illustrated by an example from *Troilus and Cressida*. On the occasion of his first undisturbed meeting with Cressida, Troilus avers the trueness of his love—later "swains in love", he says, will measure the fidelity of their love by Troilus:

> when their rhymes,
> Full of protest, of oath and big compare,
> Want similes, truth tired with iteration,
> As true as steel, as plantage to the moon,
> As sun to day, as turtle to her mate,
> As iron to adamant, as earth to the centre,
> Yet, after all comparisons of truth,
> As truth's authentic author to be cited,
> "As true as Troilus" shall crown up the verse,
> And sanctify the numbers.   (III. ii. 181)

This sequence of pretty comparisons is continued by Cressida in the same manner. It is as if we had before us two courtly lovers from the early comedies, where such agglomeration of clever comparisons was the fashion. But these two passages have their special dramatic significance within the framework of the whole play. Before the course of the play brings the tragic termination of their love, Shakespeare shows the two lovers in a mood of lyric ardour which stands in greatest contrast to the sceptical coolness and the bitter disillusionment of the following scenes. In order to enhance this effect, and to emphasize the unsuspecting, unconcerned and almost playful mood of the lovers, Shakespeare lets both speak here in a style which recalls the imagery of the early comedies. "The illusion must convince before it is pricked and shown to be a bubble", says Sir Edmund Chambers, referring to this passage.[1]

[1] *Shakespeare, A Survey*, p. 194.

In a previous chapter on the early plays, we spoke of Shakespeare's habit of embellishing certain general themes appearing in the conversation with metaphorical epithets and definitions. The resulting imagery was undramatic; it was rhetorical decoration and no integral part of the dramatic structure. But let us examine the famous words of Macbeth on sleep:

> Methought I heard a voice cry "Sleep no more!
> Macbeth does murder sleep", the innocent sleep,.
> Sleep that knits up the ravell'd sleave of care,
> The death of each day's life, sore labour's bath,
> Balm of hurt minds, great nature's second course,
> Chief nourisher in life's feast,— (II. ii. 35)

Viewed from the outside, this series of metaphorical expressions for sleep is in no way different from the earlier type. Nevertheless, we scarcely need to say that the imagery of this passage is of the greatest dramatic suitability. For sleep is in this case no "theme of conversation", but a dramatic issue of first importance. That Macbeth has murdered Duncan while asleep is what is especially fearful in his deed. The wrong has been done, as it were, not only to Duncan, but also to the sacred nature of sleep. And "wronged sleep" rises in the conscience of the murderer like a real power. The rich imagery therefore is no digression. It is no burst of fine-sounding words and names, no interruption of the action. It is a vital, throbbing expression of what is taking place at this moment in Macbeth's soul. Macbeth perceives again and again what he has done with a strange clarity, and expresses this in imagery (cf. I. vii. 19). *Sleep* runs like a key-word throughout the whole play and is the occasion of many metaphors of which the above passage is the climax.

A comparison of this passage with the words of the sleepless King Henry IV appealing to sleep, may show how Shakespeare's power of metaphorical expression has in the meantime grown in depth and concentration.

> O sleep, O gentle sleep,
> Nature's soft nurse, how have I frighted thee,
> That thou no more wilt weigh my eyelids down
> And steep my senses in forgetfulness?

8

Why rather, sleep, liest thou in smoky cribs,
Upon uneasy pallets stretching thee
And hush'd with buzzing night-flies to thy slumber,
Than in the perfumed chambers of the great,
Under the canopies of costly state,
And lull'd with sound of sweetest melody?
O thou dull god, why liest thou with the vile
In loathsome beds, and leavest the kingly couch
A watch-case or a common 'larum-bell?
                                    (*B Henry IV*, iii. i. 6)

In the earlier play, the King reviews in almost epic contemplation the effect of sleep among the different levels
and classes of his subjects (the rich, the poor, the sailors on
the high seas and himself), but here in *Macbeth*, instead of
a concrete picture executed in twenty-six lines (of which
only the first half was quoted here), we have compressed
into four lines a summary of the fundamental, timeless,
eternally valid attributes of sleep.

The most important standard, accordingly, whereby to
judge the imagery of the tragedies, is the degree of harmony
existing between the image and the dramatic situation
producing it. It may be that the dramatic situation admits
of a richer expansion of the imagery; on the other hand,
the speed of the play, or of the scene, may not permit the
development of the whole image, so that as a result, the
image merely flashes up for a moment. This latter case is
more frequent than the former, because the insertion of a
wholly executed image would mean retarding and interrupting the rapid progress of the dramatic action. Shakespeare
must bring in the image without making more words of it.
"Shakespeare smuggles in the images" we might say of
many passages of the tragedies in which the image is only
touched upon and hinted at. In *Troilus and Cressida* Ulysses
says of Achilles:

                    the seeded pride
        That hath to this maturity blown up
        In rank Achilles must or now be cropp'd,
        Or, shedding, breed a nursery of like evil,
        To overbulk us all.   (i. iii. 316)

This passage may serve as an example of how Shakespeare
merely lets his diction take on the *colour* of the image in

mind, the image being implicit, no longer expressly uttered. "Macbeth is ripe for shaking" says Malcolm at the end of the fourth act (IV. iii. 238), quite aware of the way things will end. This image, too, is suggestive, awakening the notion of the ripe fruit which must be shaken from the tree. At an earlier stage Shakespeare would have given us the whole image. Thus in *Richard II*, we read:

> The ripest fruit first falls, and so doth he;
> His time is spent,   (II. i. 153)

or in the *Merchant of Venice*:

> The weakest kind of fruit
> Drops earliest to the ground; and so let me:
>   (IV. i. 115)

Thus the development towards dramatic imagery is a development towards condensation and suggestiveness. Shakespeare compresses into one short sentence an astonishing wealth of associations. No matter what he is writing, he is always accompanied by pictorial conceptions and associations. No longer is there purposeful "hunting" for suitable images, as in the early plays; the matter of which he wishes to speak has already appeared to him in a metaphorical form. If we see or read a tragedy for the first time, we scarcely notice to what unbelievable degree imagery is employed. This is in part due to the fact that much of it belongs to the type of the merely suggested, implied and concealed imagery that has unobtrusively melted into the language. But it is also because the imagery is so wholly adapted to the situation and the emotion of the speaker, that we fail to feel anything unusual in it. Mr. Middleton Murry, discussing the poetic and dramatic value of the conceit, quotes a passage from *Antony and Cleopatra* (IV. ix. 15–18) and notes how little we are disturbed by this difficult and extravagant language; on the contrary, how much we are moved by it. He writes convincingly: "The dramatic intensity of the situation in which they [the words] are spoken is such that it seems to absorb the violence of the imagery, without need to modify the image itself. The conceit becomes the natural extravagance of a depth of

emotion that would also go unuttered.''[1] Shakespeare's
use of the single metaphor calling forth a more comprehensive image has become much bolder in the tragedies in
comparison with the plays discussed in previous chapters.
A few examples only may be quoted. Coriolanus says:

> I mean to stride your steed, and at all times
> To undercrest your good addition
> To the fairness of my power. (i. ix. 71)

Coriolanus is here expressing his thanks for the charger
which has been presented to him. By undercrest Shakespeare
makes Coriolanus say that he will wear this present as
proudly as an embellishment of a helmet. A single metaphor
suffices for what we needs must explain in many words.
Hamlet bids Horatio:

> Observe mine uncle: if his occulted guilt
> Do not itself unkennel in one speech, (iii. ii. 85)

By association occulted leads to unkennel, and thus a whole
picture is lit up in our imagination. But ordinary words,
too, if employed in a new and figurative sense, may have a
surprising freshness. When Gloucester gives Edmund the
order to sound Edgar, he simply says: "wind me into him",
a phrase which with its vigorous simplicity remains unforgettable. By such unusual metaphors the audience are
more startled than by an ordinary phrase which may pass
unnoticed. We "prick up our ears" at such passages, the
picture fastens on our imagination and we are less likely to
skip such a line.

A study of the imagery in Shakespeare's tragedies helps
us to appreciate them as an organism in which all the parts
are interrelated and mutually attuned. Each tragedy has its
own unmistakable individual nature, its own colour; it has
its own landscape, its own atmosphere, its own diction.
All details are closely connected, as in a finely meshed web;
they are mutually dependent and point ahead or hark
back. It is amazing to observe what part the imagery plays
in helping to make the dramatic texture coherent as well
as intricate. The same motif which was touched upon in the

---

[1] Shakespeare, p. 273.

first act through the imagery, is taken up again in the
second; it undergoes a fuller execution and expansion,
perhaps, in the third or fourth. As Professor Spurgeon has
demonstrated, these *leitmotifs* of the imagery run through
the play like a brightly coloured thread. Of *Macbeth* it
has been noted with acumen that Shakespeare substitutes
the unity of atmosphere for the dramatic unities of time and
action.[1] This is true of many of the Shakespearian tragedies.
This unity of atmosphere and mood is no less a "dramatic
unity" than the classical dramatic unities. And the imagery
of a tragedy plays an important part, not only in creating a
dramatic unity of the atmosphere, but also in binding the
separate elements of the play together into a real organic
structure.

[1] Max Deutschbein, *Macbeth als Drama des Barock*, Leipzig, 1936.

HAMLET

THE surprisingly new possibilities of language which make this play appear a turning-point in the development of Shakespeare's style[1] seem to have their origin in the personality of Hamlet. The new language comes from him, in him it attains to perfection. The language of the King and the Queen, of Laertes and Polonius, although subtly adapted to their character, still treads the well-worn paths; it is less novel, because the people by whom it is spoken are not in need of a new form of expression—on the contrary, they may be more aptly characterized by a conventional mode of speech. But Hamlet's nature can only find expression in a wholly new language. This also applies to the imagery in the play. It is Hamlet who creates the most significant images, images marking the atmosphere and theme of the play, which are paler and less pregnant in the speech of the other characters. Hamlet's way of employing images is unique in Shakespeare's drama. When he begins to speak, the images fairly stream to him without the slightest effort—not as similes or conscious paraphrases, but as immediate and spontaneous visions.[2] Hamlet's imagery shows us that whenever he thinks and speaks, he is at the same time a visionary, a seer, for whom the living things of the world about him embody and symbolize thought. His first monologue may show this; the short space of time which lies between his father's death and his

---

[1] On the style in *Hamlet* see L. L. Schücking, *The Meaning of Hamlet*, London, 1937, I. i. and I. iv.

[2] The spontaneous and unpremeditated character of Hamlet's imagery will become obvious through a comparison with Claudius' language. Claudius' speeches are studied and give the impression of having been previously prepared. His images often are consciously inserted. Dr. Schmetz notes that while Claudius often uses comparisons, linking object and image by "as" or "like", Hamlet's imagination fuses both into a metaphor (cf. IV. i. 40–44, IV. v. 94–96 with III. 83–84, III. 407–408). Further examples for Claudius' comparisons: III. iii. 41; IV. vii. 15; IV. xx. 88. This is, of course, only one aspect of the manifold differences between Claudius' and Hamlet's language. The whole problem has been exhaustively dealt with in Dr. Schmetz's study. For the difference between the imagery of Claudius' public and that of his private language, and for further distinguishing features in Claudius' imagery see Una Ellis-Fermor, *The Frontiers of Drama*, London, 1945, p. 88.

mother's remarriage is to him a series of pictures taken from
real life:

> A little month, or ere those shoes were old
> With which she follow'd my poor father's body,
> Like Niobe, all tears: (I. ii. 147)

> Ere yet the salt of most unrighteous tears
> Had left the flushing in her galled eyes, (I. ii. 154)

or a little later, addressed to Horatio:

> the funeral baked meats
> Did coldly furnish forth the marriage tables. (I. ii. 180)

These are no poetic similes, but keen observations of reality.
Hamlet does not translate the general thought into an
image paraphrasing it; on the contrary, he uses the opposite
method: he refers the generalization to the events and
objects of the reality underlying the thought. This sense of
reality finds expression in all the images Hamlet employs.
Peculiar to them all is that closeness to reality which is
often carried to the point of an unsparing poignancy.[1]
They are mostly very concrete and precise, simple and, as
to their subject matter, easy to understand; common and
ordinary things, things familiar to the man in the street
dominate, rather than lofty, strange or rare objects.[2]
Illuminating in this connection is the absence of hyperbole,[3]
of great dimensions in his imagery. In contrast to Othello
or Lear, for example, who awaken heaven and the elements
in their imagery[4] and who lend expression to their mighty

[1] This, as Dr. Schmetz notes, gives to Hamlet's language sometimes a brutal violence
that expresses itself in the use of forceful metaphors: "For I mine eyes will rivet to his face"
(III. ii. 90), "Let me wring your heart" (III. iv. 35).

[2] After completion of the manuscript, the author became acquainted with Professor
Mikhail M. Morozow's article, "The Individualization of Shakespeare's Characters through
Imagery" (*Shakespeare Survey, II*, Cambridge, 1949, pp. 83–106). Professor Morozow's
more systematic and comprehensive examination of the content of all of Hamlet's images
can throw new light on the statements made above and adds a number of acute observations,
which have a bearing on the theory put forward in this chapter. Morozow also emphasizes
the realistic, common and popular nature of Hamlet's imagery, his faculty to "see right
through people" and his closeness to the common people which does not exclude his scholarship and humanist education.

[3] If he makes use of hyperbole in v. i. 304 (at Ophelia's grave) it is to parody Laertes'
hyperbolic diction.

[4] Hamlet, too, invokes God and the heavenly powers, but these invocations never take
the form of grandiose images, they are mostly brief and often restricted to mere references
(cf. I. ii. 132, 150, 195; I. v. 92; I. iv. 85; v. ii. 343, 355).

passions in images of soaring magnificence, Hamlet prefers
to keep his language within the scope of reality, indeed,
within the everyday world. It is not spacious scenery and
nature which dominate in Hamlet's imagery, but rather
trades and callings, objects of daily use, popular games and
technical terms; his images are not beautiful, poetic,
magnificent, but they always hit their mark, the matter in
question, with surprisingly unerring sureness. They do not
waft the things of reality into a dream-world of the imagination; on the contrary, they make them truly *real*, they
reveal their inmost, naked being. All this, the wealth of
realistic observation, of real objects, of associations taken
from everyday life, is enough to prove that Hamlet is no
abstract thinker and dreamer. As his imagery betrays to us,
he is rather a man gifted with greater powers of observation
than the others. He is capable of scanning reality with a
keener eye and of penetrating the veil of semblance even
to the very core of things. "I know not seems."

At the same time, Hamlet's imagery reveals the hero's
wide educational background, his many-sidedness and the
extraordinary range of his experience.[1] That metaphors
taken from natural sciences are specially frequent in
Hamlet's language again emphasizes his power of observation, his critical objective way of looking at things.[2] But
Hamlet is also at home in classical antiquity or Greek
mythology,[3] in the terminology of law,[4] he is not only
familiar with the theatre and with acting—as everyone
knows—but also with the fine arts,[5] with falconry and
hunting,[6] with the soldier's trade and strategy,[7] with the
courtier's way of life. All these spheres disclosing Hamlet's
personality as that of a "courtier, soldier and scholar"
(in Ophelia's words, III. i. 159) are evoked by the imagery
which, however, turns them to living account by a fit
application to situations, persons and moods. Hamlet

---

[1] For the following cf. Dr. Schmetz's study and Professor Morozow's article.
[2] Cf. III. i. 119; I. v. 22, 27, 29; III. iv. 147. For the disease-imagery see below.
[3] E.g. I. ii. 140, 149, 153; III. ii. 89, 294; III. iii. 56–58; v. i. 306, 315.
[4] v. i. 107 sqq.
[5] E.g. his images taken from musical instruments, III. ii. 75.
[6] II. ii. 397; III. ii. 361; II. ii. 458.
[7] Hamlet speaks of the "pales and forts of reason" (I. iv. 28), wonders whether his mother's
heart is "proof and bulwark against sense" (III. iv. 37; cf. III. iv. 208).

commands so many levels of expression that he can attune his diction as well as his imagery to the situation and to the person to whom he is speaking. This adaptability and versatility is another feature in Hamlet's use of language which can also be traced in his imagery.

At the same time, this wide range of imagery can, in certain passages, serve to give relief to his conflicting moods, to his being torn between extremes and to the abruptness of his changes of mood. This characteristic which has been particularly emphasized and partly attributed to "melancholy" by L. L. Schücking and John Dover Wilson,[1] also expresses itself in the sudden change of language and in the juxtaposition of passages which are sharply contrasted in their diction. With no other character in Shakespeare do we find this sharp contrast between images marked by a pensive mood and those which unsparingly use vulgar words and display a frivolous and sarcastic disgust for the world.[2]

Let us consider further how Hamlet's use of imagery reflects his ability to penetrate to the real nature of men and things and his relentless breaking down of the barriers raised by hypocrisy. Many of his images seem in fact designed to unmask men; they are meant to strip them of their fine appearances and to show them up in their true nature. Thus, by means of the simile of fortune's pipe, Hamlet shows Rosencrantz and Guildenstern that he has seen through their intent, and thus he unmasks Rosencrantz when he calls him a "sponge", "that soaks up the king's countenance" (IV. ii. 16). He splits his mother's heart "in twain", because he tells her the truth from which she shrinks and which she conceals from herself. And again it is by means of images that he seeks to lead her to a recognition of the truth. He renews the memory of his father in

---

[1] Cf. L. L. Schücking, *The Meaning of Hamlet*, London, 1937. Hamlet edition (English-German), Leipzig, 1941. J. D. Wilson, *What Happens in Hamlet*, Cambridge, 1935.

[2] There are many instances for these contrasts in Hamlet's language. Cf. the transition from the famous monologue in III. i. 56 to his conversation with Ophelia in the same scene (a parallel change in III. ii.) or cf. IV. iii. 22; v. i. 230 sqq. Dr. Schmetz notes the following instances of Hamlet's use of vulgar words: "truepenny" (I. v. 150); "old mole" (I. v. 161); "drab" (II. ii. 623); "carrion" (II. ii. 184); "Jowls it to the ground" (v. i. 82); "Knocked about the mazard" (v. i. 95). For further instances of Hamlet's use of coarse and common images see Morozow's article, *loc. cit.*, p. 95.

110 THE GREAT TRAGEDIES

her by means of that forceful description of his outward appearance which could be compared with Hyperion, Mars and Mercury. On the other hand, another series of comparisons seeks to bring home to his mother the real nature of Claudius:

> a mildew'd ear,
> Blasting his wholesome brother.   (III. iv. 64)

> a vice of kings;
> A cutpurse of the empire and the rule,
> That from a shelf the precious diadem stole,
> And put it in his pocket!

> .   .   .   .   .

> A king of shreds and patches,   (III. iv. 98)

So Hamlet sees through men and things. He perceives what is false, visualizing his recognition through imagery.

Hamlet's imagery, which thus calls things by their right names, acquires a peculiar freedom from his feigned madness. Hamlet needs images for his "antic disposition". He would betray himself if he used open, direct language. Hence he must speak ambiguously and cloak his real meaning under quibbles and puns,[1] images and parables. The other characters do not understand him and continue to think he is mad, but the audience can gain an insight into the true situation. Under the protection of that mask of "antic disposition", Hamlet says more shrewd things than all the rest of the courtiers together.[2] So we find the images here in an entirely new rôle, unique in Shakespeare's drama. Only the images of the fool in *King Lear* have a similar function.

Hamlet suffers an injustice when he is accused of merely theoretical and abstract speculation which would lead him away from reality. His thoughts carry further than those of

[1] Through John Dover Wilson's edition of *Hamlet* (Cambridge, 1934) many of these puns and quibbles which so far had remained unintelligible (or were falsely understood) have been cleared up. On the importance of quibbles in *Hamlet* see John Dover Wilson's Introduction, p. xxxiii. sqq.

[2] Edward Dowden noted this: "Madness possesses exquisite immunities and privileges. From the safe vantage of unintelligibility he can delight himself by uttering his whole mind and sending forth his words among the words of others, with their meaning disguised, as he himself must be, clothed in an antic garb of parable, dark sayings which speak the truth in a mystery" (*Shakespeare, His Mind and Art*, 1877, p. 145). Cf., too, John Dover Wilson's Introduction to *Hamlet*, p. xl.

others, because he sees more and deeper than they, not
because he would leave reality unheeded. It is true that his
is a nature more prone to thought than to action; but that
signifies by no means, as the Hamlet critics would often
have us believe, that he is a philosopher and dreamer and
no man of the world. When, in the graveyard scene, he
holds Yorick's skull in his hand, he sees *more* in it than the
others, for whom the skull is merely a lifeless object. And
precisely because he is more deeply moved by the reality
and significance of these earthly remains, his fantasy is
able to follow the "noble dust of Alexander" through all
its metamorphoses. The comparisons which spring from
this faculty of thinking a thing to the end, as it were, derive
in fact from a more intense experience of reality.

It is a fundamental tenet of Hamlet criticism that
Hamlet's over-developed intellect makes it impossible for
him to act. In this connection the following famous passage
is generally quoted:

> And thus the native hue of resolution
> Is sicklied o'er with the pale cast of thought,
> And enterprises of great pith and moment
> With this regard their currents turn awry,
> And lose the name of action.—   (III. i. 85)

The customary interpretation of this passage, "reflection
hinders action", does it an injustice. For Hamlet does not
say "reflection hinders action", he simply utters this image.
The fact that he does not utter that general maxim, but this
image, makes all the difference. For this image is the unique
and specific form of expression of the thought underlying
it, it cannot be separated from it. If we say "reflection
hinders action", we make a false generalization; we replace
a specific formulation by an apothegm. And thereby we
eradicate in this passage that quality which is peculiarly
Shakespeare's or, what is more, peculiarly Hamlet's. Here
the image does not serve the purpose of merely casting a
decorative cloak about the thought; it is much rather an
intrinsic part of the thought.

"Reflection hinders action"—this phrase carries in it
something absolute, something damning. We sense a

moralizing undertone. Action and reflection are thus conceived of as two mutually inimical abstract principles. But not so in Shakespeare's metaphorical language. "Native hue of resolution" suggests that Shakespeare viewed resolution as an innate human quality, not as a moral virtue to be consciously striven after. But the Hamlet-criticism of the nineteenth century saw the problem in this light of a moral virtue. We see, then, that a careful consideration of Shakespeare's imagery may sometimes correct false interpretations.[1]

"Reflection hinders action." Polonius, the sententious lover of maxims, could have said this, for a general saying carries no sense of personal obligation; it places a distance between the speaker and what he would say. But just as it is characteristic of Polonius to utter banalities and sententious effusions,[2] so, too, it is characteristic of Hamlet, to express even those things which would have permitted of a generalizing formulation, in a language which bears the stamp of a unique and personal experience.

Hamlet sees this problem under the aspect of a process of the human organism.[3] The original bright colouring of the skin is concealed by an ailment. Thus the relation between thought and action appears not as an opposition between two abstract principles between which a free choice is possible, but as an unavoidable condition of human nature. The image of the leprous ailment emphasizes the malignant, disabling, slowly disintegrating nature of the process. It is by no mere chance that Hamlet employs just this image. Perusing the description which the ghost of Hamlet's father gives of his poisoning by Claudius (I. v. 63) one cannot help being struck by the vividness with which the process of poisoning, the malicious spreading of the disease, is portrayed:

[1] Cf. Spurgeon, *Shakespeare's Imagery*, pp. 318–319.

[2] Cf. Edward Dowden: "his wisdom is not the outflow of a rich or deep nature, but the little, accumulated hoard of a long and superficial experience. This is what the sententious manner signifies" (*Shakespeare, His Mind and Art*, p. 142). Professor John W. Draper, reviewing the divergent interpretations of Polonius' character, gives him a far more favourable treatment and considers him "not far removed from the Elizabethan ideal of what a courtier, what a father, what a 'Worthie Priuie Counceller' should be" (*The Hamlet of Shakespeare's Audience*, Durham, 1938, p. 53).

[3] For the contemporary scientific background of the disease-imagery in *Hamlet* see John W. Draper, *The Humors and Shakespeare's Characters*, Durham, N.C., 1945.

> And in the porches of my ears did pour
> The leperous distilment; whose effect
> Holds such an enmity with blood of man
> That swift as quicksilver it courses through
> The natural gates and alleys of the body,
> And with a sudden vigour it doth posset
> And curd, like eager droppings into milk,
> The thin and wholesome blood: so did it mine;
> And a most instant tetter bark'd about,
> Most lazar-like, with vile and loathsome crust,
> All my smooth body.   (I. v. 63)

A real event described at the beginning of the drama has exercised a profound influence upon the whole imagery of the play. What is later metaphor, is here still reality. The picture of the leprous skin disease, which is here—in the first act—described by Hamlet's father, has buried itself deep in Hamlet's imagination and continues to lead its subterranean existence, as it were, until it reappears in metaphorical form.

As Miss Spurgeon has shown, the idea of an ulcer dominates the imagery, infecting and fatally eating away the whole body; on every occasion repulsive images of sickness make their appearance.[1] It is certain that this imagery is derived from that one real event. Hamlet's father describes in that passage how the poison invades the body during sleep and how the healthy organism is destroyed from within, not having a chance to defend itself against attack. But this now becomes the *leitmotif* of the imagery: the individual occurrence is expanded into a symbol for the central problem of the play. The corruption of land and people throughout Denmark is understood as an imperceptible and irresistible process of poisoning. And, furthermore, this poisoning reappears as a *leitmotif* in the action as well—as a poisoning in the "dumb-show", and finally, as the poisoning of all the major characters in the last act. Thus imagery and action continually play into each other's hands and we see how the term "dramatic imagery" gains a new significance.

The imagery appears to be influenced by yet another event in the action underlying the play: Hamlet feels

---

[1] Spurgeon, *Shakespeare's Imagery*, p. 316 sqq.

himself to be sullied by his mother's incest which, according to the conception of the time, she committed in marrying Claudius. For him this is a poisoning idea which finds expression in his language. Professor Dover Wilson has defended the reading of the Second Quarto with convincing arguments:[1]

> O, that this too too sullied flesh would melt,
> Thaw and resolve itself into a dew!   (i. ii. 129)

It is therefore probable that this idea is present in Hamlet's mind at many moments when images of decay and rot appear in his language.

The *leitmotif* occasionally appears in a disguised form at a point where it seems to have no real connection with the main issue of the play, for instance, in the following passage:

> So, oft it chances in particular men,
> That for some vicious mole of nature in them,
> As, in their birth—wherein they are not guilty
> Since nature cannot choose his origin—
> By the o'ergrowth of some complexion,
> Oft breaking down the pales and forts of reason,
> Or by some habit, that too much o'er-leavens
> The form of plausive manners, that these men,
> Carrying, I say, the stamp of one defect,
> Being nature's livery, or fortune's star,
> Their virtues else—be they as pure as grace,
> As infinite as man may undergo—
> Shall in the general censure take corruption
> From that particular fault: the dram of eale
> Doth all the noble substance of a doubt
> To his own scandal.   (i. iv. 23)

Hamlet has spoken of the excessive revels and drinking-bouts among his people and has said that this was disparaging to the Danes in the eyes of the other peoples. Then

---

[1] Cf. the note on this passage on p. 151 of John Dover Wilson's edition of *Hamlet* (Cambridge, 1934): " 'Sullied flesh' is the key to the soliloquy and tells us that Hamlet is thinking of the 'kindless' incestuous marriage as a personal defilement. Further, 'sullied' fits the immediate context as 'solid' does not. There is something absurd in associating 'solid flesh' with 'melt' and 'thaw'; whereas Shakespeare always uses 'sully' or 'sullied' elsewhere (cf. *Henry IV*, ii. iv. 84; *Winter's Tale*, i. ii. 326) with the image, implicit or explicit, of dirt upon a surface of pure white; and the surface Hamlet obviously has in mind here is snow, symbolical of the nature he shares with his mother, once pure but now befouled."

follows this general reflection. The question arises: why does Hamlet speak in such detail of these matters here? For at this point in the play he has as yet heard nothing of his uncle's murderous deed. And still he touches in this speech upon that *leitmotif* of the whole play; he describes how human nature may be brought to decay through a tiny birth-mark, just as from one "dram of evil"[1] a destructive effect may spread over the whole organism. *O'er-leavens* already points to *sicklied o'er*, and, as in the passage discussed, the notion of the human body is in the background. As in later passages, the balance of the powers in man is the theme here, and "corruption", a basic motif in the whole play, already makes its appearance. This general reflection on gradual and irresistible infection is made in passing, as it were. Thus Shakespeare makes use of every opportunity to suggest the fundamental theme of the play. When the King says to Laertes in the fourth act:

> There lives within the very flame of love
> A kind of wick or snuff that will abate it;

the same motif occurs again: corruption through a "dram of evil".

The following passage, too, from Laertes' words of warning to his sister, has never been examined for its value as "dramatic presaging".

> The canker galls the infants of the spring,
> Too oft before their buttons be disclosed,
> And in the morn and liquid dew of youth
> Contagious blastments are most imminent. (I. iii. 39)

It is no mere chance that this sententious little image,[2] which is so neatly woven in and so conventional, touches upon a motif later to be worked out more clearly. The worm in the bud, like ulcer and eruption, is also an irresistible force destroying the organism from within. Light is cast upon this early passage when, in the last act, it is said of

---

[1] The emendation *evil* has been accepted by several editors, e.g. by John Dover Wilson in the *New Shakespeare* edition.

[2] Dr. Schmetz points out that this use of sententious diction betrays a certain immaturity in Laertes, just as his apostrophes at the sight of the mad Ophelia in IV. v. 155 reveal a hollow pathos, or as his hyperboles at Ophelia's grave impress us as theatrical bombast (v. i. 274).

Claudius: "this canker of our nature" (v. ii. 69). But here
we still know nothing of the coming developments. The
image is a faint warning, preparing the way, together with
other hints, for the future.

The Pyrrhus episode[1] which the first Player recites
before Hamlet contains features which are also of importance for the theme of the play. For here it is related of
Pyrrhus with vigorous emphasis how "Aroused vengeance
sets him new a-work" (ii. ii. 510). For Hamlet it must be
a gentle warning that vengeance calls forth so bloody a deed
in another without delay. On the other hand, the previous
lines described Pyrrhus as being in suspense, unable to act,
"neutral to his will" as Hamlet still is:

> So, as a painted tyrant, Pyrrhus stood,
> And like a neutral to his will and matter,
> Did nothing.   (ii. ii. 502)

The mention of "strumpet Fortune" and the picture of her
broken wheel rolled "down the hill of heaven" at the end of
this passage, is likewise a hint; in the third act this image
of the wheel plunging down from the height, reappears in
the conversation between Rosencrantz and the King:

> The cease of majesty
> Dies not alone; but, like a gulf, doth draw
> What's near it with it: it is a massy wheel,
> Fix'd on the summit of the highest mount,
> To whose huge spokes ten thousand lesser things
> Are mortised and adjoin'd; which, when it falls,
> Each small annexment, petty consequence,
> Attends the boisterous ruin.   (iii. iii. 15)

Through these images, which are also spun out from a more
general reflection, the coming catastrophe is already
significantly foreshadowed.

The imagery in Shakespeare's tragedies often shows
how a number of other images are grouped around the
central symbol which express the same idea, but in quite
other terms. Several degrees, as it were, of the metaphorical
expression of a fundamental idea may be distinguished.

---

[1] A new and important interpretation of the "Player's Speech" is given by Harry Levin,
"An Explication of the Player's Speech", *The Kenyon Review*, XII, 2, 1950.

Besides images which express a motif with the greatest clarity and emphasis, we find others which utter the thought in a veiled and indirect manner. An examination of the way in which the images are spread over the play, can reveal how subtly Shakespeare modifies and varies according to character and situation.

The most striking images of sickness, which Miss Spurgeon has already listed, make their first appearance, significantly enough, in the second half of the play, and most notably in the scene in which Hamlet seeks to bring his mother to a change of heart. Here the plainness and clarity of the images is meant to awaken the conscience of the Queen; they can scarcely be forceful enough; "let me wring your heart", Hamlet has said at the beginning of the meeting. In the first part of the play the atmosphere of corruption and decay is spread in a more indirect and general way. Hamlet declares in the first and second acts how the world appears to him:

> . . . Ah fie! 'tis an unweeded garden,
> That grows to seed; things rank and gross in nature
> Possess it merely.   (I. ii. 135)

> . . . and indeed it goes so heavily with my disposition that this goodly frame, the earth, seems to me a sterile promontory, this most excellent canopy, the air, look you, this brave o'erhanging firmament, this majestical roof fretted with golden fire, why, it appears no other thing to me than a foul and pestilent congregation of vapours.   (II. ii. 309)

The image of weeds, touched upon in the word "unweeded", is related to the imagery of sickness in Shakespeare's work. It appears three times in *Hamlet*. The ghost says to Hamlet:

> And duller shouldst thou be than the fat weed
> That roots itself in ease on Lethe wharf,   (I. v. 32)

In the dialogue with his mother, this image immediately follows upon the image of the ulcer:

> And do not spread the compost on the weeds,
> To make them ranker,   (III. iv. 151)

9

Images of rot, decay and corruption are especially numerous in the long second scene of the second act. There are, for example, Hamlet's remarks on the maggots which the sun breeds in a dead dog (ii. ii. 181), on the deep dungeons in the prison Denmark (ii. ii. 249), on the strumpet Fortune (ii. ii. 240), who reappears in the speech of the first Player (ii. ii. 515), his comparison of himself with a whore, a drab and a scullion (ii. ii. 614).

Seen individually, such images do not seem to be very important. But in their totality they contribute considerably to the tone of the play.

OTHELLO

IN this chapter we shall try to show Shakespeare's art of adapting imagery to the character using it, so that imagery becomes a means of characterizing the dramatis personae. *Othello* furnishes a particularly good example for a study of this kind, in that it turns upon the relation between two opposite and contrasted characters, Iago and Othello.

The growing connection between imagery and character is a particularly important aspect of the process by which the images become more closely related to the drama. It is part of the more comprehensive development, traceable throughout Shakespeare, whereby each character is eventually given his own language.[1] In the early comedies, as we have seen, the language used by the characters is suited to the atmosphere of the play, but does not grow directly out of their own individual nature. We only find, here and there, an adaptation of the language to the various groups of characters: servants speak a language different from that of courtiers, etc. In Shakespeare's "middle period" we discover the beginning of a more subtle differentiation. But this differentiation is as yet restricted to certain outstanding types such as Falstaff and Parolles, the Nurse and Shylock, Mrs. Quickly and Doll Tearsheet. Furthermore it is modified, as in *Romeo and Juliet* or in the *Merchant of Venice*, by Shakespeare's tendency to give to whole scenes a certain stylistic pattern which often overrides the consistent individualization of single characters through language. The individualization of characters through language in the above-mentioned cases, moreover, mostly consists in the regular and recurrent use of certain obvious features of style and syntax, easy to comprehend and usually few in number. Compared to later plays, Shakespeare uses

[1] Tolstoy's assertion that all characters in a Shakespearian play speak the same language was refuted by L. L. Schücking, *Character Problems in Shakespeare*, London, 1922. For a full treatment of Shakespeare's art of adapting language to character see Dr. Lotte Schmetz, *Sprache und Charakter bei Shakespeare*, Munich thesis, 1949.

in general rather simple devices and does not avail himself of all the resources offered by language and style for differentiation. A more subtle and complex characterization through language and imagery could be seen in *Richard II*. Here, however, it was only the dominant figure of the king who was thus individualized. In the great tragedies we find Shakespeare's technique of characterizing his persons through imagery fully developed. In *Hamlet*, each character was given his own mode of speech, and from *Hamlet* to *Antony and Cleopatra* this discrimination of language applies to all tragedies until, in the romances, we find a notable modification of this technique—indeed, to a certain extent, a decline.

There are several ways of studying imagery as a revelation of character. One is to consider the subject matter of the images, and to ask whether the objects and themes occurring in the imagery stand in a significant relation to the character of the person using the image. Another method of approach is to inquire into the form in which the images appear, and to ask whether the syntax, the context and similar factors might give us a hint of the nature of that relationship. It may also be illuminating to examine the frequency or recurrence of images in the speech of the several persons and the occasion on which they use imagery. The investigation of whether a character adjusts his imagery to his partner in the dialogue may also yield revealing results. Finally, the question whether the imagery of a character runs on the same lines up to the end of the play or undergoes a noticeable change in the course of the drama, may throw some light upon the function of the imagery in indicating a spiritual change in the character.

Othello and Iago have entirely different attitudes towards their images. Iago is consciously looking for those which best suit his purpose. With Othello, however, the images rise naturally out of his emotions. They come to him easily and unconsciously whenever he is talking. He is a character endowed with a rich imagination; it is part of his very nature to use imagery. Iago, on the contrary, is not a person with an imaginative mind; his attitude towards the world is rational and speculative. We find fewer images in his language than in Othello's. When he is alone, he uses scarcely any imagery, a fact which proves that the use of imagery is not natural to him, but rather a conscious and studied device by which he wishes to influence those to whom he is speaking. Iago selects his images with deliberate intent, he "constructs" them in the very same manner as he constructs his whole language. It is not without significance that Iago introduces many of his images with *as* and *like*, which we rarely find in Othello's language. The particles *as* and *like* show that the speaker is fully conscious of the act of comparing; the comparison is added to the object to be compared as something special. In metaphorical language, however, both elements melt into one; the object itself appears as an image, as a metaphor. This differentiation should not be carried too far, but in this case the preference for comparisons is suited to Iago's conscious and studied manner of speech. Furthermore, Iago's images scarcely ever refer to himself, whereas Othello in his images continually has himself in mind. Iago likes the form of general statement; he places a distance between himself and his images. He does not care to identify himself with what he says; he would rather have his utterances understood as being as objective, neutral and general as possible. In Othello's language, however, the personal pronoun *I* is predominant; he is almost always talking of himself, his life and his feelings. And thus his imagery serves also to express his own emotions and his own nature. This becomes increasingly clear from the very beginning: for instance, in the third scene of the first act, when Othello relates his life to the Duke; in ii. i., deeply moved at seeing Desdemona again when he cries out, "O my soul's joy!" and finds that magnificent image (quoted on p. 123); when he compares his own thoughts to the "Pontic sea" (iii. iii. 453); when, finally, he speaks of his love for Desdemona and of his disillusionment in terms of immeasurable passion (ii. ii.). In these cases, as in others, with the innocence and frankness characteristic of strong natures who live within themselves, he always takes *himself* as the point of departure.

In contrast to this, Iago seeks to achieve an effect upon the other characters with his similes and images. He measures his words with calculating guile, attuning them to the person he has to deal with. Consider, for instance, the images which he employs with Roderigo and Cassio in I. iii. or II. i. from this point of view; we find that they are devised to kindle in the brain of the other man a notion that will further his own plans; they are a means of influencing, or they may also be a means of dissimulation. The whole diction then appears attuned to the mood and sphere of the other character.[1] Iago seeks to poison the others with his images; he aims to implant in the minds of his victims a *conceit* which will gradually assume gigantic proportions.

The fact that Iago speaks so much in prose is likewise characteristic of him. Let us look at his imagery in the following passages:

If the balance of our lives had not one scale of reason to poise another of sensuality, the blood and baseness of our natures would conduct us to most preposterous conclusions: but we have reason to cool our raging motions, our carnal stings, our unbitted lusts, whereof I take this that you call love to be a sect or scion.   (I. iii. 330)

the food that to him now is as luscious as locusts, shall be to him shortly as bitter as coloquintida.   (I. iii. 354)

you are but now cast in his mood, a punishment more in policy than in malice; even so as one would beat his offenceless dog to affright an imperious lion: (II. iii. 274)

Shakespeare lets Iago clothe his comparisons here in euphuistic style. This shows how conventional stylistic patterns are employed in the tragedies as a means of individual characterization. For precisely this euphuistic style, with its combination of antithesis, consonance and parallelism, corresponds to the cool, and at the same time hypocritical nature of Iago. It would be wholly foreign to

---

[1] Thus, in speaking to Roderigo, Iago assumes, as Dr. Schmetz has observed, the bombastic euphuistic diction, abounding in latinisms which is characteristic of Roderigo himself (I. iii. 312, 374; II. 262 sqq., 288; IV. ii. 175 sqq.). When, however, he addresses Montano, he switches over from prose to verse, using high-sounding metaphors and terms taken from astronomy ("'Tis to his virtue a just equinox", II. iii. 129; "horologe", II. iii. 136). The only time Iago apostrophizes solemnly the heavenly lights and elements is also in a dissembling, imitating manner by which he wants to adjust himself to Othello's preceding vow "by yond marble heaven" (III. iii. 463–467).

the spontaneous and unconscious Othello to force imagery into such an artificial mould of parallelisms and symmetrically constructed periods. The euphuistic pattern of style presupposes that the sentences are carefully prepared, and that they are balanced one against the other, *before* their utterance. The euphuistic style is an intellectual, hyperconscious child of the brain, combining skilful ingenuity with calculation. All these elements are typical of Iago himself.

The difference between Othello's and Iago's imagery —like everything else in Shakespeare—cannot be reduced to a simple formula. But of all the contradistinctions which might at least give us a hint of this difference, that existing between the concept of the static and of the dynamic comes closest to the real heart of the matter. Iago's images are static, because they are incapable of further inner growth, because the objects appear in a dry and lifeless manner, because—as in those euphuistic passages we have spoken of—a narrow pattern of stylistic construction hinders the further development of the image. The prosaic brevity of Iago's images stands in contrast with the swelling opulence and poetic force of Othello's imagery. This is Iago's way of speaking:

IAGO.   but indeed my invention
          Comes from my pate as birdlime does from frize;
                              (II. i. 126)

          He'll be as full of quarrel and offence
          As my young mistress's dog.   (II. iii. 52)

     ∜   Our bodies are our gardens, to the which our
          wills are gardeners;   (I. iii. 323)

And this is Othello's language:

OTHELLO.   O my soul's joy!
          If after every tempest comes such calms,
          May the winds blow till they have waken'd death!
                              (II. i. 187)

          And let the labouring bark climb hills of seas
          Olympus-high and duck again as low
          As hell's from heaven!   (II. i. 189)

> Like to the Pontic sea,
> Whose icy current and compulsive course
> Ne'er feels retiring ebb, but keeps due on
> To the Propontic and the Hellespont,
> Even so my bloody thoughts, with violent pace,
> Shall ne'er look back, ne'er ebb to humble love,
> Till that a capable and wide revenge
> Swallow them up.   (III. iii. 453)

Iago would be wholly incapable of the moving poetic language uttered by Othello; and, likewise, Othello could never be the author of Iago's cold and cynical utterances. In Othello's imagery everything is in movement, because everything springs from his own emotion. His images always appear at crucial points of his inner experience; the forcefulness and agitation of his images is an expression of his own passionate nature. Iago, on the other hand, stands not in an emotional, but in a rational relationship to his images.

✗   Through the imagery Othello's emotional nature is revealed to us as highly sensuous, easily kindled and interpreting everything through the senses. Othello's metaphors show us this peculiar activity of all his senses, his tendency to *sense* all abstract matters as palpable, tastable, audible and visible things.[1] He can only think, even of his retaliation, in terms of extraordinary physical pain:

> Blow me about in winds! roast me in sulphur!
> Wash me in steep-down gulfs of liquid fire!
>   (v. ii. 279)

---

[1] Cf. Dr. Schmetz *op. cit.* Dr. Schmetz quotes the following instances:

> or, at the least, so prove it,
> That the probation bear no hinge nor loop
> To hang a doubt on;   (III. iii. 365

> no, my heart is turned to stone; I strike it, and
> it hurts my hand.   (IV. i. 192)

> Had it pleased heaven
> To try me with affliction; had they rain'd
> All kinds of sores and shames on my bare head,
> Steep'd me in poverty to the very lips,   (IV. ii. 47)

> O thou weed,
> Who art so lovely fair and smell'st so sweet
> That the sense aches at thee,   (IV. ii. 67)

This last passage may also once again reveal the heightened
poetical nature of Othello's imagery,[1] his preference for
bright, colourful, intense pictures.[2] This feature can, of
course, be also related to Othello's race, and these images
thus link up with another group of metaphors, to be
discussed later, which reproduce the peculiar colour and
atmosphere of Othello's sphere of life.

A closer examination of the content of Othello's and
Iago's imagery reveals further characteristic differences.
The objects named by Iago belong to a lower and purely
material world, whereas the things alive in Othello's
imagination generally belong to a higher sphere. Iago's
imagery teems with repulsive animals of a low order;[3]
with references to eating and drinking and bodily functions[4]
and with technical and commercial terms. In Othello's
language, however, the elements prevail—the heavens, the
celestial bodies, the wind and the sea—the forces of nature,
everything light and moving that corresponds best to his
nature. At moments of intense emotion his imagery links
heaven and hell together, bearing out his inner relation to
the cosmic powers, and revealing the enormous dimensions
and power of his imaginative conceptions.[5] Hyperbole is
therefore more often found in Othello's imagery than in
that used by other Shakespearian heroes. Othello's already
quoted welcoming words to Desdemona in Act II may again
serve as an example for the breadth of his imaginative world:[6]

> And let the labouring bark climb hills of seas
> Olympus-high, and duck again as low
> As hell's from heaven!   (II. i. 189)

---

[1] In his article on "The Individualization of Shakespeare's Characters through Imagery"
(*Shakespeare Survey*, II, 1949) Professor Mikhail M. Morozow sees the characteristic feature
of Othello's imagery in its being *lofty* and *poetic*. He illustrates by a number of well-chosen
examples, how Othello instead of using the common or usual expressions, always chooses
lofty, poetic or solemn imagery.

[2] Dr. Schmetz notes in this connection the wealth of sensuous colourful epithets in
Othello's language: "flinty and steel couch of war" (I. iii. 231); "bright swords" (I. ii. 59);
"sweet body" (III. iii. 347); "balmy slumbers" (II. iii. 260); "balmy breath" (v. ii. 16); "liquid
fire" (v. ii. 279); "burning hell" (v. ii. 127); "marble heaven" (III. iii. 461).

[3] Iago refers to asses, cats, spiders, flies, dogs, goats, monkeys, wolves, these creatures
occurring mostly in obscene, low, guileful connection or activity.

[4] E.g. " . . . you are eaten up with passion" (III. iii. 391) or "her delicate tenderness
will find itself abused, begin to heave the gorge, disrelish and abhor the Moor;" (II. i. 235).

[5] See Introductory chapter, p. 92 seq.

[6] For further examples of this kind of imagery see below, p. 131.

But the contrast between Othello's and Iago's imagery will perhaps become most clear by comparing how differently the same theme is expressed in the language of each. Miss Spurgeon has already pointed out how differently the sea appears in Othello's and Iago's speech. Iago employs technical maritime terms, and colours some of his images with sailor's jargon. But the sea as a whole does not appear in his imagery. He looks at the sea only from a professional point of view. He is at home on the sea, but only in a practical way.[1]

In Othello's imagination, on the other hand, the sea lives in its whole breadth and adventurous power. In his language it appears as a force of nature and as scenery. Again and again it occurs to Othello for the expression of his inner emotions through vivid, connected images.

We may compare, too, the different ways in which Othello and Iago speak of war and martial life. Iago speaks of the "trade of war" (i. ii. 1) whereas Othello thinks of the "Pride, pomp and circumstance of glorious war" (iii. iii. 354). The life of a soldier is for Iago not an ideal, but a sort of business, in which everything is weighed according to material advantage and recompense. This mercenary attitude betrays itself when he introduces expressions taken from the language of commerce, as in the following passage:

> And I, of whom his eyes had seen the proof
> At Rhodes, at Cyprus and on other grounds
> Christian and heathen, must be be-lee'd and calm'd
> By debitor and creditor.   (i. i. 28)

Othello's conception of war is worlds apart. He won Desdemona with the simple telling of his adventures and brave deeds as a soldier:

> Of moving accidents by flood and field,
> Of hair-breadth scapes i' the imminent deadly breach,
>   (i. iii. 135)

and when, at the climax of the action, he loses his inner balance, it is the life of the soldier, it is war, which appears

---

[1] Cf. Spurgeon, p. 337: " . . . complaining that Othello had passed him over for Cassio, he describes himself as 'be-lee'd and calm'd', he knows the state has not another of Othello's 'fathom'; he says he must 'show out a flag and sign of love'; that Brabantio will take action against Othello to whatever extent the law 'will give him cable' . . .", etc.

in his mind. In moving words he takes leave of his beloved
element:

> Farewell the plumed troop, and the big wars,
> That make ambition virtue! O, farewell!
> Farewell the neighing steed, and the shrill trump,
> The spirit-stirring drum, the ear-piercing fife,
> The royal banner, and all quality,
> Pride, pomp and circumstance of glorious war!
>
> (III. iii. 349)

Thus in *Othello* the imagery has the function of making
visible to us the contrasting life-sphere and background of
the chief characters. In the tragedies Shakespeare treads
new paths in order to bring home to us the nature of a
character. The sources from which our conception of a
character in the drama was formed and fed, were, apart
from the action of the play, the character's behaviour in
different situations and the words, through which he
informs us of his plans, thoughts and feelings, and finally
how the other characters react to him and what they say
of him. These means of characterization naturally remain
effective up to the last plays. But in the great tragedies
Shakespeare creates with a greater fullness and differentiation the atmosphere typical of each central character.
Othello brings with him the magic spell of distant lands and
exotic things; his language is tinged with the lustre and
strangeness of this other world out of which he comes.
Shakespeare will have him understood from the very
beginning as the "wheeling and extravagant stranger" (as
Roderigo terms Othello in the first scene, I. i. 137). Already
Othello's first long speech before the Venetian Senate is
suffused with such touches. In the dramatic structure, this
speech not only gives us the immediate proof of Othello's
innocence, but it also presents us with a colourful picture
of the world of Othello's origin. Othello tells of "Cannibals"
and "Anthropophagi" and of

> antres[1] vast and deserts idle,
> Rough quarries, rocks and hills whose heads touch heaven,
>
> (I. iii. 140)

---

[1] Dr. Schmetz notes that Othello uses rare and strange words: "antres" for "caves",
"agnize" for "confess" (I. iii. 232); he speaks of "Ottomites" (I. iii. 235; II. iii. 173), where
the others simply say "Turk".

in his images we hear further of the "Pontic sea", of the "Propontic", "Hellespont", Ottomites, of Sibyls and strange myths, of a "sword of Spain", the "icebrooks' temper" (v. ii. 253), and of "Arabian trees" (v. ii. 351).[1]

Iago, too, betrays his nature in his language, and this not only when he sets forth his base plans and intentions, or when he tries to entangle and to deceive the other characters. Even those words which at first glance seem to have no bearing upon the immediate issue, can reveal his personality to us. We need only examine what Iago thinks about other people, about love and general human values, in order to know what kind of man he is. If he is thinking of love, the image of rutting animals always makes its appearance in his imagination (I. i. 89; I. i. 112; III. iii. 403).[2] He drags all higher values down to his low level. Whereas Othello characteristically never discusses general human values, Iago delights in defining them in a derogatory way. Love—according to his definition—is only "a sect, or scion" of "our carnal stings, our unbitted lusts" (I. iii. 336). "Virtue! a fig!" he cries, shortly before (I. iii. 322), "honesty's a fool and loses what it works for" (III. iii. 382), and "Reputation is an idle and most false imposition", we read in another passage (II. iii. 268).

Iago betrays to us his own cunning method towards his victims in two characteristic images. He views his action against Othello, Desdemona and Cassio as an ensnaring with the net and as a poisoning:

> . . . with as little a web as this will I
> ensnare as great a fly as Cassio . . .   (II. i. 169)

> And out of her own goodness make the net
> That shall enmesh them all.   (II. iii. 368)

This image is echoed in Othello's desperate question at the end of his life: "Why he hath thus ensnared my soul and body?" (v. ii. 302). The idea of poisoning is quite conscious in Iago, when he seeks to awaken that false suspicion in Othello:

[1] For a full list of passages of this kind see G. Wilson Knight, *The Wheel of Fire*, London, 1949, p. 100.
[2] Iago is so obsessed by sexual images that they creep into his speech even when there is nothing of the kind at stake. Cf. I. iii. 377; II. i. 128; II. iii. 180.

I'll pour this pestilence into his ear,
That she repeals him for her body's lust;
(II. iii. 362)

The Moor already changes with my poison:
Dangerous conceits are, in their natures, poisons,
Which at first are scarce found to distaste,
But with a little act upon the blood
Burn like the mines of sulphur.   (III. iii. 325)

Almost everything Iago says—not only his imagery—is
marked by this conscious and purposeful quality. Iago
always adapts himself to his partner in conversation, he
uses his language as a chief means of influence and ensnare-
ment. He is no stranger in this life, like Othello, but is
indeed well informed about the abilities and the behaviour
of men of the most various states and classes. This already
becomes clear in the first sixty-five lines. Here he contrasts
types of men and characterizes them with biting comparisons:

You shall mark
Many a duteous and knee-crooking knave,
That, doting on his own obsequious bondage,
Wears out his time, much like his master's ass,
For nought but provender, and when he's old, cashier'd:
(I. i. 44)

Such passages show how much he is accustomed to observe
others and how he goes through life with critical and open
eyes. In fact, the best and most appropriate judgement of
Othello is uttered by him:

The Moor is of a free and open nature,
(I. iii. 405)

The Moor, howbeit that I endure him not,
Is of a constant, loving, noble nature, (II. i. 297)

It is precisely this very "open nature" which is revealed
in Othello's imagery and causes it to differ so decidedly
from Iago's imagery. Othello does not measure his imagery
by the effect which it is to have upon others; he speaks
what is in his heart. Iago, on the other hand, speaks as it
seems expedient to him. Othello's images can therefore be

looked upon as a genuine self-revelation, and we quote again the famous passage from the third act:

> Like to the Pontic sea,
> Whose icy current and compulsive course
> Ne'er feels retiring ebb, but keeps due on
> To the Propontic and the Hellespont,
> Even so my bloody thoughts, with violent pace,
> Shall ne'er look back, ne'er ebb to humble love,
> Till that a capable and wide revenge
> Swallow them up.   (III. iii. 453)

This image appears at the critical turning-point of the play: Iago has supplied him with the evidence of the handkerchief, Othello's suspicion is now hardened. The image is a marvel of language in this scene; at the same time, it is premonitory, casting light upon the following, often hardly comprehensible events. Here, in a simile, the tempestuousness and absolute nature of Othello's character finds clear expression, a nature, which, when once seized by a real suspicion, rushes violently along this new path, incapable of every half-heartedness, of a return, or of any compromise. To this absoluteness of his character Othello gives metaphorical expression once again in a later passage, when he faces Desdemona in the hour of final decision. The images by which he here reveals to us the fundamental law of his nature no longer have anything in common with "poetic diction"; no language other than the language of imagery could express what is moving Othello at this moment in terms more poignant, more forceful or more convincing.

> But there, where I have garner'd up my heart,
> Where either I must live, or bear no life;
> The fountain from the which my current runs,
> Or else dries up; to be discarded thence!
> Or keep it as a cistern for foul toads
> To knot and gender in! Turn thy complexion there,
> Patience, thou young and rose-lipp'd cherubim,—
> Ay, there, look grim as hell!   (IV. ii. 58)

The repulsive image of the "cistern for foul toads" is followed by the magnificent vision of "Patience, thou young and rose-lipp'd cherubim"—this bold sequence symbolizes the tremendous tension in Othello's soul and points to the abrupt change which is taking place within him.

It is indeed imagery which announces and accompanies the change that is taking place in Othello. In the third act Othello suffers the first great shock to his feeling of security and—like all of Shakespeare's tragic heroes in such moments—he, too, now calls upon the heavenly powers. He swears "by yond marble heaven" (iii. iii. 460) and exclaims:

> Arise, black vengeance, from thy hollow cell!
> (iii. iii. 446)

From this point on the heavens, the stars and the elements appear again and again in his language. He calls upon all the elements as witnesses and accusers of Desdemona's supposed unfaithfulness:

> Heaven stops the nose at it and the moon winks,
> The bawdy wind that kisses all it meets
> Is hush'd within the hollow mine of earth,
> And will not hear it.   (iv. ii. 77)

It is not merely chance that in the final scene (v. ii.) the words *heaven* and *heavenly* occur seventeen times and that this scene is particularly rich in mighty adjurations of heaven. Himself near the beyond, Othello's imagination seems to be spellbound with the idea of heaven:

> Methinks it should be now a huge eclipse
> Of sun and moon, and that the affrighted globe,
> Should yawn at alteration.   (v. ii. 99)

> If heaven would make me such another world
> Of one entire and perfect chrysolite,
> I'ld not have sold her for it.   (v. ii. 144)

> . . . Are there no stones in heaven
> But what serve for the thunder?   (v. ii. 234)

> when we shall meet at compt,
> This look of thine will hurl my soul from heaven,
> And fiends will snatch at it.   (v. ii. 273)

It is furthermore characteristic of the way in which the imagery portrays Othello's inner alteration, that from that third scene of the third act on, Othello's fantasy is filled with images of repulsive animals such as were up to that point peculiar to Iago.[1] Iago's endeavour to undermine and poison Othello's imagination by his own gloomy and low conceptions has been successful.

Thus an examination of the imagery in Othello has been able to reveal the connection existing between the image-motif and the time of its appearance.

[1] "Toad" (III. iii. 270); "aspics' tongues" (III. iii. 449); "the raven o'er the infectious house" (IV. i. 21); "goats and monkeys" (IV. i. 274); "cistern for foul toads" (IV.ii. 61); "summer flies are in the shambles" (IV. ii. 66). Both Dr. Schmetz and Professor Morozow emphasize that after the famous words "Chaos is come again" (III. iii. 92), "Iago gains the ascendancy over Othello's soul, so that the latter begins to think in Iago's images, to see the world with Iago's eyes" as Professor Morozow puts it. Dr. Schmetz has convincingly shown how Iago's disintegrating influence over Othello expresses itself also in various other features of style.

14

KING LEAR

AN attempt to interpret a Shakespearian play solely on the basis of its imagery—a risky undertaking—would have the greatest chance of success if *King Lear* were the play in question. The imagery here seems to be more fully integrated into the structure of the drama and for that reason to play a more meaningful rôle than in other plays. Not only do the various sequences of imagery offer important clues to what Shakespeare sought to represent in *King Lear*, but the distribution of the images among the characters, their interrelation and their significance for the illumination of certain themes and trends of the action also help us to a better insight into the meaning of the drama. In *King Lear*, action and imagery appear to be particularly closely dependent upon each other and are reciprocally illuminating; the imagery, in fact, seems to have taken over some functions which so far—in Shakespeare's earlier plays—belonged to other mediums of dramatic expression. In the development of Shakespeare's imagery, *King Lear* therefore represents an important new stage. The present chapter tries to investigate only some of these new aspects. To explore it fully would demand a study of greater length than the scope of the present book allows.[1]

At the very first glance we perceive that the form of most of the images and their connection with the context differ from those in the earlier plays. Formerly, the images

[1] After completing this chapter the present writer became acquainted with the book by R. B. Heilmann, *This Great Stage, Image and Structure in King Lear*, Louisiana State University Press, 1948. This book, so far the most outstanding full-length study of the imagery in a single Shakespearian play, is of great importance and interest for our own investigation. Heilmann's book can throw light on several points made in this chapter, in that it develops and examines more comprehensively some of the ideas upon which we here have merely touched. On the other hand, the present writer's view and approach differ in several important respects from that put forward by R. B. Heilmann, so that it was not thought necessary to cancel or rewrite this chapter in spite of certain similarities the two studies may offer. Whereas Heilmann's chief concern is with "patterns" or "areas" of meaning created by recurrent and interrelated imagery, which, in his view, embody "a good deal of what the drama has to say", the present writer's aim has been to examine the different functions, the distribution and the form of imagery as well as its cooperation with the other elements of dramatic art.

were used as illustrations, or the metaphorical element was fused with the train of thought as a means of enhancement or elucidation. In *King Lear* we can seldom speak of such an illustrative function. The image is presented as if it existed for its own sake; it serves no other aim but to speak for itself alone. Let us look at Lear's speeches in III. ii. or in IV. vi. from this point of view: he sets image after image as independent, direct visions. The same thing holds true of the fool. Up to now, we have found characters speaking exclusively in imagery only in moments of the greatest excitement. In *King Lear*, however, this is the case throughout many scenes; imagery is for Lear his most characteristic form of utterance.

The reason for this becomes clear if we trace Lear's development during the early scenes. The first shows us Lear still in possession of his power; he is still a member of society. He makes decisions, gives orders and makes plans, addresses the other characters of this scene, his daughters, Kent, France, etc. But the very first scene gives us a hint of how Lear is going to lose contact with this natural relation to his environment. The dialogue which he carries on with his daughters is at bottom no true dialogue, that is, a dialogue based on a mutual will to mutual understanding. Lear determines in advance the answers he will receive; he fails to adapt himself to the person with whom he is speaking. Hence his complete and almost incomprehensible misunderstanding of Cordelia. Lear takes no pains to understand what Cordelia is really trying to say; he does not consider whether her words could not have quite another meaning. He catches up only their superficial form and, because he had expected another answer, different from this, he repels the one person who in reality is nearest and dearest to him. More and more Lear loses contact with the outside world; words become for him less a means of communication with others than a means of expressing what goes on within himself. His utterances, even when addressed to other persons, take on, increasingly, the character of a monologue and become less and less part of the dramatic dialogue, although Lear (which is typical) never speaks an actual monologue himself.

The wealth of images in his speech results from this process and gives it expression; we have seen that in Shakespeare, the monologue is always the form of utterance richest in imagery. Lear gazes within himself; he no longer sees people nor what goes on about him. In madness a man is alone with himself; he speaks more to his own person than to others; where he does not speak to himself, he creates for himself a new and imaginary partner. Lear speaks to people not present, he speaks to the elements, to nature, to the heavens. Men have forsaken him; so he turns to the non-human, superhuman powers. It is one of the functions of the imagery in *King Lear* to awaken these elemental forces and to open to them the way into the play.

The characters around Lear, too, the Fool, Edgar and Kent, speak a language rich in imagery. We shall discuss later the significance of the image in their utterances. If we glance, however, at the other group of characters, Edmund, Goneril, Regan, Cornwall, we note how seldom they employ images, how different is their whole language. In contrast to Lear and his followers, we never find that peculiar form of "monologic dialogue" between them. They speak rationally; they address their words to their partner, and converse in a deliberate and conscious manner. They have a goal which they seek to attain and everything they have to say is bent upon this. Their language does not betray to us what is taking place within them—in the form of "imaginative visions"; it reveals to us solely their aims and attitudes, and how they intend to put these into practice. Thus their language scarcely changes throughout the course of the play, whereas Lear's, Edgar's and Kent's way of speaking is constantly varied. Goneril, Regan and Edmund are the calculating,[1] cool and unimaginative people who are incapable of "creative" imagery. They have no relationship to nature, to the elemental powers. Their world

---

[1] Gundolf notes that Goneril, while expressing her feelings towards her father, uses the terminology of "possession and calculation". She asserts her love in terms of "negative measurements" (I. i. 61) (Fr. Gundolf, *Shakespeare, Sein Wesen und Werk*, Berlin, 1928, vol. II, p. 235). Dr. Schmetz (*op. cit.*) notes the frequent occurrence of quantitative and mercantile terms as well as the use of calculating comparatives in the language of the two sisters (cf. "disquantity", "remainder", "want", "need", "scanted", "prize", "use", "business", "safe and politic", "expense and waste of his revenues" (I. i. 72, 281–282; I. iv. 272–273, 348, 353; II. i. 102; II. ii. 121–130; II. iv. 241, 264, 266)).

is the world of reason; they live and speak within the narrow
limits of their plans, within the limits drawn by the plot and
the given moment of the action. Lear's language continually
points beyond these limits. Thus the distribution of the
images among the characters also gives us a hint as to their
position within the play.

The middle acts of the tragedy, Acts II.–IV., are the
richest in imagery. The outer action is less important here
and is relegated to the background. The main emphasis
does not fall upon the outer course of events, upon what
Regan or Goneril are planning, or what Edmund is about,
but rather upon what is passing in Lear himself.[1] The outer
drama has become an inner drama. Beneath the surface of
the plot lies the deeper level of inner experience which
gradually frees itself more and more from the sparse events
of the action. The latter becomes a frame and an occasion
in order that the former may take on living reality. In truth,
Shakespeare has not treated this outer action with the same
thoroughness and care as he usually employed in the construction of the plot. As Bradley has already pointed out,[2]
the plot displays a number of inconsistencies and is not
carried out clearly. Goethe found the action of *Lear* full of
improbabilities, and "absurd". But Shakespeare was concerned not with the "outer", but with the "inner" drama.
The important thing is not what Lear does, but what he
suffers, feels and envisions with his inner eye. One of the
greatest and deepest truths of this play is that we must
first go through suffering before we can recognize our real
selves and the truth. "I stumbled when I saw", Gloucester
cries out (IV. i.); he first learned to see, when he was blind.
Thus Lear, too, sees through the world of appearances not
with his physical eyes; it is rather with his inner eye—in
madness—that he penetrates to the very bottom of things
and recognizes their true nature, whereas he formerly let
himself be blinded by their outward appearance. It is
obvious that imagery is the only adequate form of expression
for such an inner process.

[1] Granville-Barker says about some of these scenes: "They pass beyond the needs of the
plot, they belong to a larger synthesis" (H. Granville-Barker, *Prefaces to Shakespeare, First
Series*, London, 1927).
[2] Bradley, *Shakespearean Tragedy*, p. 256.

But the term "inner drama" is not sufficient to describe accurately the peculiar shifting of emphasis—from the level of human action to another level. Much of what Lear utters in the central scenes points beyond the limits of his personal fate. Indeed, Lear's suffering and experience, although represented to us as an individual case, is meant to signify much more than something merely personal; it is meant to be an archetype of the universal. More than in any other play, the human events in *King Lear* are related to the happenings of the whole world. Bradley speaks of the "feeling which haunts us in *King Lear*, as though we were witnessing something universal—a conflict not so much of particular persons as of the powers of good and evil in the world".[1] Behind Lear's personal suffering stands the suffering of the whole world; behind the severing of the bond between Lear and his daughters stands the breakdown of all the hard-and-fast limits of the universe. This inclusive action is made clear to us by means of the imagery. The imagery gives the horizon of the individual occurrence a comprehensive perspective; it transforms human matters into mighty universal events. The elemental forces and the things of nature, as they appear so profusely in the language of Lear and his followers from the second act on, often seem to grow beyond the speakers. They assume, as it were, an individual existence, they become almost independent of the speakers. The imagery becomes the means by which these forces of nature enter into the play and take part therein as active agents. These sequences of imagery, such as are to be found, for example, in Edgar's long list of animals and plants, are not to be interpreted as the "expression" of individual inner experiences, but rather as the appearance of independent forces which belong to the play just as much as to the people. The words "atmosphere", "background", no longer suffice to designate what of nature, landscape and animal world is evoked by the imagery. This "atmosphere" here becomes a world in itself; we almost forget that it is only through the words of certain characters that life is given to this world of nature.

The non-human nature-world enters into the play in

[1] *Shakespearean Tragedy*, p. 262.

the same measure as the human world breaks down and falls to pieces. This occurs when the father is expelled by his daughters, when the son is persecuted by the father and madness dissolves human order; the firm bonds and laws of human society are destroyed; so now non-human powers, heavenly forces, lightning, thunder, rain and wind, animals and plants, enter in rich variety. This interrelationship is to be seen clearly in the structure of the play; the first act contains relatively little nature-imagery; in the second act it begins to grow, and it attains to its height in the third and fourth acts, which show us the forsaken Lear in his madness.

In the first scene of the play we may study the peculiar nature of "dramatic imagery", consisting in preparing for later issues and giving hints of the further development of the action. For the reasons explained above, the first scene is relatively poor in images; but where they do occur, their appearance is significant.

When Lear appears for the first time upon the stage and communicates to the assembled court and to his daughters his intention to divide the kingdom, he says:

> and 'tis our fast intent
> To shake all cares and business from our age;
> Conferring them on younger strengths, while we
> Unburthen'd *crawl* toward death.   (i. i. 39)

crawl awakens a definite notion. Taken from the realm of animal life, crawling suggests a wounded, tired, perhaps hunted animal dragging itself nearer to death. Lear, at this point still in full possession of his royal authority, employs the metaphor ironically; he has as yet no knowledge of the fate which will actually cast him out and bring him down to the level of the animals.

We find the next metaphorical passage of this scene when Lear irrevocably disinherits Cordelia:

> Let it be so; thy truth, then, be thy dower:
> For, by the sacred radiance of the sun,
> The mysteries of Hecate, and the night;
> By all the operation of the orbs
> From whom we do exist, and cease to be;
> Here I disclaim all my paternal care,   (i. i. 110)

Lear's security is shaken for the first time by Cordelia's misunderstood renouncement. It is no mere chance that Lear at just this moment should turn to the non-human powers, call upon them and repudiate his fathership in their name. This reveals his relationship to the elemental powers: it is awakened when his relationship to the human world is shaken, and it is intensified, as if by a law of nature, by every further wound and repulse he receives from this quarter. On this first occasion we have not yet the form of the direct apostrophe, but the formula of the oath. When Goneril—some scenes later—expels him, Lear again turns to those powers of the underworld. We have a preparatory abrupt flash in "Darkness and devils! Saddle my horses;" (I. iv. 274), and a few lines later, the first great explosion of this feeling in the apostrophe to nature (I. iv. 297). When Goneril reappears, we hear: "Blast and fogs upon thee", and when finally his other daughter also rejects him, the elemental forces are called upon once again:

> You nimble lightnings, dart your blinding flames
> Into her scornful eyes! Infect her beauty,
> You fen-suck'd fogs, drawn by the powerful sun,
> To fall and blast her pride! (II. iv. 167)

The great apostrophes to the elements in the heath scene are the culmination of this sequence; we shall discuss them later. Thus light is thrown from these later passages upon the passage in the first scene.

When Kent in the first scene repeatedly takes the part of the unjustly treated Cordelia, Lear answers impatiently:

> The bow is bent and drawn, make from the shaft.
> KENT. Let it fall rather, though the fork invade
> The region of my heart: (I. i. 145)

This is the first independent image of the scene; the more excited Lear becomes, the more often do images appear in his language. The form of the comparison, such as we still have in the simile of the barbarous Scythian (I. i. 118), is soon replaced by more direct and forceful metaphorical language in "Come not between the dragon and his wrath" (I. i. 123). By the well-known image of the bent bow Lear seeks to warn Kent of continuing in his contradiction; twenty lines later he seizes the sword. But beyond the significance of the moment, this image simultaneously contains dramatic irony: with the transfer of the crown to his daughters Lear has surrendered his own position and power; at this moment, without being aware of it, he has delivered himself up to his coming fate. Nothing can now recall the arrow.

When Lear threatens Kent with the sword, Kent replies:

> Kill thy physician, and the fee bestow
> Upon thy foul disease.   (i. i. 166)

This designation as physician is also premonitory, for the title comes to full realization only in Kent's rôle in the last acts. "The foul disease", too, is forewarning; it points to the ungrateful daughters and to what they are later to signify for Lear's own feelings. Here, in this first scene, Kent is the only one who has a presentiment of this; but soon, in the second act, Lear himself will say to Goneril:

> But yet thou art my flesh, my blood, my daughter;
> Or rather a *disease* that's in my flesh,
> Which I must needs call mine: thou art a boil,
> A plague-sore, an embossed carbuncle,
> In my corrupted blood.   (ii. iv. 223)

A final example may serve to show how here, at the beginning of the play, short metaphors and hints suggest what is more fully unfolded by the imagery of the later scenes. France, the future husband of Cordelia, uses the following words in speaking to Lear of Cordelia:

> Sure, her offence
> Must be of such unnatural degree,
> That monsters it, or your fore-vouch'd affection
> Fall'n into taint: (i. i. 221)

France employs the metaphor "monsters" in regard to Cordelia's alleged attitude, wherein lies a reproach against Lear, but at the same time dramatic irony as well. For in the course of the play the word "monster" will have its

specific application to the ingratitude and the inhuman
behaviour of the two other daughters.[1]

Thus many images in this first scene are prophetic.
What Herder, speaking more generally, said of the first
scene also applies to the imagery: "Lear . . . in the very
first scene of his appearance on the stage already bears
within himself all the seeds of his destinies for the harvest
of the darkest future".[2]

The figure in the play for whom the image is an even
more characteristic form of expression than for Lear, is that
of the Fool. The Fool never speaks in blank verse, indeed he
never comes near the more conventional, measured and
dignified manner of speech such as we find, for example, in
the first part of the first scene. From the very beginning he has
his own peculiar way of expressing himself, a manner which
marks him as an outsider. In the speech of the Fool, Shakespeare has given the images wholly new functions. But what
is the significance of the image in his case?

We have already stated that in the very first scene Lear
loses the capacity for really understanding others in conversation; he cannot carry on a real dialogue. The words of
the others no longer reach him or, if they do, in an ill-
conveyed meaning. Lear shuts himself off; he becomes
isolated in his speech, which from now on, even in the
dialogue, bears the stamp of a monologue.[3] The usual
manner of speech can therefore no longer move him;
such words can neither help nor heal Lear who, in his
madness, needs help more and more. The Fool knows this
from the very beginning, and he speaks to the King in
simile, proverb and image and in rhymed adages and
sayings which have the same purpose as his images. Much

---

[1] To take a few examples from this image-group which was first noticed by Miss Spurgeon
(*Shakespeare's Imagery*, p. 341): to the King "ingratitude" appears as "monster" (I. iv. 281;
I. v. 41); Albany says of Goneril that she "be-monsters" her countenance, and Albany says
of all humanity:

> Humanity must perforce prey on itself,
> Like monsters of the deep. (IV. ii. 48)

"Women will all turn monsters" cries Cornwall's angry servant after Gloucester's blinding
(III. vii. 102). The symbolic meanings and ramifications of this "pattern of imagery" have
been further explored and interpreted by R. B. Heilmann *op. cit.*, pp. 93–98 *et passim*.

[2] "Shakespeare" (Section 5) in *Von deutscher Art und Kunst, Einige fliegende Blätter*,
Hamburg, 1773. Reprinted in all complete editions of Herder's works.

[3] Cf. J. Gurland, *Das Gestaltungsgesetz von Shakespeares König Lear*, Würzburg, 1938.

of what the Fool says Lear neither hears nor grasps, for much is indeed spoken more to the audience than to the King. But part comes home to him and this he does comprehend. Even if Lear replies to only a few of the Fool's utterances, that is still no proof of what Lear may really have heard and understood. For much of the Fool's talk expects no answer. He inserts his sayings and comparisons between the speeches of the others, and he sings his little songs as an outsider, as it were—in this respect his position[1] is often similar to the chorus of the classical tragedy—and formulates most of what he says not as if it were coined to fit a particular case, or were directed at a particular person. "He that hath ears to hear let him hear!" It is the image which makes this unobtrusive parenthetical way of speaking possible. The image clothes the individual and particular case in a more general form; it may take away the sting. Between Lear and the Fool a new form of the dialogue develops which is no longer based upon rational communication, upon the simple play of question and answer, but which is a finer and more subtle interplay of shifting meanings and hints.

The more Lear becomes a victim of self-delusion and madness, the more it becomes the task of the Fool to express in epigrammatic images the unreality of Lear's behaviour, his self-deception and his error. The images of the Fool are the dry and almost trivial language of reality which is continually contrasted with Lear's separation from the outside world. In the great scenes on the heath Lear reaches heights of fantasy and emotion which far transcend human proportions; he becomes a gigantic superhuman figure whose huge dimensions threaten to overstep the limits of what may be represented upon the stage and within the scope of a drama. Here the Fool has the continual function "to keep the scene in touch with reality" (Granville-Barker).[2] For no matter how tremendously the horizon spread out before us in these scenes may widen, the presentation of

[1] In almost every Shakespearian tragedy there is the figure of the objective observer who interprets the action from a standpoint outside the dramatic action. In *King Lear* there is, in addition to the Fool, Kent, who serves as an objective observer, as does also in a certain manner Edgar.

[2] "King Lear" (H. Granville-Barker, *Prefaces to Shakespeare, First Series*, London, 1927).

the play never loses itself in a sphere of the fantastic-
ally unreal. Lear himself, as Granville-Barker has shown,
returns again and again to intimate, earthly things, he again
and again resorts to simplicity and actuality.[1] But it is
especially the little sayings and similes of the Fool pertaining
to the triviality of every day which counterbalance the
gigantic dimensions of Lear's feelings and ideas. The Fool
understands how to reduce Lear's behaviour to the simplest,
most uncomplicated images of actuality, so that the state of
affairs becomes perfectly obvious. Thus, for example, by
means of the trivial simile of the egg which Lear has divided
to give away both halves (the two crowns) he shows how
simple is the division of the kingdom and the relinquish-
ment of the royal power (I. iv. 173). In spite of this simplicity,
the Fool's images may have a complex meaning and may
give us hints of things still hidden.[2] This passage, thirty
lines later, harks back to the image just mentioned: "thou
hast pared thy wit o' both sides and left nothing i' the middle.
Here comes one o' the parings" (I. iv. 206). The voluntary
dispossession of property is seen as a relinquishing of
reason. The ceding of both halves of the land without
leaving anything for himself was like the paring of reason
on both sides without leaving anything in the middle—so
blind and foolish. Thus the rapid transition to "paring"
becomes comprehensible; Goneril represents the half of the
kingdom given away and at the same time, through her,
Lear will go mad. Thus many of the Fool's other images
serve to light up the situation with a single flash and, furthermore, to draw the obvious conclusion and to clothe in the
universally intelligible language of the proverb what the
language of the action is unable to epitomize so convincingly
(cf. I. iv. 124; I. v. 8; I. v. 30; II. iv. 7; II. iv. 68; III. vi. 13).

At first glance, the images of the Fool, gathered as they
are from the unexciting sphere of everyday common sense
and often expressing trivial commonplaces, seem to stand
in contrast to the great issues of the Lear drama. Fateful

---

[1] "Shakespeare has, besides, to carry us into strange regions of thought and passion, so
he must, at the same time, hold us by familiar things", *op. cit.*, p. 158.

[2] How many hidden meanings are suggested by the utterances of the Fool is shown by
Edmund Blunden in his essay, "Shakespeare's Significances", in A. Bradby, *Shakespeare
Criticism*, 1919-1935, London, 1937.

predestinations, even aberrations of such tragic weight and such great pathos—thus we could argue—may not be viewed from a merely utilitarian or common-sense stand-point. But it is precisely these simple, uncomplicated conclusions which form the path by which Lear and we, the audience, are led to a deeper and more moving recognition of the ultimate truth.

The effect of image, rhymed proverb and maxim is different from the effect of the direct admonition. Images as well as proverbs can convey a meaning in a manner more impersonal and universally valid. Images, as they are employed by the Fool, free the action from the narrow restrictions of the moment—they assist in producing a detached attitude of mind. The little songs which the Fool sings, further enhance this quieting effect which liberates us and creates this detachment: "the greater the force of the truth, the lighter, the calmer and the more detached appears the form".[1] The songs of the Fool as well as his images indicate a relaxation and a diminution of the suspense in the structure of the scenes—this being, indeed, to a large degree the function of the Fool. If we recall to mind the early Elizabethan tragedies, the *Spanish Tragedy* or *Titus Andronicus*, we see that such relaxation and counter-balancing are there entirely wanting: everything moves in extremes, every gesture, every word, every action is aimed at achieving the highest possible degree of glaring and bloody effect. In the later Elizabethan drama the Fool with his songs belongs, of course, to the conventions. But nowhere else are he and his forms of utterance employed in so profound a manner, at one and the same time creating detachment and pointing beyond the immediate issue, as here in *King Lear*.

The dramatic quality of the imagery also becomes apparent in the way the dynamic presence of nature in the heath scenes is prepared for very early through allusions and hints; on the other hand, the raging storm continues to sound in the words of the characters long afterwards in later scenes. As early as Edgar's monologue in ii. iii. we have an introduction to the great heath scene. Edgar's

---

[1] Gurland, *Das Gestaltungsgesetz von Shakespeares König Lear*, Würzburg, 1938, p. 60.

language—from the moment he begins to play the madman —is full of references to the world of nature, and in this respect differs greatly from the unimaginative utterances characteristic of Edmund. His monologue displays many a little touch which summons to the mind the picture of the heath-landscape: happy hollow of a tree; pins, wooden pricks, nails, sprigs of rosemary; poor pelting villages, sheep-cotes and mills—to select just a few lines out of the scene. In the following act also his deliberately confused talk greatly assists the creation of a powerful nature-atmosphere. To quote two examples:

> through ford and whirlipool, o'er bog and quagmire
>
> (III. iv. 53)

or:

> who drinks the green mantle of the standing pool

When he says that he is ready "to outface/The winds and persecutions of the sky" (II. iii. 14), his words are parallel to, and anticipate Lear's assertion in the next scene:

> No, rather I abjure all roofs, and choose
> To wage against the enmity o' the air;
> To be a comrade with the wolf and owl,
>
> (II. iv. 211)

In Lear's language, too, the forces of nature make their appearance before they become grim reality in the third act: "You nimble lightnings" (II. iv. 167). Especially the following line is already suggestive of the atmosphere of the heath:

> You fen-suck'd fogs, drawn by the powerful sun.

The Fool sings:

> That sir which serves and seeks for gain,
>   And follows but for form,
> Will pack when it begins to rain,
>   And leave thee in the storm.   (II. iv. 79)

At the end of the scene the coming of the storm is announced more definitely: "'twill be a storm" (II. iv. 290); "the night comes on, and the black winds do sorely ruffle:"

(II. iv. 304). In the next scene Lear is not yet shown us in person, but we are first apprised by the Gentleman of how the King fares:

KENT. Where's the king?
GENTLEMAN. Contending with the fretful element;
Bids the wind blow the earth into the sea,
Or swell the curled waters 'bove the main,
That things might change or cease;

tears his white hair,
Which the impetuous blasts, with eyeless rage,
Catch in their fury, and make nothing of;
Strives in his little world of man to out-scorn
The to-and-fro conflicting wind and rain.

(III. i. 3)

The dramatic value of this brief description is apparent. Lear's appearance in the following scene is so overwhelming, and so far surpasses, in every respect, what we are accustomed to seeing and hearing upon the stage, that we must be prepared for this moment. The great heath-scene (III. ii.) demands the utmost of our own creative powers of imagination; unprepared, we would be unable to comprehend it. Lear's apostrophes to the elements transform the detached description of the Gentleman into living dramatic dialogue:

Blow, winds, and crack your cheeks! rage! blow!
You cataracts and hurricanoes, spout
Till you have drench'd our steeples, drown'd the cocks!
You sulphurous and thought-executing fires,
Vaunt-couriers to oak-cleaving thunderbolts,
Singe my white head! And thou, all-shaking thunder,
Smite flat the thick rotundity o' the world!
Crack nature's moulds, all germens spill at once,
That make ingrateful man! (III. ii. 1)

In this series of images, Lear's relation to the elements finds its most direct expression. Lear can scarcely be said to be still speaking to the Fool or to Kent; his real partners in converse are the forces of nature. In this act, through Lear's words, they become acting characters. It is interesting to note that single motifs of this apostrophe to the elements appeared previously, but that they now achieve a more universal significance; in the first act Lear had asked nature[1] to make Goneril forever barren. Now all mankind shall become unfruitful, everything shall be destroyed. To Lear's prophetic fantasy, the breaking of the natural bond between himself and his daughters, appears as a rent running through the whole of the universe.[2] Just as human nature overstepped its limits, so do the elements now transcend their boundaries—this is a fundamental idea, which appears in the imagery again and again. Thus the Gentleman had already said: at Lear's command, the waters should overflow the earth and the earth should sweep into the sea. At the end of the act we again find an image of this kind, this time used by Gloucester:

> The sea, with such a storm as his bare head
> In hell-black night endured, would have buoy'd up,
> And quench'd the stelled fires. (III. vii. 59)

The storm is reflected by the individual characters of this scene in various ways. For Lear it has the greatest symbolical significance and reality; hence he speaks of "the tempest in my mind". What passes outside, goes on within himself. Kent stands aside, he is the observer, who, with experience and quiet contemplation, takes note of all that occurs:

> Since I was man,
> Such sheets of fire, such bursts of horrid thunder,
> Such groans of roaring wind and rain, I never
> Remember to have heard: (III. ii. 46,

> The tyranny of the open night's too rough
> For nature to endure. (III. iv. 2)

The Fool strikes the note of the storm in his little song:

> With hey, ho, the wind and the rain, (III. ii. 75)

and, finally, Edgar mirrors the weather in the twice repeated "Through the sharp hawthorn blows the cold wind" (III. iv. 47). And even after this tempest scene is long

---

[1] For the different meanings of "nature" in *King Lear* and in sixteenth-century literature see John F. Danby, *Shakespeare's Doctrine of Nature, A Study of King Lear*, London, 1949. For further comment on the significance of "nature" in *King Lear* cf. Heilmann *op. cit.*, p. 115, and George Gordon, *Shakespearean Comedy and other Studies*, London, 1944, p. 124.

[2] The symbolic implications of the imagery relating to this theme have been explored by R. B. Heilmann in his chapter on "The Breach of Nature", *op. cit.*, p. 89.

past, it still lives on in the memory. Thus Lear's recollection: "When the rain came to wet me once, and the wind to
make me chatter; when the thunder would not peace at my
bidding;" (iv. vi. 102), or Cordelia's words in the next scene:

> Was this a face
> To be opposed against the warring winds?
> To stand against the deep dread-bolted thunder?
> In the most terrible and nimble stroke
> Of quick, cross lightning?   (iv. vii. 32)

The elements of nature not only help to create the
atmosphere, but they also have symbolical significance and
a definite "function". This also holds true of the animal-
imagery. The wealth of animal-images in *King Lear* has
often been emphasized. Thus Bradley sums up the effect
of these animal-images: "As we read, the souls of all the
beasts in turn seem to have entered the bodies of these
mortals; horrible in their venom, savagery, lust, deceitful-
ness, sloth, cruelty, filthiness; miserable in their feebleness,
nakedness, defencelessness, blindness; and man, 'consider
him well', is even what they are". Miss Spurgeon, in her
subtle analysis of the "dominating image" in *King Lear*,[2]
shows how these animal-images, too, "because portrayed
chiefly in angry or anguished action, very distinctly augment
the sensation of horror and bodily pain". G. Wilson Knight,
in his chapter on "The Lear Universe",[3] explains at length
how the animal-imagery helps to illustrate the "revulsion
from humanity" and other basic themes of the tragedy. It
is interesting to note how these animal-images make their
appearance in considerable numbers from a definite moment
in the play on. That is in the heath-scenes of the third act.
Nature and landscape, the world of animals come to life
after the world of man has failed; since his fellow-men
have cast him out, the aged king turns to nature. But this
involves an increasing influence of the low and animal

---

[1] First by J. Kirkman in *New Shakespeare Society Transactions*, 1877; Bradley, *Shakespearean Tragedy*, p. 266 sqq.; Spurgeon, *Shakespeare's Imagery*, p. 342; G. Wilson Knight,
The Wheel of Fire, p. 194 sqq. For further comment on the animal-imagery in *King Lear*
see Heilmann, *op. cit.* p. 93 ("The Animal in Man"). Audrey Yoder's book, *Animal Analogy
in Shakespeare's Character Portrayal* (New York, 1947), became accessible to the author only
after completion of this book.

[2] *Shakespeare's Imagery*, p. 342.   [3] *The Wheel of Fire*, p. 194 ff.

element in contrast to the dimming of the human mind and
consciousness, as we are to see it represented to us in Lear's
insanity and Edgar's madness. We must discriminate,
however, between the low and repulsive animal-images,
such as are uttered by Edgar and the Fool, and the higher
animals, which populate the forest. Lear's prophecy, "to
be a comrade with the wolf and the owl" (II. iv. 213) is the
cue for their coming to life.

The beasts of prey, to which the thankless daughters
are frequently compared,[1] often appear without any definite
reference to characters of the play, but nevertheless have
the significance outlined above. Edgar's seemingly irrelevant
list has surely this meaning: "hog in sloth, fox in stealth,
wolf in greediness, dog in madness, lion in prey" (III. iv. 96).
Likewise this statement of the Fool: "He's mad that trusts
in the tameness of a wolf" (III. vi. 20). Another thought
which is expressed by the animal-imagery, is: in such
fearful weather even the animals of the forest would fare
better than Lear (III. i. 12), some shelter would have been
offered even to the howling wolves or the enemy's dog
(III. vii. 63; IV. vii. 36). It is significant that Lear, too,
when he seeks a comparison with his own state, draws
upon animal-imagery:

> Thou'ldst shun a bear;
> But if thy flight lay toward the raging sea,
> Thou'ldst meet the bear i' the mouth. (III. iv. 9)

One act later Lear is called:

> a gracious aged man,
> Whose reverence the head-lugg'd bear would lick,
> (IV. ii. 41)

Edgar's language fairly teems with repulsive, low
animals: "Poor Tom, that eats the swimming frog, the
toad, the tadpole, the wall-newt and the water; . . .
swallows the old rat and the ditch-dog" (III. iv. 137).
Mice, rats, salamander and mongrel (III. vi. 71) complete
the list. Not only in his outward appearance but also in
his language Edgar is meant to impress us as an image

---

[1] Cf. Bradley, *op. cit.* p. 207.

II

of bestiality. The fact that Lear meets with him on the
heath has symbolical meaning. Himself cast out and
left defenceless to the untrammelled winds, he meets in
Edgar the worst extremity of the outcast. His own condition,
and above and beyond that, the insignificance of man in
general, his similarity to the animal, become apparent to
Lear:[1] "unaccommodated man is no more but such a poor,
bare, forked animal as thou art" (III. iv. 111).

This comparison of man with the lowly animal finds
its most significant expression in Gloucester's words,
culminating in the well-known comparison:

> I' the last night's storm I such a fellow saw;
> Which made me think a man a worm: . . .
>
> As flies to wanton boys, are we to the gods,
> They kill us for their sport.   (IV. i. 36)

Many animal-comparisons of the Fool, too, are meant
to stress the fact that men may fare no better than the
animals: when he sees Kent in the stocks, he remarks:
"Horses are tied by the heads, dogs and bears by the neck,
monkeys by the loins, and men by the legs" (II. iv. 7).
Otherwise, however, most of the animal comparisons
employed by the Fool are aimed to show how dumb
animals, in spite of their want of reason, still fare better
and act more sensibly than unintelligent human beings.
Even animals would not be so foolish and devoid of instinct
as Lear, when he gave his kingdom away (cf. I. iv. 124, 177,
235, 244; I. v. 26).

Lear's inner development is portrayed in images more
than that of any other character in Shakespeare.[2] The great

---

[1] This recurrent theme in the imagery has been further traced and interpreted by R. B.
Heilmann, *op. cit.* p. 67 sqq.

[2] We must distinguish here between the rôle of the imagery to denote certain characteristic traits in a person and its function to give expression to a change in his mind. Whereas
the latter function, as shown above, is very marked and noteworthy, the former, i.e. the
characterization of a person through consistent features of the imagery, is less important in
King Lear, than, for instance, in *Othello* or *Hamlet*. As was shown in the last passage, certain
fundamental themes of the play are taken up in the imagery of several characters who all
in turn contribute to the progressive disclosure of the play's meaning through imagery and
action.

For certain features in Lear's personality (his manifold interests, his classical education,
his love of English scenery and his knowledge of hunting, tournament and warfare) as revealed
through his imagery see Edmund Blunden, "Shakespeare's Significances" in *Shakespeare
Criticism*, 1919–1935, ed. A. Bradby, London, 1937.

apostrophes to the elemental forces of nature in the scenes
on the heath have already revealed a significant change in
Lear. The images of the next scenes, in which the King
goes mad, are again illuminating for Lear's state of mind.
The swiftly passing images, logically unconnected with
each other, which we hear Lear utter, correspond to the
abnormal mental state of the King; they are the adequate
form of perception and expression of a lunatic. "It is his
mind which is laid bare", Charles Lamb said as an interpretation of these strange speeches—especially in the fourth
act. Lear's insanity should not be dismissed as simple
craziness. It is rather another manner of perception, by
means of which, however, Lear now sees and recognizes
what formerly remained concealed to him, as long as he
was sane. These images are the fragments of his inner
visions, which have not yet attained to the form of
thoughts; they have not yet been transformed, ordered
and connected in logical sequence and in the service of
clear statement.[1] Many images in the fourth act become
more comprehensible if light is thrown upon them from
previous passages. In the great scene on the heath we hear
Lear cry out:

> Let the great gods,
> That keep this dreadful pother o'er our heads,
> Find out their enemies now. Tremble, thou wretch,
> That hast within thee undivulged crimes,
> Unwhipp'd of justice: hide thee, thou bloody hand;
> Thou perjured, and thou simular man of virtue
> That art incestuous: (III. ii. 50)

The sins of earth pass before Lear's inner eye as visionary
images—the thanklessness of his daughters brings him to
the thanklessness and unrighteousness of the whole world.
At first judge of his daughters (cf. the judgement scene
played in madness with the Fool and Kent, III. vi.), Lear
becomes in the fourth act the judge of all creatures. From

---

[1] Regarding these passages A. Somerville says in his book *Madness in Shakespearean Tragedy*, London, 1929: "What really happens, however, is that the thoughts from his subconscious mind run too rapidly for expression in words, and sentences that should appear as associating links necessary to make the whole speech coherent, are left out." In general, however, it is a rather dubious procedure to seek to judge Shakespeare's characters from the point of view of modern psychology.

the passage quoted above there runs a connecting link to
IV. vi. 165:

> Thou rascal beadle, hold thy bloody hand!
> Why dost thou lash that whore? Strip thine own back;

Lear, having experienced in his personal world the destruction of human right and order, thus gains insight into the
common injustice and frailty of all mankind. His fancy now
sees examples of this everywhere in the world. License
appears to him in the form of animal-images (IV. vi. 114)
and in the vision of the "simpering dame" (IV. vi. 120);
injustice and mendacity in the image of the railing judge
(IV. vi. 154), of the beggar running from the farmer's dog
(IV. vi. 158), of the hypocritical beadle, and of the magnificent robes which cover vice (IV. vi. 168). In madness
Lear has won eyes for reality. His inner eye pierces
the outer appearance and penetrates to the true nature
of things. Lear's recovery in the fifth act, too, is clearly reflected
in the imagery. Peaceful and delicate things have taken the
place of the unclean and repulsive images, and his language
is connected, musical and gentle:

> We two alone will sing like birds i' the cage:
> When thou dost ask me blessing, I'll kneel down,
> And ask of thee forgiveness: so we'll live,
> And pray, and sing, and tell old tales, and laugh
> At gilded butterflies,   (V. iii. 9)

This mood, however, is again interrupted by the terrible
and painful experience of Cordelia's death. The fourfold
"Howl" when Lear "re-enters with Cordelia dead in his
arms" recalls the animal-imagery, and in the next lines
spoken by Lear the gigantic and powerful nature of Lear is
once again given expression through imagery:

> Had I your tongues and eyes, I'ld use them so
> That heaven's vault should crack.   (V. iii. 258)

Lear translates all feelings into bodily terms. His imagery
thus conveys to us the impression of immense physical

force[1] or, if mental suffering is to be expressed, of immense physical pain. The imagery thus helps to intensify and sharpen the poignancy of the spiritual experience through which Lear has to pass.[2] The above image is the last link in a chain which runs through the whole drama.[3]

---

[1] After having been told that Regan and her husband refuse to appear, Lear threatens:

> bid them come forth and hear me,
> Or at their chamber-door I'll beat the drum
> Till it cry sleep to death. (II. iv. 118)

[2] This also applies to the perhaps most famous image used by Lear:

> . . . but I am bound
> Upon a wheel of fire, that mine own tears
> Do scald like molten lead. (IV. vii. 46)

[3] The frequency of metaphors and images expressing bodily pain and tension was first noted by Miss Spurgeon (*op. cit.* p. 338). She goes so far as to consider these images of "bodily and generally anguished motion" as the "one overpowering and dominating continuous image" in *King Lear*.

15

CORIOLANUS

THE imagery in *Coriolanus*, compared with that in *Macbeth* or *Antony and Cleopatra*, is less intricate and complex. It is simpler, runs on few and obvious lines, is easier to survey, and more concise. The images are mostly clear, short, obvious and illustrate a plain theme. This definiteness and simplicity of imagery corresponds to the play's mood. The warlike atmosphere, the vigorous and active mind of Coriolanus, the speed of the action, the absence of meditative or sentimental scenes, all these combine to call forth brevity and clarity of diction,—a "Roman distinctness" determines plot and style. Moreover, the plot involves a sharp and clearly marked contrast that could well be brought out by the imagery.

The function of the imagery to emphasize and repeat the play's main theme is particularly interesting in *Coriolanus*. For here the imagery throws much light on Shakespeare's attitude towards a general problem, to which he gave dramatic life. We cannot draw deductions and inferences from every play of Shakespeare's as to his own attitude towards certain problems. He even seems to conceal what he himself thinks of his characters. This is, of course, betrayed to us by the play taken as a whole; it is seldom explicitly said in this or that passage. But while Shakespeare rarely expresses his opinions in his plays, he frequently implies very subtly his attitude towards certain problems. And imagery is one of the subtlest and most effective methods he employs for this purpose.

The contrast between the commanding figure of Coriolanus and the baseness of the "rabble" is vividly brought out by a series of images which, at the same time, reveal Shakespeare's intense dislike of the masses, of the never-to-be-trusted rabble.

As early as the first scene, Coriolanus uses comparisons which bear upon the fundamental theme of the play and

are at the same time significant for what is going to happen
in the next acts:

> He that trusts to you.
> Where he should find you lions, finds you hares;
> Where foxes, geese; you are no surer, no,
> Than is the coal of fire upon the ice,
> Or hailstone in the sun.   (i. i. 174)

> He that depends
> Upon your favours swims with fins of lead
> And hews down oaks with rushes.   (i. i. 184)

In the third act, Coriolanus warns the senate even more
emphatically against the "cockle" of the rabble:

> In soothing them, we nourish 'gainst our senate
> The cockle of rebellion, insolence, sedition,
> Which we ourselves have plough'd for, sow'd, and scatter'd,
> By mingling them with us, the honour'd number,   (iii. i. 69)

Our unconscious imagination is, however, still more
influenced by the numerous short metaphors and nouns
characterizing the rabble. These epithets may be found on
almost every page. Taken as a whole, they represent the
most intense characterization by means of imagery ever
attempted by Shakespeare.

Of animal names applied to the rabble we have *dogs,
cats, curs, hares, geese, camels, mules, crows, minnows, goats.*
All these animals (some of them occurring repeatedly) are
represented as cowardly creatures which are to be hunted,
which know nothing but their greedy feeding, which may
be packed and commanded, beaten as one pleases, etc.
More particular and rare names are *clusters* (iv. vi. 122),
multiplying spawn (ii. ii. 82), *those measles, which we disdain
should tetter us* (iii. i. 79), *scabs* (i. i. 169). The disgust for
the rabble finding expression in this disease-imagery is
also apparent in epithets like *musty superfluity* (i. i. 230),
musty chaff (v. i. 26, 31), *fusty plebeians* (i. ix. 7). This list
may be completed by epithets like *monster* (iii. iii. 265),
beast with many heads (iv. i. 1), *woollen vassals* (iii. ii. 9),
fragments (i. i. 226), and *shreds* (i. i. 212).

Shakespeare must have been particularly struck by the
greediness of the rabble, as this feature is repeatedly

emphasized. Thus Coriolanus, in the first scene of the play, in growing anger cries:

> They said they were an-hungry; sigh'd forth proverbs,
> That hunger broke stone walls, that dogs must eat,
> That meat was made for mouths,   (I. i. 209)

The rabble, unless kept in awe by the senate, would, in Coriolanus' phrase, "feed on one another" (I. i. 192), their "affections are a sick man's appetite" (I. i. 182).

We now turn from these images of disdain and disgust to their antithesis, namely those describing Coriolanus. It is Shakespeare's admiration for great and heroic men that leads him to characterize them by means of images of boldness and force. Their impressive and victorious appearance on the stage is re-echoed and enhanced in imagery. Antony, Caesar, Othello are examples of this art of characterization, Antony being the most forceful. Coriolanus is another important example. In contrast with the timorous and insignificant animals which characterize the common people, we find brave and noble animals as symbols of the heroic nature of Coriolanus. He is a dragon (IV. i. 30; IV. vii. 23; V. iv. 12), an eagle (V. vi. 115), a steed (I. ix. 12) and a tiger (V. iv. 32). Volumnia compares him to the bear from which enemies flee like children (I. iii. 34), and Aufidius likens him to the osprey who takes the fish "by sovereignty of nature" (by *fish* Rome is meant) (IV. vii. 35). There are other images which embody the irresistible, victorious and at the same time terrible character of his warlike nature: he strides along like a harvestman who must mow all or else lose his hire (I. iii. 39); the effect of his personality on the flying soldiers is thus described:

> as weeds before
> A vessel under sail, so men obey'd
> And fell below his stem: (II. ii. 109)

And thus is his coming depicted by Volumnia:

> Before him he carries noise, and behind him he leaves tears:
> Death, that dark spirit, in's nervy arm doth lie;
> Which, being advanced, declines, and then men die.   (II. i. 173)

He is the "god" of his soldiers, a thing not made by nature:

> He is their god: he leads them like a thing
> Made by some other deity than nature,
> That shapes man better; . . .   (IV. vi. 90)

On the other hand, Shakespeare counterbalances these grandiose images by another type of imagery which, through ironical exaggeration, suggests a more critical point of view. It is Menenius who characterizes Coriolanus in the following words:

When he walks, he moves like an engine, and the ground shrinks before his treading: he is able to pierce a corslet with his eye; talks like a knell, and his hum is a battery. He sits in his state, as a thing made for Alexander. . . . He wants nothing of a god but eternity and a heaven to throne in.   (V. iv. 19)

This, to be sure, is a final reaction to Coriolanus' overbearing nature of which the tragic destiny disclosed itself in the course of the action. In the first acts it had been the purpose of the imagery to convey as fully as possible Coriolanus' imposing greatness, as in this passage:

> Thou art left, Marcius:
> A carbuncle entire, as big as thou art,
> Were not so rich a jewel. Thou wast a soldier
> Even to Cato's wish, not fierce and terrible
> Only in strokes; but, with thy grim looks and
> The thunder-like percussion of thy sounds,
> Thou madest thine enemies shake, as if the world
> Were feverous and did tremble.   (I. iv. 55)

In characterization of such comprehensiveness Shakespeare displays an extraordinary fertility of invention. The imagery is drawn from almost every quarter: Coriolanus is "Flower of warriors" (I. vi. 32), "The rock", "the oak not to be wind-shaken" (V. ii. 117), "a great sea-mark" (V. iii. 73), "he waxed like a sea" (II. ii. 103), he is "a thing of blood" (II. ii. 113). His sword is called "death's stamp" (II. ii. 111). The nobles "bended, as to Jove's statue" (II. i. 282) and he is compared even with Hercules: "He will shake/Your Rome about your ears/As Hercules/Did shake down mellow fruit." (IV. vi. 98). In another passage we read:

> He would not flatter Neptune for his trident,
> Or Jove for's power to thunder.   (III. i. 256)

and to his mother, too, he appears as an imitator and emulator of the gods (v. iii. 149). And, finally, Shakespeare grants him the highest praise with which he occasionally distinguishes his kings and great generals; he terms him "planet" (ii. ii. 118). After his death, all these epithets are summed up in the magnificent lines:

> The man is noble and his fame folds in
> This orb o' the earth.   (v. vi. 127)

In this play Shakespeare indeed realized what one of the tribunes bitterly remarked: "All tongues speak of him" (ii. i. 221). Coriolanus is present in every scene, his personality is reflected in almost every utterance of the other characters.

The technique of characterizing the hero by means of images used by other characters began with the repulsive animal-images which surround the figure of Richard III; but as early as *Richard II* we can discern how the range of these images has widened. Certain comparisons, however, appear again and again and may be traced throughout all the histories: the symbol of the sun or of the star for the king; plant-imagery or the image of the ship for human existence. In *Antony and Cleopatra* the images of light, and the cosmic-imagery characterizing Antony, are linked up with the symbols accompanying the common catastrophe. Thus *Antony and Cleopatra* marks a climax in the combined use of characterizing and symbolic imagery; but *Coriolanus* represents an achievement in another respect. For in no other play did Shakespeare honour his hero with such a wealth of imagery. The omnipresence of Coriolanus produces one of the most powerful dramatic effects of this play.

Such omnipresence of the hero in a Shakespearian drama cannot be demonstrated simply by listing all the passages referring to the hero. Such an enumeration must remain more or less of an approximation; by this method we can at most divine something of that which will always be a secret.

16

ANTONY AND CLEOPATRA

WE have already observed in earlier chapters that the imagery creating atmosphere soon began to express other abstract things as well. In *Antony and Cleopatra*, we now note that the imagery which is chosen to express abstract ideas seems itself to be derived from the atmosphere of the play. To take one example: the sea constitutes an important element of the "scenery" of this tragedy. The sea lies between the two main scenes of action, Egypt and Rome; battles are fought on it, Antony and Caesar are continually crossing it. By allusions and references, the sea is therefore constantly present to the mind. But Shakespeare heightens the omnipresence of this peculiar sea-atmosphere even further by drawing metaphors to express abstract issues from the sea and the terminology of navigation. Caesar, paraphrasing the fickleness of popular favour, draws upon sea and seafare several times:

> And the ebb'd man, ne'er loved till ne'er worth love,
> Comes dear'd by being lack'd. This common body,
> Like to a vagabond flag upon the stream,
> Goes to and back, lackeying the varying tide,
> To rot itself with motion.　　　　　　(I. iv. 43)

We have the same thing, when Enobarbus says: "My reason sits in the wind against me" (III. x. 36); when he identifies Antony, abandoned by fate, with a leaking ship which must be left to sink (III. xiii. 63); or when Euphronius compares himself to the morning dew and Antony to the "grand sea" (III. xii. 10). We find another such image creating atmosphere in this indirect way when Enobarbus says, speaking of Cleopatra's tears: "We cannot call her winds and waters sighs and tears; they are greater storms and tempests than almanacs can report" (I. ii. 152), and when Antony warns Lepidus: "these quick-sands, Lepidus, keep off them, for you sink" (II. vii. 65). The last passage contains dramatic irony as well, for, as we have heard, Antony himself will be termed a sinking ship in the next act—a gentle hint of his descending curve of fortune. To Cleopatra, Antony also applies the terminology of the sea, when he says:

> Egypt, thou knew'st too well
> My heart was to thy rudder tied by the strings,
> And thou shouldst tow me after: . . .   (III. ii. 56)

We meet with this sea-terminology even in the words which are spoken after Antony's death:

> A rarer spirit never
> Did steer humanity!   (v. i. 32)

We are indebted to Miss Spurgeon for the listing of those images in *Antony and Cleopatra* which strike the key-note of the play—the expanse of the world and the tremendous consciousness of power on the part of the characters—and which elevate the figures of these great rulers to the level of demi-gods. These images, too, generally fulfil a double function: in the first place, they are a means of expressing Antony's greatness, but at the same time they create atmosphere by summoning to our minds again and again the image of the wide ocean and of the immeasurably vast world:

> I, that with my sword
> Quartered the world, and o'er green Neptune's back
> With ships made cities—   (IV. xiv. 58)

The native scenery lives in the words of its people. And since such expressions appear to us entirely natural in their place, we are generally quite unaware of the fact that they create atmosphere.

One striking example of this is Shakespeare's use of the Nile which, with its creatures, its snakes and adders, introduces into the drama the intimate interplay of person and scene.[1] We notice that in moments of angry emotion, Cleopatra envisions the Nile with its vipers. Thus three times in that scene in which, beside herself with rage, she

[1] For illuminating remarks on the significance of the Nile-imagery see also G. Wilson Knight, *The Imperial Theme*, Oxford, 1931, p. 231.

receives the messenger's news from Rome. She greets the messenger:

> Thou shouldst come like a Fury crown'd with snakes
>
> (II. v. 39)

and curses her Egypt:

> Melt Egypt into Nile! and kindly creatures
> Turn all to serpents! (II. v. 77)

> So half my Egypt were submerged and made
> A cistern for scaled snakes! (II. v. 94)

Again this motif enters her mind, when Antony doubts her love (IV. xiii. 164). And one last time, when she is faced with the frightful possibility of being taken captive to Rome:

> Rather a ditch in Egypt
> Be gentle grave unto me! rather on Nilus' mud
> Lay me stark naked, and let the water-flies
> Blow me into abhorring! (V. ii. 58)

The motif of the snake also appears in the conversation between Lepidus and Antony on Pompey's galley. They are talking about the Nile flood[1] and its fertility, and, as if born of the landscape, Cleopatra enters as a serpent of the Nile mud:

LEPIDUS. You've strange serpents there.
ANTONY. Ay, Lepidus.
LEPIDUS. Your serpent of Egypt is bred now of your mud by the operation of your sun: so is your crocodile. (II. vii. 27)

The use of this image for her occurs as early as the first act, when Cleopatra imagines Antony addressing her: "Where's my serpent of old Nile" (I. iv. 25). Now, this whole sequence of imagery gains powerful dramatic relevance through the fact that Cleopatra at the end commits suicide by means of one such Nile serpent:

CLEOPATRA. Hast thou the pretty worm of Nilus there,
That kills and pains not? (V. ii. 244)

---

[1] It is significant of the suggestive force of this image that Hazlitt, in his characterization of the play, closes with the words, "Shakespeare's genius has spread over the whole play a richness like the overflowing of the Nile", probably without being conscious of the fact that this selfsame image appears in the play (*Characters of Shakespeare's Plays*, London, 1817–1818, chapter on *Antony and Cleopatra*).

Thus Shakespeare's imagery, which at first glance seems only to create the atmosphere of the play, actually effects more than this. It is symbolically related to the characters, serves their self-interpretation and the expression of their feelings.

This symbolical meaning of certain sequences of imagery becomes apparent when we examine how the main theme of the play, the fall of the great lovers, is metaphorically expressed. From the very beginning, we find for Antony images suggesting his relation to the stars and emphasizing his equality with the gods. Already in the second line of the play we read:

> . . . those his goodly eyes,
> That o'er the files and musters of the war
> Have glow'd like plated Mars. . . . (I. i. 2)

He is the "Herculean Roman" (I. iii. 84), "the God of Jupiter" (III. ii. 10), and, when he compares himself with mythological figures,[1] we have an illustration of this high self-esteem. Enobarbus expresses the luminous nature of his character in the words: "He'll outstare the lightning" (III. xiii. 195), and Lepidus says:

> His faults in him seem as the spots of heaven,
> More fiery by night's blackness; (I. iv. 11)

Cleopatra's encomium in the last act heightens this effect. Here the different motifs are combined in a magnificent characterization:

> His face was as the heavens; and therein stuck
> A sun and moon, which kept their course, and lighted
> The little O, the earth. (V. ii. 79)

This sequence of imagery describing Antony's nature is now joined with another sequence of figurative expressions which prepare and accompany Antony's fall. Just as Antony himself is conceived of as partaking of the nature of light, so does his death appear as the quenching of this light.[2] He seemed allied with the stars; hence they too grow dim

---

[1] These images especially are a good example of the frequent self-characterization of the figures of the play by means of comparison, with which we meet in the later plays. "Let me lodge Lichas on the horns o' the moon;" (IV. xii. 45), "O, that I were upon the hill of Basan, to outroar the horned herd!" (III. xiii. 127), cf. also IV. xiv. 38; IV. xii. 44.

[2] G. Wilson Knight notes this point, too, but deals with it in a different connection. Cf. *The Imperial Theme*, p. 242.

at his death; hence the whole world darkens. As early as the second act we have a hint of this possibility, namely, that Antony's brilliance might once fade; characteristically enough, it is the Soothsayer who tells this to Antony. "Thy lustre thickens, when he shines by" (he = Caesar) (II. iii. 27). Foreboding are Antony's words in the next act: "I am so lated in the world, that I have lost my way for ever" (III. xi. 3).[1]

Two scenes later we find another allusion to the quenching of the light, when Antony says:

> When my good stars, that were my former guides,
> Have empty left their orbs, and shot their fires
> Into the abysm of hell.   (III. xiii. 145)

and again:

> Alack! our terrene moon
> Is now eclipsed; and it portends alone
> The fall of Antony!   (III. xiii. 153)

Antony's apostrophes to sun, moon and stars are also to be understood as expressions of this consciousness of a relation to the heavenly bodies. These appeals are occasioned by the greatest shocks to his feeling of earthly security: "Moon and stars!" (III. xiii. 95), "O sun, thy uprise shall I see no more" (IV. xii. 18), and this image links up with a later appeal by Cleopatra to the sun:

> O sun,
> Burn the great sphere thou movest in! darkling stand
> The varying shore o' the world.   (IV. xv. 9)

The appropriateness of this image to the action is clear, because at this moment the mortally wounded Antony is carried in.

In the two last acts, those hints and images which presage Antony's fall, under the common sign of approaching darkness, become more and more frequent. In IV. xii., we have the important scene between Antony and Eros, in which Antony imagines he sees omens of his death in the cloud-pictures:

> Thou hast seen these signs;
> They are black vesper's pageants. (IV. xiv. 7)

---

[1] "Darkness" is only implied here, for a man who is belated goes astray because of darkness.

but both the guards, too, choose this language for Antony's approaching death:

> The star is fall'n.
> And time is at his period. (IV. xiv. 106)

A scene later, Cleopatra employs the image of the spent lamp:

> Ah, women, women, look,
> Our lamp is spent, it's out! (IV. xv. 85)

And in the fifth act we find a further light-symbol for Antony:

> Finish, good lady; the bright day is done,
> And we are for the dark.   (V. ii. 193)

On the other hand, this light-symbolism is also used in reference to Cleopatra's death. She, who appeared to Antony as "day o' the world" (IV. viii. 13), to Charmian as "eastern star" (V. ii. 310), is conceived of by Antony in her death as light extinguished.

> Since the torch is out, . . .   (IV. xiv. 46)

"Light extinguished" had always been a symbol of death with Shakespeare.[1] A comparison with earlier examples makes clear to what degree Shakespeare's imagery has developed along this particular line. In *Henry VI* the dying Mortimer declares before his death:

> These eyes, like lamps whose wasting oil is spent,
> Wax dim, as drawing to their exigent;
> (*A Henry VI*, II. v. 8)

while his death is stated by Plantagenet in the same intentional and circumstantial manner:

> Here dies the dusky torch of Mortimer,   (II. v. 122)

In the tragedies, "descriptive imagery" becomes "dramatic imagery".[2] The same motif is now adapted to the natural emotions of the characters and is made an organic feature

---

[1] Cf. *Richard II*, I. iii. 321; *Comedy of Errors*, V. i. 315; *C Henry VI*, II. vi. 3; *All's Well that Ends Well*, I. ii. 59; *Romeo and Juliet*, IV. ii. 96; *Sonnet*, lxxiii. 5.

[2] The distinction between "descriptive" or "poetic" and "dramatic" imagery appears to have first been worked out by George Rylands in his book *Words and Poetry*, London, 1930. See also the same writer's article "Shakespeare the Poet", *A Companion to Shakespeare Studies*, ed. by H. Granville-Barker and G. B. Harrison, Cambridge, 1934.

of the course of action. Macbeth's "Out, out, brief candle!" (v. v. 23), Othello's "Put out the light, and then put out the light" (v. ii. 7), may suffice here as examples. But in no other play is this darkness-symbol of death so closely associated with the whole characterization of the persons as in *Antony and Cleopatra*. These images may justly be called symbolical; they reveal that Shakespeare viewed the life of his great characters as being in harmony with the cosmic powers. Cosmic events and human events run parallel in *Antony and Cleopatra*. What occurs in the one sphere must have its counterpart in the other.

The dramatic preparation of coming events in which imagery plays a part is, in *Antony and Cleopatra*, pervaded by a strong sense of destiny. Such a great life as Antony's has its curve of destiny, its "kairos", its fated end. The numerous passages alluding to Fortune illustrate this. At the very beginning of the play, in a more casual way (i. ii.), Fortune appears in the conversation of the Soothsayer with the women attendants, to whom he makes prophesies. In the next act, however, Antony himself asks the Soothsayer:

ANTONY. Say to me, whose fortunes shall rise higher,
Caesar's or mine?
SOOTHSAYER. Caesar's.
Therefore, O Antony, stay not by his side:
Thy demon, that's thy spirit which keeps thee, is
Noble, courageous, high, unmatchable,
Where Caesar's is not; but, near him, thy angel
Becomes a fear, as being o'erpower'd: . . .
(ii. iii. 16)

At this early moment Antony's words of assent which follow sound strange: "Be it art or hap,/He hath spoken true;" (ii. iii. 32). From now on Fortune will accompany Antony's path.

The imagery relating to "fortune" may help to bear out the various meanings of "fortune" in Shakespeare's dramas, although any such interpretation based solely on the imagery must necessarily remain incomplete. If, for instance, after he believes himself betrayed by Cleopatra, Antony cries:

Fortune and Antony part here; even here
Do we shake hands. (iv. xii. 20)

it would be false to infer from this passage that "fortune" always means good fortune abandoning the hero when he has run the course allotted to him in life.

We occasionally find a condemnation of "Fortune". It is an inherent feature of the self-estimation of Shakespeare's great characters that they protest against Fortune again and again, mock her, and also even believe her vanquished. Such passages naturally contain a fine dramatic irony when the audience knows that the curve of destiny is already taking a downward trend:

ANTONY.   Fortune knows
             We scorn her most when most she offers blows.
                                                    (III. xi. 73)

CLEOPATRA.   Let me rail so high,
             That the false housewife Fortune break her wheel
             Provoked by my offence.   (IV. xv. 43)

The allegiance of others to a great man appears not only as devotion to his person, but, at the same time, as adherence to his star of fortune. If this star begins to fade, the bond which ties the faithful servant to his master grows looser. This is betrayed by Enobarbus' words, who, to be sure, rates personal loyalty highly at the beginning but who also ends by forsaking Antony.

             I'll yet follow
        The wounded chance of Antony, though my reason
        Sits in the wind against me.   (III. x. 35)

The same is suggested by the words of Menas alluding to Pompey (II. vii. 88), and from Dercetas' statement (IV. xiv. 111). Man's dependency upon "Fortune" is expressed in the words of Enobarbus, when he says:

             I see, men's judgements are
             A parcel of their fortunes;   (III. xiii. 31)

And, finally, it is not the man himself who corrupts others, but his "Fortune". Thus Antony exclaims:

             O, my fortunes have
             Corrupted honest men!   (IV. v. 16)

In his illuminating chapter on this play,[1] Mr. G. Wilson Knight has fully shown how Antony and Cleopatra

[1] *The Wheel of Fire*, London, 1931.

mutually characterize each other. When we have read the whole tragedy we see before us the gleaming multi-coloured image of the changeable queen, now whore, now courtesan, now royal lover. This "Infinite variety" (II. ii. 241), how-ever, is to be easily gathered from the different terms applied to Cleopatra. On the lowest level she appears as a tempting morsel to be coveted:

> I was a morsel for a monarch! (I. v. 31)

she says of herself, and Antony returns to this image:

> I found you as a morsel cold upon
> Dead Caesar's trencher; (III. xiii. 116)

In Enobarbus' words she is Antony's *Egyptian dish* (II. vi. 134). She often appears as *witch*. "*Avaunt, thou spell*" (IV. xii. 30), Antony cries to her; he calls her *great fairy* (IV. viii. 12), *gipsy* (IV. xii. 28), *witch* (IV. xii. 47), and he himself appears as *a strumpet's fool* (I. i. 13), as *the bellows and the fan to cool a gipsy's lust* (I. i. 9), and as *the noble ruin of her magic* (III. x. 19). Further, she is *triple-turn'd whore* (IV. xii. 13), *girl* (IV. viii. 19), *trull* (III. vi. 95), *ribaudred nag* (III. x. 10), *my chuck* (IV. iv. 2), *my nightingale* (IV. viii. 18). But this scale is wider and embraces her royal nature as well: *Royal wench* (II. ii. 231) shows the mingling of both elements, *Royal Egypt* (IV. xv. 70), *Rare Egyptian* (II. ii. 223), *Sovereign of Egypt* (I. v. 34), *most noble Empress* (V. ii. 71), and, finally, *day o' the world* (IV. viii. 13), *eastern star* (V. ii. 311) display other features of her nature. The dying Cleopatra feels herself related to the very elements: *I am fire and air* (V. ii. 292).

Cleopatra's enigmatic character has repeatedly baffled the critics, and the question has been raised how Shake-speare really wanted Cleopatra to be understood. As is evinced, however, by the many-coloured mosaic of terms applied to Cleopatra, he saw all these qualities combined in her. She is neither solely queen, nor solely harlot, nor solely witch, but unites in her person all these contrasting natures.

17

TIMON OF ATHENS

WHEN the style of a drama begins to become rich in imagery from a certain point on, this must suggest fundamental changes in the characters themselves. The relationship existing between the dramatic structure and the distribution and frequency of the images in the individual scenes and acts has been discussed in the chapter on *King Lear*. *Timon of Athens* displays similar structural relationships. For the language both of Lear and Timon underwent the same change when their inner mood changed: not only does it all at once become suffused with images, but closely related series of symbolical images make their appearance accompanying that inner metamorphosis and giving it verbal expression. The imagery of these scenes in which Timon's spiritual withdrawal from his environment takes place, derives from a spiritual situation similar to that in *Lear* and fulfils similar functions. The conjecture that *Timon* was composed shortly after *Lear* may find corroboration through these similarities in the employment of imagery.

The whole play gives the unsatisfactory impression of not being entirely completed.[1] The imagery, too, seems somehow unfinished. We miss the ardour, the poetic wealth and complexity characteristic of the imagery in *Antony and Cleopatra*. Only a few themes are underlined and illustrated by the imagery in *Timon*; its motifs are simple and easy to grasp. But truly Shakespearian is the way in which it is employed as dramatic preparation and a mirroring of the action.

In the first scene we find the subject presented in a manner partly symbolical and partly allegorical. The poet describes to the painter an allegorical poem which he has composed in honour of Lord Timon, and which represents Fortune enthroned on a high mountain, and below, at the

---

[1] E. K. Chambers believes that the play has remained only a sketch and an outline (*Shakespeare, A Survey*, London, 1935, p. 273).

foot of the mountain among the supplicant throng, Timon,
graced above all by Fortune who beckoned him to her.
But the continuation of the allegory anticipates the real
meaning of the play. For when the painter asks how the
crowds of flatterers following Timon will behave later on,
the poet replies:

> When Fortune in her shift and change of mood
> Spurns down her late beloved, all his dependants
> Which labour'd after him to the mountain's top
> Even on their knees and hands, let him slip down,
> Not one accompanying his declining foot.   (I. i. 84)

That the theme of the play is thus anticipated by this
allegory throws light on the peculiar nature of *Timon of
Athens*.[1] As Gundolf has pointed out the theme of the drama
—the friend of mankind becoming the enemy of all men
and the untrustworthiness of flattering friends—has been
clearly worked out by Shakespeare, but the characters,
especially the minor characters, are lacking in real vitality.
The characters affect us as types; they are treated allegoric-
ally; they are representatives of characteristics, but they are
not real people. This emphasis on the central theme becomes
apparent in the allegory of the first scene.

As we have seen in the preceding chapters, things taking
place in reality can be viewed more intensively as well as
formulated more pointedly and with greater emphasis when
expressed by a metaphor. In the first scenes we see how the
flatterers crowd around Timon and partake of his viands.
Shakespeare presents this as if the flatterers were eating
Timon *himself*. He makes clear from the very start that the
adulatory relationship of the flatterers to Timon is based
solely upon the materialist enjoyment of his bounty. The
imagery makes us realize, in an early phase of the play, that,
in spite of the apparently trustworthy attitude of the friends,
the core of the relationship between them and Timon is
unsound. In the second scene Apemantus cries out:

. . . 'O you gods, what a number of men eat Timon, and he sees 'em
not! It grieves me to see so many dip their meat in one man's blood;
                                                            (I. ii. 41)

---

[1] Gundolf, *Shakespeare, Sein Wesen und Werk, II*, Berlin, 1928, p. 372.

and a hundred lines later he puts it even more drastically, using the same motif:

> And spend our flatteries, to drink those men
> Upon whose age we void it up again,
> With poisonous spite and envy.   (i. ii. 142)

This motif is carried on subterraneously, and when the First Stranger says: "I never tasted Timon in my life" (iii. ii. 84), he, too, unconsciously identifies Timon's food with Timon himself. When, finally, Timon is hard pressed by his insolent creditors, his words repeat the earlier simile. In the bitter mockery of despair he offers himself as payment: "Cut my heart in sums. . . . Tell out my blood" (iii. iv. 93). When Timon's old and faithful servant curses one of those false friends he also sees him under this aspect:

> . . . this slave,
> Unto his honour, has my lord's meat in him:
> Why should it thrive and turn to nutriment,
> When he is turn'd to poison?
> O, may diseases only work upon't!
> And, when he's sick to death, let not that part of nature
> Which my lord paid for, be of any power
> To expel sickness, but prolong his hour!   (iii. i. 59)

Another series of images may show how an image makes its first appearance merely as presentiment; when, however, reality has made this image "come true", how it is taken over by the leading character and applied in its full, poignant significance. Timon's impoverishment is seen under the image of approaching winter. As early as the second act Flavius puts it this way:

> Feast-won, fast-lost; one cloud of winter showers,
> These flies are couch'd.   (ii. ii. 181)

In the third act Lucius states "'Tis deepest winter in Lord Timon's purse" (iii. iv. 14). Two scenes later this image has wandered into the consciousness of Timon himself. At the last feast a lord remarks: "The swallow follows not summer more willingly than we your lordship". Timon answers with an aside: "Nor more willingly leaves winter; such summer-birds are men" (iii. vi. 33). He further develops this image when, in the fourth act, he thinks of

himself and his forsakenness as a tree stripped of its leaves
in winter, and says of his false friends:

> That numberless upon me stuck as leaves
> Do on the oak, have with one winter's brush
> Fell from their boughs and left me open, bare
> For every storm that blows: (iv. iii. 264)

Timon's fate is illuminated by imagery from the most
different angles. In the second act the Senator prophesies
that Timon will soon appear as a naked "gull", whereas he
is still flashing like a phoenix (ii. i. 32). He is compared
to the setting or the no longer rising sun (i. ii. 150; iii. iv.
13), to a leaking ship (iv. ii. 19) and to the moon which
has no more light wherewith to shine and cannot renew itself
(iv. iii. 68).

It is in the last two acts that the imagery fulfils its most
important mission. In these acts it becomes the principal
means of dramatic presentation for disclosing to us the
changes in Timon. The significant rôle played by the
images here must be seen in connection with the alteration
in the whole style. For at the moment when Timon leaves
Athens the entire style of the play undergoes a remodelling.
Instead of the consistently quiet manner of speaking only
occasionally interrupted by exclamations of uneasiness, we
have from the fourth act on, a new form of utterance
vehement in tone, loose in structure as to syntax and
increased in speed. The very first monologue is characteristic
of this new style in which imagery forms so important a
component. This monologue consists of eighteen consecu-
tive exclamations, loosely stringing curses and wishes
together, images and disconnected thoughts. Almost every
one of these eighteen exclamations contains a new image;
from now on, we note a great frequency of images. At
least three-quarters of what Timon utters from now on is
clothed in images which supply an important clue to his
character. If we try to interpret them and to understand
their pattern, their themes and their significance, we at the
same time best describe what is going on in Timon himself.
We may recall *King Lear* in this respect. In both plays we
find a striking similarity as to the inner situation; hence

the correspondence in the function and subject of the imagery. Both Lear and Timon are outcasts; in both plays, the wealth of imagery expands from the very moment in which Timon and Lear as outcasts are thrown upon their own resources. Their language brings inner visions to light in the same measure as their relations to the world of men are cut off. The growing predominance of the monologue also accounts for this process. And, furthermore, Timon, as well as Lear, now that all human relationships have failed, seeks a relationship to superhuman forces (in *Lear*, the elements; in *Timon*, nature, the earth). Finally, we may compare how in *Lear* as well as in *Timon* the curses heaped upon their personal enemies are extended to cover all mankind. As in *King Lear*, earthly institutions pass before Timon's inner eye, and one after the other is damned.

In the long row of images in these two acts some central themes may be clearly distinguished. The fundamental theme for the first monologue (iv. i.), which is continued in the later scenes, is Timon's will to destroy everything. Starting from the wish that the walls of Athens should crumble, his thoughts turn to the field of human nature: "Matrons, turn incontinent!/Obedience fail in children!" (iv. i. 3). All values were to change into their opposites: chastity into licence, honesty into theft, justice into injustice; and thus curses are heaped upon each other in unheard-of vehemence:

> Maid, to thy master's bed;
> Thy mistress is o' the brothel! Son of sixteen,
> Pluck the lined crutch from thy old limping sire,
> With it beat out his brains!   (iv. i. 13)

The transition to the appeal to disease is significant, for disease is the strongest force of destruction:

> Plagues, incident to men,
> Your potent and infectious fevers heap
> On Athens, ripe for stroke!   (iv. i. 21)

The motif of disease is by far the most powerful. A wealth of maledictions invoking disease, plague-summoning curses and revolting images of sickness are spread over the last two acts. The frequency of the images of disease in the later tragedies is well known. Compared with the disease-images of the histories, these images are much more realistic and of a keen and poignant nature.[1] *Timon* presents the most intense expression of this symbolism of sickness. His language teems with such images: ulcers, plague,[2] fever, consumption, crippling, poisoning, leprosy and sciatica are among them.

This disease-motif also finds expression in the real action upon the stage: in the fourth act Timon meets with two harlots whom he bids transmit their diseases to all classes and conditions of men (IV. iii. 151). Finally, he wishes the very air to be plagued and poisoned, when he says to Alcibiades:

> Be as a planetary plague, when Jove
> Will o'er some high-viced city hang his poison
> In the sick air: (IV. iii. 108)

This atmosphere of sickness, decay and rot, lying like a dark veil above many plays of the later period, has been the occasion of the most diverse interpretations. Whether we have a right to draw any conclusions regarding Shakespeare's personal life from this increase in sickness-imagery is an open question. It is certain, however, that Shakespeare employed[3] the symbol of disease for all conditions in which the natural, harmonious order of things had given place to unnaturalness, disorder and corruption. We should not forget this specific significance of the sickness-images, although may it be admitted that the conspicuous employment of these images in the later plays perhaps suggests some connection with Shakespeare's own increasingly pessimistic outlook.

Apart from the sickness-images, "nature-imagery" plays the most important part in the last acts. Nature takes the place of people for Timon. Instead of conversing with men, he now holds converse with nature:

> O blessed breeding sun, draw from the earth
> Rotten humidity; below thy sister's orb
> Infect the air! (IV. iii. 1)

---

[1] Cf. Spurgeon, *Shakespeare's Imagery*, p. 129 sqq.

[2] Plague appears thirteen times, leprosy three times, consumption twice, poison six times.

[3] Professor Spurgeon has convincingly shown how the numerous sickness-images in *Hamlet* reflect Shakespeare's own view of the Hamlet problem (*Shakespeare's Imagery*, p. 318).

This recalls Lear and his appeals to the elements. The passage is the beginning of a new train of thought which itself finds expression in images; in nature, too, Timon sees strife, contempt and lack of harmony. In the simultaneous existence of sun and moon he sees opposition—a mutual scorn and a mutual flattery. Thus all his thoughts appear here in the form of imaginative images and plastic visions. Only the last lines return to a more abstract language and draw the logical conclusion from that chain of images:

> . . . all is oblique;
> There's nothing level in our cursed natures,
> But direct villany.   (iv. iii. 18)

In Shakespeare's great tragedies we can observe time and again how the imagery takes its cue from some real event taking place on the stage, this event then being symbolically interpreted by the imagery. In *Timon*, *gold* is one such real element of great symbolical force which for Timon himself is repeatedly the occasion of new chains of images (iv. iii. 26; iv. iii. 83; v. i. 50). How an unbroken series of images rises from a real situation may best be shown by the third scene of the fourth act. Timon is digging in the ground for roots and thus addresses the earth:

> . . . Common mother, thou,
> Whose womb unmeasurable, and infinite breast,
> Teems, and feeds all; whose self-same mettle,
> Whereof thy proud child, arrogant man, is puff'd,
> Engenders the black toad and adder blue,
> The gilded newt and eyeless venom'd worm,
> With all the abhorred births below crisp heaven
> Whereon Hyperion's quickening fire doth shine;
> Yield him, who all thy human sons doth hate,
> From forth thy plenteous bosom, one poor root!
> Ensear thy fertile and conceptious womb,
> Let it no more bring out ingrateful man!
> Go great with tigers, dragons, wolves, and bears;
>   (iv. iii. 177)

Here Timon turns to the earth, to nature; just as Lear turned to nature after men had failed him. But at the same time these verses produce that new nature-atmosphere dominating the last two acts and spreading ever wider. The world of animals and plants (v. 193) is called to life and from now on informs the language of the play.[1] This background of nature in the last acts stands in contrast to the symbolical atmosphere of the first three acts: there the basic tone was struck by representations of sumptuousness, festivity and culture (jewelry, gold, costly vessels, presents). Furthermore, the last two acts take place in the open air and thus the real situation is reflected in the imagery. As a result, many of the images are ambiguous. When Timon compares his false friends to the leaves dispersed by the winter storm and says that they left him behind "open, bare/For every storm that blows", we may note that this image at the same time refers to his own situation of being deserted in the forest—a situation of which Apemantus had shortly before reminded us when he said to Timon:

> Call the creatures . . .
> Of wreakful heaven, whose bare unhoused trunks,
> To the conflicting elements exposed,
> Answer mere nature;   (iv. iii. 227)

In the speeches which Timon makes in these last acts we find a trend of thought entirely different from that in the opening dialogues. The action of these final acts is in itself not very important; it is far more important that Timon's fundamental spiritual attitude—his hatred of mankind, his negation, his will to destruction—continually receives new nourishment and can encompass ever new fields of imagination. View Timon's encounter with the prostitutes, with Alcibiades, with the thieves, in this light. Each one of these individual encounters expands in Timon to a chain of imagery which spins itself along by pure association and which soon forsakes its concrete occasion. These encounters are an opportunity for Timon to proclaim anew his desire for a universal inversion of all values, a theme which was

---

[1] The world of animals is widely represented in Timon's long list (iv. iii. 329). We hear of lion, fox, lamb, ass, wolf, unicorn, bear, horse, leopard. Nature becomes vivid through Apemantus' reference to "these moss'd trees, that have outlived the eagle", "the cold brook, candied with ice" (iv. iii. 223); through the comparison with the oak tree (iv. iii. 442); through Timon's little description: "The oaks bear mast, the briers scarlet hips;/The bounteous housewife, nature, on each bush/Lays her full mess before you." (iv. iii. 422); through the description of the sea-shore, etc.

characteristic of the first monologue in iv. i. Thus matron, virgin and child reappear in his speech to Alcibiades in motifs which we have noted in iv. i. The encounter with the thieves gives Timon an opportunity to view the whole world now as a manifestation of thievery, and thus there results a new chain of "image examples":

> I'll example you with thievery:
> The sun's a thief, and with his great attraction
> Robs the vast sea: the moon's an arrant thief,
> And her pale fire she snatches from the sun:
> The sea's a thief, whose liquid surge resolves
> The moon into salt tears: (iv. iii. 438)

Such speeches, though set in dialogue, are scarcely addressed to the partner in the dialogue. The heaping up of the images here shows again that the emphasis lies on this inner complex of representations. The other characters are merely an occasion for such imaginative flights. Such "thinking-in-images" which makes itself almost wholly free from the given situation of converse we have already observed in *King Lear*. In *Lear* such general reflections were still closely connected with the action. But in *Timon* there is a perceptible loosening of the firm guidance of the dramatic action; these debates which Timon holds with the general and the universal powers and elements often appear to us as digressions and parentheses. Thus in this respect also, *Timon* impresses us as a play that is not quite perfect and complete.[1]

[1] Cf. Una Ellis-Fermor, "*Timon of Athens:* An Unfinished Play" *RES XVIII*, 71, 1942.

Part III

THE IMAGERY IN THE "ROMANCES" (*THE TEMPEST, THE WINTER'S TALE, CYMBELINE*)

18

INTRODUCTORY

IT was possible to generalize as to the use and style of imagery in Shakespeare's early plays. But the further our study advanced in examining the imagery in the dramas of Shakespeare's middle and tragic period, the more difficult did it become to pass any general judgement on the imagery, not of single plays, but of a whole group of plays. One feature of the development of Shakespeare's imagery has been an increase in variety and richness. Shakespeare found more and more dramatic uses to which he could turn the imagery, and, simultaneously, more and more types, patterns and subdivisions of imagery developed. The ways of combining and interconnecting the images, too, became, as we have seen, more intricate and varied. If, therefore, the attempt is made to say a few words in general on Shakespeare's use of imagery in the romances, before entering into a discussion of single plays, all due caution must be observed, and a broad margin must be left for exceptions to those general rules.

A close scrutiny of the imagery in the "romances" will certainly help to refute the often-made observation that Shakespeare's last plays show a weakening of imagination, of power of expression, a loss of vitality and a growing lack of interest in craftsmanship. This theory has already been convincingly rejected and disproved by recent studies on Shakespeare's last plays, notably by E. M. W. Tillyard, G. Wilson Knight and S. L. Bethell,[1] to each of which the following chapters are much indebted. Among the various aspects discussed by these three authors, imagery takes a prominent part.

Generally, it may be said of the romances that the tempo of the speech and of the action has slowed down. We have only a very few examples of that breathless and

[1] E. M. W. Tillyard, *Shakespeare's Last Plays*, London, 1938; G. Wilson Knight, *The Crown of Life*, Oxford University Press, 1947; S. L. Bethell, *The Winter's Tale*, 1948.

vehement dialogue which we frequently find in the tragedies
(the first scenes with Leontes in *The Winter's Tale* and
Iachimo's great scene with Imogen come near it, but are
nevertheless not the same). Consequently we find more
seldom that type of impassioned, abrupt and supremely
concentrated imagery, in which the images seem to run
into one another, and in which, according to Dowden's
still valid phrase "the thought is more rapid than the
language". Instead, the slower pace of action and speech
allows better for fully executed imagery, even for elaboration
of images which, sometimes, as we shall see in *Cymbeline*,
even recall the manner of Shakespeare's early plays. We
also have more of descriptive and graphic imagery which
helps to create the rich nature-atmosphere in these plays.
The serenity and beauty pervading at least large parts of
these plays finds its equivalent in poetical imagery of finest
delicacy and subtlety, such as, for instance, occurs in the
fourth act of *The Winter's Tale*, or in a few scenes of *The
Tempest*. That peculiar and poetic blend of remoteness and
sensuousness, strangeness and reality as denoting some
images of Prospero, Ariel, Perdita and Imogen, seems
typical of the climate of the romances, and could not fit into
any other group of plays.

As to the distribution of imagery over the plays we have,
compared to the tragedies, a stronger contrast between
scenes which contain scarcely any imagery at all and other
scenes where we find long passages packed with imagery
like colourful carpets. The action seems almost suspended
while these carpets are spread out, and the images are not
auxiliary or secondary, but the whole life and essence of
the scene speaks through them. *The Tempest* and *The
Winter's Tale* will furnish examples for this peculiar concentration and density of imagery. On the whole, however,
there is less density and continuity of imagery in the
romances. In *King Lear* and *Macbeth* Shakespeare continually thought in images which are charged with symbolic
meaning to such a degree that we could not understand
the tragedy's significance and import without a proper
understanding of its image-patterns. This cannot be said
with like emphasis of the romances. The imagery, in

Shakespeare's last plays, offers in some respects different problems and consequently demands an approach different from that to the tragedies. The following discussion again selects from the multitude of aspects a few points which seem to deserve closer examination and may throw some light on the relation existing between the imagery on the one hand and the structure and particular character of the plays on the other. Of the three romances *The Tempest*, though the last, shall be discussed first as it will best illustrate some new functions of imagery.

19

THE TEMPEST

IN reading or watching *The Tempest* we feel that there is more at stake in this play than man and man's fate; nature and the elements seem to be included in the action which thus extends beyond the characters on the stage. In a play of this kind, as was shown by the example of *King Lear*, the imagery is to give expression to these accompanying superhuman powers and realms. The imagery is therefore more than a means of creating atmosphere and background, or of emphasizing the main theme of the play. Besides, *The Tempest* is one of the plays where the supernatural plays a considerable rôle. These plays have strong resemblances as regards the imagery. For the imagery is an essential mediator of these supernatural powers which do not enter the play only through certain characters, as e.g. Ariel. In *The Tempest*, the natural scene of action also has a deeper significance. The enchanted island which becomes vivid through such a wealth of single features and of concrete touches is more than merely a well-chosen locality for the play. And to say that the tempest has a meaning beyond that of being a mere background is a commonplace.[1] It is, however, through imagery that we are made to see these deeper significances.

The distribution of images in the individual scenes and their function in the structure of the drama bear out the pattern on which *The Tempest*, differing in this respect from the tragedies, is built up. In *The Tempest*, the actual catastrophe is at the beginning, and not at the end or in the middle of the play. And everything derives and develops from this beginning. Thus the images in this first scene that act as links with the previous events have not the function of preparing or foreboding what is to come; they are rather a reminiscence, an echo, an afterthought, they

---

[1] For a comprehensive discussion of the tempest-imagery in Shakespeare see G. Wilson Knight, *The Shakespearian Tempest*, London, 1932.

keep awake our remembrance of what has happened. The manner in which an actual event, by means of the imagery, pervades and overcasts the whole play is a good instance of Shakespeare's technique, sometimes employed by him in his later plays, of transforming frequently used symbolic imagery into actual incident.[1]

The "sea-storm" lingering in our memory, together with the recollection of wind, water and conflicting elements, thus constitutes one of the main streams of imagery which, from the second scene onwards, flow through the play. Merely to enumerate all these passages, however, would not be enough.[2] It is more illuminating to recognize the varying and devious methods that Shakespeare uses in order to introduce this imagery, often referring to the sea and to the elements in a very indirect and unobtrusive manner. It is also interesting to note how storm and sea are reflected in a quite different manner through the speech of the various characters. Lastly, the way Shakespeare distributes this imagery among the acts and scenes throws some light on his dramatic technique.

In the second scene, we are still under the impression of what we have witnessed just before; and, accordingly, the imagery is full of echoes recalling the first scene. Shakespeare, however, now modifies the theme by awakening the recollection of another tempest in the far-distant past.[3] After Miranda, by her first words, had referred to the events immediately preceding, Prospero leads her memory back to "the dark backward and abysm of time" (i. ii. 49), and thus arises the remembrance of another tempest, endured by Prospero and Miranda when they were expelled by his brother:

> there they hoist us,
> To cry to the sea that roar'd to us, to sigh
> To the winds whose pity, sighing back again,
> Did us but loving wrong. (i. ii. 148)

The two tempests thus become connected by a relation between guilt and redemption, this connection adding to

[1] Cf. G. Wilson Knight, *The Crown of Life*, 1947, p. 203 and *passim*.
[2] In this connection one could note, for instance, the frequency of compounds with *sea* in *The Tempest*: sea-sorrow, sea-swallowed, sea-change, sea-nymph, sea-marge, sea-water, etc.
[3] On the two storms in *The Tempest* see Dr. Tillyard, *op. cit.* p. 79.

the significance of the tempest-imagery in this scene.
Shakespeare then returns to the present through Miranda's
asking for Prospero's "reason/For raising this sea-storm"
(I. ii. 175). Shortly afterwards we see a being who is himself
a kind of storm-spirit and, through his spirit-like nature,
is related to the airy elements. The words and images
which characterize Ariel (and by which he characterizes
himself) at the same time thus revive, in a most natural and
organic manner, the world of the sea, of the winds and
waves. Ariel's description of his activity during the sea-
storm subsequently makes it clear that there were supernatural powers behind it. But if we compare his description
with Miranda's first words on the tempest, subtle differences
again are revealed:

> Jove's lightnings, the precursors
> O' the dreadful thunder-claps, more momentary
> And sight-outrunning were not; the fire and cracks
> Of sulphurous roaring the most mighty Neptune
> Seem to besiege and make his bold waves tremble,
> Yea, his dread trident shake.   (I. ii. 201)

Ariel's experience and vision of the storm is from *above*,
from the regions of the sky, and his reference to Jupiter
and Neptune suggests his own god-like rôle in this storm.[1]
Only fifty lines later in the scene, this spirit-like elemental
nature of Ariel is again expressed by suggestive and pregnant
imagery.

> PROSPERO. Thou dost, and think'st it much to tread the ooze
> Of the salt deep,
> To run upon the sharp wind of the north,[2]
> To do me business in the veins o' the earth
> When it is baked with frost.   (I. ii. 253)

In these lines, the fourth element, the "earth", is added to
the three elements of water, fire and air suggested by the
first passage referring to Ariel.[3] In the conversation between
Prospero and Caliban the vegetation and scenery of the

---

[1] See the note on I. ii. 4 by Mr. Morton Luce, editor of *The Tempest* in the "Arden
Shakespeare".

[2] Cf. the words Prospero speaks to Ariel at the end of the scene: "Thou shalt be as free/
As mountain winds" (497).

[3] See Morton Luce's note on l. 190.

island is evoked, whereas the following two famous songs
of Ariel again remind us of the sea. But meanwhile the sea
has calmed down, as Ariel's songs make clear; his line
"The wild waves whist" (379) is endorsed by Ferdinand's
ensuing narration:

> This music crept by me upon the waters
> Allaying both their fury and my passion.   (I. ii. 392)

The next verses, however, direct the eyes of our imagination
into that depth which, like "the veins o' the earth", is
solely accessible to Ariel. The depth of the sea, the corals
and pearls, the sea-change, remove us into a region of magic.
The sea-imagery in these songs thus opens up a deeper
level of nature, and we thus can trace throughout the scene
a gradual development. The imagery not merely repeats
the same theme, but it deepens and intensifies; the picture
of the world of nature which is formed in our imagination
gradually becomes more complex.

From a very different angle the sea is powerfully evoked
in the next scene. Francisco describes the desperate struggle
of Ferdinand against the hostile sea.[1] We shall see that this
aspect of nature as a hostile force which threatens man's
existence is repeatedly emphasized through the imagery.
But also by quite indirect means we are reminded of the
moist element in this scene. The dialogue between Sebastian
and Antonio, trying to sound each other's thought, is
tinged by sea-imagery.[2]

> SEBASTIAN. Well, I am standing water.
> ANTONIO.   I'll teach you how to flow.
> SEBASTIAN.   Do so: to ebb
> Hereditary sloth instructs me.
>
> (II. i. 222)

---

[1]
> I saw him beat the surges under him,
> And ride upon their backs; he trod the water,
> Whose enmity he flung aside, and breasted
> The surge most swoln that met him; his bold head
> 'Bove the contentious waves he kept, and oar'd
> Himself with his good arms in lusty stroke
> To the shore, that o'er his wave-worn basis bow'd,
> As stooping to relieve him: (II. i. 115–121)

[2] Cf. Prospero's words in the play's last scene:
> Their understanding
> Begins to swell, and the approaching tide
> Will shortly fill the reasonable shore
> That now lies foul and muddy.   (v. i. 79)

And, similarly, the image, shortly before applied by Gonzalo
to the bad humour of Antonio, is in keeping with the
tempest-imagery:

> GONZALO. It is foul weather in us all, good sir,
> When you are cloudy.   (II. i. 141)

The next scene contains another striking variation of the
tempest-imagery. Trinculo's vision of the storm with his
picture of the "black cloud" that "looks like a foul bombard
that would shed his liquor" (II. ii. 21), shows how very
differently the stor   is reflected in the speech of the characters, according to their nature and mood. Trinculo here
reads his own drunkenness into the shapes of the sky.[1]

In III. iii. Alonso's remark "and the sea mocks our
frustrate search on land" (9) when his party strays over the
island is another of these minor references, whereas Ariel's
long speech in the same scene (53) summing up the situation
of the three traitors, naturally contains intenser and more
varied imagery referring to the sea, to the elements, waters
and winds. These are his world, and thus it is natural that
they should occur when Ariel embarks on a longer speech.
But, at the same time, it is in keeping with the dramatic
situation here. For before this scene ends, it seems fit that
the power of the elements and the complete "powerlessness"
of the Alonso party is again emphasized. The lines spoken
by Alonso towards the end of the scene, rich in suggestive,
poetic imagery add other features to this picture of the sea
and the elements, and form an organic continuation of
Ariel's speech.

While the imagery in the fourth act runs on different
lines, in the last act the elements are again awakened and
are blended in the magnificent valedictory speech of
Prospero. Viewed within the structure of the drama, this
speech has the function of evoking once again the powers
of nature and the elements which continually accompanied
the action, modifying it every now and then. This speech
marks a climax and a final summing-up which interweaves
into a poetic vision the four elemental worlds of earth, fire,

---

[1] That the sea again occurs in Stephano's songs, later in this scene (II. ii. 44–56) may also
be noted.

water and air. But also in their music and colour these lines are among the most beautiful and rich in Shakespeare's romances.

> I have bedimm'd
> The noontide sun, call'd forth the mutinous winds,
> And 'twixt the green sea and the azured vault
> Set roaring war: to the dead rattling thunder
> Have I given fire and rifted Jove's stout oak
> With his own bolt; (v. i. 41)

Prospero's final promise of "calm seas, auspicious gales" (v. i. 316) is the last link in this chain of imagery and signifies the happy ending of the play, providing a contrast to the beginning in the first act.

We all of us are aware of the strong earthy atmosphere pervading the play. Except for *A Midsummer Night's Dream* and *King Lear* there is no other play of Shakespeare's in which so many plants, fruits and animals appear. Compared to the nature-world of *A Midsummer Night's Dream*, however, the world of flora and fauna in *The Tempest* is less lovely, less "Elizabethan", less poetic and aesthetic, especially if we look at Beaumont and Fletcher for comparison. There are fewer flowers, more weeds, roots and fruits of the country.

Again, it is illuminating to trace how Shakespeare creates this intense earthy atmosphere, how he infiltrates this world of animals and plants. Caliban, of course, is a main agent in this connection. From him, who at his very first appearance is called "thou earth" a penetrating earthy atmosphere really does emanate. While Ariel, being an "airy spirit", is related to the moving elements, Caliban, on the other hand, is at home in a lower animal world. His imagination is ruled by the primitive needs of life, and this is expressed in his language.

The dialogue between Prospero and Caliban, at Caliban's first appearance, will be discussed in another connection. But it should be noted how much sensuous and concrete detail is contained in those six lines spoken by Caliban towards the end of the second act:

> I prithee, let me bring thee where crabs grow;
> And I with my long nails will dig thee pig-nuts;

> Show thee a jay's nest and instruct thee how
> To snare the nimble marmozet; I'll bring thee
> To clustering filberts and sometimes I'll get thee
> Young scamels from the rock. Wilt thou go with me?
>
> (II. ii. 171)

Thus the vegetation and the animal-world of the island
are called up through Caliban's language. He does not,
however, speak of these only, but also of the mysterious
voices and noises on the enchanted isle which, as Professor
Spurgeon has shown, constitute one of the leading motives
in the play's imagery.[1] But there are more indirect ways
through which Shakespeare, from the very beginning of the
play, forms in our minds the picture of the island-soil with
its strange and rich vegetation. Gonzalo's wish, pronounced
at the end of the first scene "for an acre of barren ground,
long heath, brown furze, any thing" (I. i. 70), may be
quoted in this connection as well as Prospero's threat to
Ferdinand

> thy food shall be
> The fresh-brook muscles, wither'd roots and husks
> Wherein the acorn cradled.   (I. ii. 462)

The words by which Gonzalo, at the beginning of the second
act, describes the grass on the island as "lush and lusty"
could in fact be put as a motto over the sensuous imagery-
passages spoken by Iris and Ceres in the well-known
masque of the fourth act. The theme of fertility and "foison",
of growth and ripening, which had been previously hinted
at, here finds its full expression in its application to the
expected marriage between Miranda and Ferdinand. Hardly
in any other passage has Shakespeare ever concentrated so
much sensuous exuberance and pregnant wealth of imagery
as in the verses exchanged between Ceres and Iris:

> IRIS. Ceres, most bounteous lady, thy rich leas
> Of wheat, rye, barley, vetches, oats and pease;
> Thy turfy mountains, where live nibbling sheep,
> And flat meads thatch'd with stover, them to keep;

---

[1] The beautiful passage in which Caliban describes these strange voices (II. ii. 144) con-
tradicts in some way the notion of Caliban as an unfeeling piece of earth. This has already
been remarked by earlier critics (see, e.g. Morton Luce's Introduction to his edition of *The
Tempest* in the "Arden Shakespeare", p. xxxvii).

Thy banks with pioned and twilled brims,
Which spongy April at thy hest betrims,
To make cold nymphs chaste crowns; and thy broom-groves,
Whose shadow the dismissed bachelor loves,
Being lass-lorn; thy pole-clipt vineyard;
And thy sea-marge, sterile and rocky-hard,
Where thou thyself dost air; . . .   (iv. i. 60)

Compared to similar passages also occurring within a framework of pastoral mythology in other contemporary dramatists, especially Fletcher, Shakespeare's imagery shows a greater density, wealth of concrete details and closeness to real earth. The diction of these passages shows again that happy balance between thought and expression which had so often been upset in the tragedies. There is a new clarity and equilibrium in these verses whose precisely chosen and singularly fitting epithets convey a full, rich and abundant picture of this earthy world. Our imagination is not called upon to supplement or add; the passages are, so to speak, self-contained. Shakespeare surely wanted us to absorb fully this impression of intense, sensuous reality and of hopeful new beginning conveyed by the imagery in this masque, in order to make us feel the more poignantly the contrast of Prospero's famous lines in which he declares the whole world as an insubstantial pageant that is to dissolve into nothing.

We have above suggested that nature in *The Tempest* does not possess an "aesthetic character", does not stand for itself, but in some way continually affects human existence. This not only applies to the storm itself, where this interrelation is quite obvious, but it also holds good of the majority of the plants and animals mentioned. For these are mostly brought into relation with physical pain, threats of punishment, trouble and distress. Thus the impression arises that nature is pervaded by hostile and adverse forces which either oppose man or are called up against him. It is only in the fourth act that this adversity is superseded by the praise of the fruitbearing blessings of nature.

The first images used by Prospero comparing Antonio to

The ivy which had hid my princely trunk,
And suck'd my verdure out on't   (i. ii. 86)

may be quoted in this connection. Later on, in the same
scene, Prospero, in recalling to Ariel his past, reminds him
of how he was confined by Sycorax "Into a cloven pine"
(I. ii. 277) and threatens, unless he keeps silence, to

> rend an oak
> And peg thee in his knotty entrails till
> Thou hast howl'd away twelve winters. (I. ii. 295)

But most of this kind of imagery develops from the curses
and threats uttered by Caliban and Prospero against each
other. This is how Caliban introduces himself:

> As wicked dew as e'er my mother brush'd
> With raven's feather from unwholesome fen
> Drop on you both! a south-west blow on ye
> And blister you all over!   (I. ii. 321)

And this is Prospero's answer:

> For this, be sure, to-night thou shalt have cramps,
> Side-stitches that shall pen thy breath up; urchins
> Shall, for that vast of night that they may work,
> All exercise on thee; thou shalt be pinched
> As thick as honey comb, each pinch more stinging
> Than bees that made 'em.   (I. ii. 324)

To this may be added Caliban's curse opening the second
scene of the second act:

> All the infections that the sun sucks up
> From bogs, fens, flats, on Prosper fall and make him
> By inch-meal a disease!   (II. ii. 1)

and his further narrative of how Prospero's spirits chased
him "sometime like apes . . . then like hedgehogs . . .",
and he concludes:

> sometime am I
> All wound with adders who with cloven tongues
> Do hiss me into madness.   (II. ii. 12)

At the end of the fourth act we see Prospero issuing new
orders to his spirits of revenge, and again new animal-
imagery creeps in:

> Go charge my goblins that they grind their joints
> With dry convulsions, shorten up their sinews
> With aged cramps, and more pinch-spotted make them
> Than pard or cat o' mountain.   (iv. i. 259)

All this and similar imagery[1] possesses a considerable
imaginative value. Not only does there enter into the play,
through these curses and threats, the atmosphere of the
island with its strange beasts and plants, but we are made
to feel at the same time that this island is haunted, and that
the persons on it are not only under an invisible spell but
may also be subject to continual harassing pains and
troubles. Shakespeare has thus contrived to make his
imagery serve several ends at once. And, moreover, all this
imagery, compared to so many passages in *A Midsummer
Night's Dream* by means of which Shakespeare also wished
to create atmosphere, always remains *appliqué*; it arises
out of a definite dramatic situation and is closely related to
what is being acted on the stage. As a last example of how
Shakespeare evokes the scenery of the island, and, at the
same time, further develops the theme of nature's hostility
against traitorous mankind, we may quote Ariel's description
of how he led astray Caliban and his companions:[2]

> so I charm'd their ears
> That calf-like, they my lowing follow'd through
> Tooth'd briers, sharp furzes, pricking goss and thorns,
> Which entered their frail shins: at last I left them
> I' the filthy-mantled pool beyond your cell,
> There dancing up to the chins, that the foul lake
> O'erstunk their feet.   (iv. i. 178)

All these passages of imagery have one feature in common:
they continually act upon our senses; our hearing, smelling,
tasting and feeling are being appealed to. This is one of
the main differences to the imagery in Shakespeare's early
comedies, where there was far less direct appeal to the
senses. The numerous images which strike our sen ≈ of

---

[1] Cf. the conversations between Caliban, Trinculo and Stephano (in iii. ii.
where things of nature also creep in through threats. Or cf. Ariel's long speed
where man and nature are represented as hostile against each other ("wound t'
. . . Incensed the seas and shores, yea all the creatures,/Against your pe
valedictory speech (v. i. 34), too, visualizes nature as being incensed agains'
[2] Dr. Tillyard quotes the whole passage in order to illustrate the f'
realism supplies to Prospero's preceding mysterious utterance, *op. cit.* '

hearing, referring to noises, have already been collected by Professor Spurgeon. But to supplement this list, the passages which appeal to our sense of smell should also be noted. For these help to create that dense atmosphere of physical sensation which surrounds the island like some curious climate and awake the sentiment not only of strangeness but also of an intense reality in which we believe that we have physically participated. (This again counterbalances the "supernatural" atmosphere of the play!) There are, to be sure, references to the air,[1] to "the quality o' the climate" (II. i. 199), especially at the beginning of the second act:

ADRIAN.   It must needs be of subtle, tender and delicate temperance.

.   .   .   .

ADRIAN.   The air breathes upon us here most sweetly,
SEBASTIAN. As if it had lungs, and rotten ones.
ANTONIO.   Or as 'twere perfumed by a fen.   (II. i. 41)

The above-quoted curses uttered by Caliban against Prospero referred to exhalations from the fen-land, and Ariel's description of the straying Caliban party had mentioned the "foul lake" that "o'erstunk their feet".[2] Compared to the great number of sensuous images, those passages in which something abstract (e.g. an intellectual quality or attitude), is interpreted by an image, are rare and occur much more seldom than in the tragedies. One passage which falls into this category may be discussed here:

SEBASTIAN. But, for your conscience?
ANTONIO.   Ay, sir; where lies that? if 'twere a kibe
           'Twould put me to my slipper: but I feel not
           This deity in my bosom: twenty consciences,
           That stand 'twixt me and Milan, candied be they
           And melt ere they molest!   (II. i. 277)

The image of the twenty consciences could occur in the tragedies where abstract things are often brought into

---

[1] Ariel himself is "but air" (v. i. 21), and when set free he exclaims "I drink the air before me" (v. i. 102).

[2] Shortly before, Ariel had said of their behaviour when they were listening to his tabor, that they "lifted up their noses/As they smelt music" (IV. i. 177). Other references to "smell" are Miranda's "The sky, it seems, would pour down stinking pitch" (I. ii. 3), the line occurring in Stephano's sailor's song, "She loved not the savour of tar nor of pitch" (II. ii. 54), and Trinculo's "Monster, I do smell all horse-piss; at which my nose is in great indignation" (IV. i. 199).

connection with wide space. The associations offered by "candied" and "melt" also refer back to earlier juxtapositions of these very words[1] and are in the manner of the suggestive and allusive imagery of Shakespeare's tragic period. Shakespeare, by inserting such an image here, wanted to impress on us this very point of Antonio's conscience. He does so by dramatic irony. For the very fact that Antonio by this unusual, wide image wants to express his disregard for his conscience makes the audience realize the actual power of conscience and Antonio's guilt. The effect of this image is strengthened by its being surrounded by others which express this contemptuous and frivolous attitude through comparisons· with the trivial everyday sphere[2] (the conscience as a kibe that would put Antonio to his slipper; the description of "all the rest who will" take suggestion as a cat laps milk (288)).

Considering the distribution of imagery to the characters in the play, we are struck by the fact that the "courtiers", especially Ferdinand, speak a language which contains very little imagery compared to Caliban and his mates and to Prospero and Ariel. Caliban, to begin with, is a person who does not think in abstract terms but in concrete objects, which consequently abound in his language. Prospero's language has the widest range. He commands the familiar, conversational, easy-flowing tones as well as the solemn poetic diction which has in it something dignified and lofty. And in this later vein, images are often used as a means of intensification. Prospero's beautiful and famous line, often quoted by critics as an example of Shakespeare's later style,[3]

The fringed curtains of thine eye advance   (I. ii. 407)

is pronounced at a moment of increased expectation and tension. It is the moment when Miranda, for the first time in her life, sees a stranger. Just before, Ariel's two famous

[1] For a full discussion of the set of images in which "candy" and "melt" occur see Spurgeon, *Shakespeare's Imagery*, p. 196.
[2] It may be noted that Sebastian shows a predilection for this kind of flippant everyday-world imagery. Cf. II. i. 10, "He receives comfort like cold porridge"; II. i. 12, "he's winding up the watch of his wit;".
[3] See Variorum Edition (particularly Coleridge) and, lately, George Rylands in *Words and Poetry*, London, 1930.

songs, rich in imagination and poetic power, had been heard and the whole tenor of the scene had grown more imaginative, more poetical. Prospero's words sustain this atmosphere, and prepare, as if a spirit was to be conjured up by the "magician",[1] the significant moment of Miranda's first encounter with Ferdinand.

Examining the distribution of imagery in the whole play we may notice that, compared to the tragedies, we find a greater number of lengthy passages which consist exclusively of images. The atmosphere which permeates the whole drama again and again concentrates and is focused into densely woven clusters of images. Several times these rich and cumulative imagery-passages occur close to the end of a scene, as if it were Shakespeare's purpose to impress upon us the setting and the peculiar atmosphere of the whole before a new part of the action is to begin.[2] Towards the end of the play such passages as are saturated in imagery grow even more frequent, especially in the great valedictory speeches of Prospero and in the masque. When the play has ended there remains in our imagination not only the remembrance of the characters which we saw on the stage, but also—and perhaps equally enduring—the vision of that strange nature-world.

The examination of the imagery in *The Tempest* showed how vividly, sensuously and precisely this nature-world was represented. As we have already said, this concreteness and realness, conveyed through the imagery, constitutes a counterpart to the world of the supernatural in this play. The supernatural, in being based on firm reality, gains probability and convincing power.

[1] See Morton Luce's note on this line.
[2] See Caliban's description of the fruits of the island (ii. ii. 171), his description "the isle is full of noises" (iii. ii. 144), Alonso's well-known passage "Methought the billows spoke . . ." (iii. iii. 96).

20

THE WINTER'S TALE

OF Shakespeare's romances *The Winter's Tale* shows the widest range of imagery. It embraces romantic and poetical imagery (as becoming to a "romance") as well as drastic and realistic imagery of the workaday world. The more intellectual types of imagery by which passion and thought express themselves are also represented, as well as the subtle and complex images that derive their effect from condensation and ambiguity. Mr. Bethell has made the acute observation (which he has illustrated by well-selected examples) that in *The Winter's Tale* we find a use of imagery and conceit more Jacobean than Elizabethan.[1] Thus Shakespeare's imagery does not only develop along the lines of Shakespeare's artistic evolution, but it also reflects the changes which we can trace in the transition of poetic style from the Elizabethan to the Jacobean period.

The Winter's Tale reveals in several respects an essentially Shakespearian tendency which we can trace throughout his whole dramatic career and which becomes more and more conspicuous towards its end: the endeavour to establish a balance between opposites, never to give only one colour without supplementing it by a complementary colour, never to yield to one specific mood without contrasting it by other entirely different moods and spheres. This desire always to create a complex, round and full picture partly accounts for Shakespeare's masterly faculty to blend various genres, sources and elements into a new organic whole. It is not only brought out by his maturer technique of characterization but becomes evident in almost all aspects and features of his art. Imagery, in this connection, is a considerable help in securing this balance and complexity of which *The Winter's Tale* is a good example.

The imagery in the first three acts of the play which so

[1] S. L. Bethell, *The Winter's Tale, A Study*, London, 1948, p. 21.

much resemble a tragedy is set off distinctly from the imagery in the "romance" of the fourth act, where we again can trace various contrasting patterns. Compared to the fourth act, the images in that first part are shorter and more thinly spread all over the text. We have more single metaphors than in the fourth act, in which the images appear more in clusters, are more compact, stand out from the context more colourfully and strikingly and (in a longer passage) often crowd so closely that the effect and the impression of this passage seems to lie solely in the imagery. In the first part, on the other hand, the imagery, being more subsidiary, has rather the function of being an expression for thought and passion, whereas in the fourth part the imagery seems largely to have been introduced for its own sake.

It could also be said that in the first acts, the imagery is more "subterranean" and subordinate; every now and then, from this hidden stream, images rise up to the surface and tinge the language, sometimes only by way of metaphor. This subterranean flow of imagery not only finds its expression in a chain of iterative imagery, but also in the associative interrelation of images. Leontes' aside, for example, in I. ii. 180, "I am angling now, . . ." gives rise, fourteen lines later, to "And his pond fish'd . . ." (I. ii. 195), which may have also been suggested by "sluic'd" in the preceding line.

In the first act Leontes' growing obsession is pictured by Shakespeare through a series of disease-images and related imagery which express poisoning, disgust and dirt. In the long passage spoken by Leontes after Polixenes and Hermione have left, Leontes confesses

> many thousand on's
> Have the disease, and feel't not (I. ii. 206)

the disease of which he had before said "Physic for't there is none" (I. ii. 200). This, at the same time, is self-revealing and possesses dramatic irony[1] as well as the other lines at the beginning of this speech:

---

[1] Another example of dramatic irony being expressed through an image occurs in II. iii. 154:
LEON. I am a feather for each wind that blows:

> and I
> Play too, but so disgraced a part, whose issue
> Will hiss me to my grave: contempt and clamour
> Will be my knell.   (i. ii. 187)

Later, in the same scene, Camillo asks him to be "cured of
this diseased opinion" (i. ii. 297) and retorts to Leontes'
false assumption of his "infected" wife "who does infect
her?" (i. ii. 307). The disease-imagery links up with the
notion of taint and stinging things. Shortly after Camillo's
question Leontes speaks the following words which also
contain dramatic irony:

> LEON.   Make that thy question, and go rot!
> Dost think I am so muddy, so unsettled,
> To appoint myself in this vexation, sully
> The purity and whiteness of my sheets,
> Which to preserve is sleep, which being spotted
> Is goads, thorns, nettles, tails of wasps,
>   (i. ii. 325)

In the next scene this collocation of disease, of stinging and
poison[1] becomes more obvious. Note the following lines
spoken by Leontes:

> There may be in the cup
> A spider steep'd, and one may drink, depart,
> And yet partake no venom, for his knowledge
> Is not infected: but if one present
> The abhorr'd ingredient to his eye, make known
> How he hath drunk, he cracks his gorge, his sides,
> With violent hefts. I have drunk, and seen the spider.
>   (ii. i. 39)

The dramatic and structural significance of this image
should be noted. For it is the first time Leontes builds up
a full image, all the more striking as Leontes' hasty diction
does not usually allow of the elaboration of images. The
directness and realism with which this image of the spider
in the cup is presented and the way Leontes turns it into a
personal experience, expressed by the laconic ending "I
have drunk, and seen the spider", bring home to us the
brutal and naked force of Leontes' self-deceiving obsession,

---

[1] It should be mentioned that previous to Leontes' above-quoted words is Camillo's
refusal to use *poison*.

14

the sudden growth of which we witnessed in the preceding
scene. This is, moreover, the first longer speech we hear of
Leontes after he has reappeared in the second act. Shakespeare could scarcely have found a more powerful means of
reminding us of what we saw in the first act and to show
that Leontes is now completely ruled by his jealousy which
has grown beyond doubt.

That the disease-metaphor creeps into the language of
other characters,[1] too, is the usual Shakespearian process.
The disease-imagery is, of course, suspended in the fourth
act, but in the fifth act there is an echo of it, though now in
a contrary sense, in Leontes' wish:

> The blessed gods
> Purge all infection from our air whilst you
> Do climate here! (v. i. 168)

As has already been said, the imagery in the first acts is
generally in the way of metaphor. In many cases we have
what may be called "sunken images". This thinned-out
imagery corresponds in some way to Leontes' barren and
restless style of arguing, to his becoming more and more
isolated from the world.[2]

There is, however, in the first three acts, one other
instance of a developed and extended image which deserves
discussion. After the news of Hermione's supposed death
Paulina exhorts Leontes to betake him

> To nothing but despair. A thousand knees
> Ten thousand years together, naked, fasting,
> Upon a barren mountain, and still winter
> In storm perpetual, could not move the gods
> To look that way thou wert. (iii. ii. 211)

---

[1] From Camillo's renewed reference to "a sickness/which puts some of us in distemper,
but/I cannot name the disease" (i. ii. 385) Polixenes takes over the image and asks: "A sickness
caught of me, and yet I well!" (i. ii. 398). The imprecation pronounced by him shortly
afterwards also derives from the disease-metaphor, "O, then my best blood turn/To an
infected jelly" (i. ii. 417). When Paulina, in the second scene of the second act, tries to get
access to Leontes, she says: "I/Do come with words as medicinal as true,/Honest as either,
to purge him of that humour/That presses him from sleep" (ii. iii. 37). To which may be
added her contrasting of Leontes' rotten opinion to the soundness of oak or stone (ii. iii. 88).
The disease-imagery even spreads over to Hermione who in iii. ii. 98 confesses: "from his
presence/I am barr'd, like one infectious". Mr. Bethell refers to the disease-image on p. 80,
op. cit., whereas Professor Spurgeon does not seem to consider it as "a leading motive",
mentioning it only incidentally (*Shakespeare's Imagery*, p. 306).

[2] Dr. Tillyard says: "Leontes' world is marvellously expressed by the hot and twisted
language he uses" (*op. cit.* p. 76).

This magnificent and terrible image marks another decisive stage of the tragic development in the first three acts, it expresses the sense of Leontes' irretrievable guilt and its effect upon us is the more forcible as it is the only fully executed image in this scene. At the same time, it forebodes the storm of the next scene.

The manner in which this storm is pictured in III. iii. also deserves attention. For it is seen from two quite different angles. The Mariner's "the skies look grimly/And threaten present blusters. . . . The heavens . . . frown upon's." (III. iii. 4), and Antigonus' similar references[1] imply the usual tempest-symbolism, whereas the Clown's prose-observations on the storm express a far more realistic point of view:

. . . now the ship boring the moon with her main-mast, and anon swallowed with yest and froth, as you'ld thrust a cork into a hogshead. . . . But to make an end of the ship, to see how the sea flap-dragoned it: . . .   (III. iii. 93)

Dr. Tillyard has noted the abrupt transition from the melo-dramatic dream-world of Antigonus to the old shepherd's world of "common humanity".[2] The imagery, to some extent, may illustrate this by the very different representation of the same thing.

To call the play a romance is fully justified only by the fourth and fifth acts. In the fourth act, nature bursts into life with extraordinary wealth and colour. But for this strong country atmosphere in its pastoral setting we are prepared during the first acts by occasional touches. The second scene opens with

Nine changes of the watery star have been
The shepherd's note since we have left our throne. (I. ii. 1)

And there is other nature-imagery spread over the first scenes[3] which can be said to prepare and forebode the pastoral romance of the fourth act.[4]

[1] "The storm begins: . . . The day frowns more and more. . . . I never saw/The heavens so dim by day . . ." (III. iii. 49, 54, 55).
[2] E. M. W. Tillyard, Shakespeare's Last Plays, p. 77.
[3] For example, G. Wilson Knight, The Crown of Life, p. 88.
[4] In this connection, especially the beginning of the third act should be noted; Mr. Bethell considers this short scene as "a turning point in the play" (op. cit. p. 82). See also Dr. Tillyard, loc. cit. p. 76.

As this fourth act (especially scene III. and IV.) has already been fully commented upon by various distinguished critics, a few remarks may suffice to recall Shakespeare's achievement here. It is, perhaps, the best example for Shakespeare's art of combining several moods and styles. Mr. Bethell has well demonstrated how that typical "juxtaposition of the timeless world of romance and the contemporary scene" is already conveyed to us in Autolycus' song which forms the beginning of scene III.[1] It not only blends various styles (Elizabethan, Jacobean and metaphysical) it also brings the "ideal world of romance" into relation with the very real world of everyday life and interconnects the contrasted spheres of natural beauty and of "the nasty sneak-thief". It is interesting to note that a similar juxtaposition recurs in the next scene. Autolycus sings:

> Lawn as white as driven snow;
> Cypress black as e'er was crow;
> Gloves as sweet as damask roses;
> Masks for faces and for noses;
> Bugle bracelet, necklace amber,
> Perfume for a lady's chamber;
> Golden quoifs and stomachers,
> For my lads to give their dears:
> Pins and poking-sticks of steel,
> What maids lack from head to heel:
> Come buy of me, come;   (IV. iii. 220)

The items from Autolycus' pedlar's pack are here compared to things which suggest the imagery of Elizabethan lyrics: white as driven snow, sweet as damask roses. And thus a romantic note is struck in this prosaic catalogue of trifles and petty stuff. But all this cheap knick-knackery, sold and broken up by Autolycus and spread all over the scene, gives much colour and a homely and realistic flavour to this peasants' idyll. Before Autolycus even enters, his wares are announced by the servant: "he has ribbons of all the colours i' the rainbow; points more than all the lawyers in Bohemia can learnedly handle, though they come to him by the gross: inkles, caddisses, cambrics, lawns . . ."

[1] Bethell *op. cit.* p. 44, *The Meaning of a Song.*

(IV. iii. 205). In a certain way, as early as in IV. iii., the Clown's enumeration of all the items he is to buy for the sheep-shearing introduces this varied and solid picture of village-life atmosphere:

> Let me see; what am I to buy for our sheep-shearing feast? Three pound of sugar, five pound of currants, rice . . . I must have saffron to colour the warden pies; mace; dates?—none, that's out of my note; nutmegs, seven; a race or two of ginger, but that I may beg; four pound of prunes, and as many of raisins o' the sun.
>
> (IV. ii. 37)

There are other small touches which help build up and sustain this atmosphere in the next scene: the references to milking-time, to the kiln-hole, to the "grange or mill", and the Servant's announcement of the "three carters, three shepherds, three neatherds, three swine-herds" who want to perform a dance "which the wenches say is a gallimaufry of gambols". Autolycus by his absurd but credulously believed ballads, adds to this picture a tinge of quaintness and strangeness, e.g. when he speaks of the usurer's wife who "longed to eat adders' heads and toads carbonadoed" (IV. iii. 267).

We become aware of the wide range of imagery in this scene if we turn from the prose[1] of these adders' heads and toads carbonadoed to the exquisite music of Perdita's and Florizel's lines. For, indeed, imagery, diction and the music of the verse here combine and go together to build up some of the most perfect pages Shakespeare has ever written. The close amalgamation of verse and imagery may best be seen in that beautiful passage where Florizel compares Perdita to a wave, this image being actually expressed by the wave-like movement of the language:

> when you do dance, I wish you
> A wave o' the sea, that you might ever do
> Nothing but that; move still, still so,
> And own no other function: (IV. iii. 140)

And has ever what we may call a conceit been uttered in a language more natural, more spontaneous and more

---

[1] Note how the change between prose and poetry in *The Winter's Tale* also helps to emphasize the contrasting of spheres.

unaffected than in these lines occurring at the end of
Perdita's famous flower-speech:

PERDITA.   O, these I lack,
          To make you garlands of; and my sweet friend
          To strew him o'er and o'er.
FLORIZEL. What, like a corse?
PERDITA. No, like a bank for love to lie and play on
          Not like a corse; or if, not to be buried,
          But quick and in mine arms. . . .   (IV. iii. 127)

We scarcely even notice that this is a conceit, for the
language flows on so naturally. But comparing this to any
conceit from the early plays we realize the development
Shakespeare has passed through until he reached this stage.

Likewise, the economical, unobtrusive use of mythological names in Perdita's and Florizel's language may be
noted. These names of antique gods, to be sure, heighten
the tone of pastoral idyll, and remind us of the fact that
both Perdita and Florizel are of princely origin. But the
allusions to mythology appear here not as rhetorical ornament,[1] for it seems the most natural thing that the lovers
should think of Flora, of the green Neptune, of "the fire-
robed god,/Golden Apollo" (IV. iv. 29), and when Perdita
apostrophizes Proserpina we entirely forget the rhetorical
origin of this device,[2] so original is the way in which it is
tied up with the context:

          Now, my fair'st friend,
    I would I had some flowers o' the spring that might
    Become your time of day; and yours, and yours,
    That wear upon your virgin branches yet
    Your maidenheads growing: O Proserpina,
    For the flowers now, that frighted thou let'st fall
    From Dis's waggon! daffodils,
    That come before the swallow dares, and take
    The winds of March with beauty;   (IV. iii. 112)

Another example of how traditional patterns of expression
falling under the heading "imagery" appear now in a much
refined manner is Florizel's declaration:

---

[1] Cf. the abundant and not always fitting use of mythological names in *Cymbeline*.
[2] Cf. the apostrophes in *Cymbeline* which are mostly in rhetorical manner. See the chapter
on *Cymbeline*, p. 207.

> I take thy hand, this hand,
> As soft as dove's down and as white as it,
> Or Ethiopian's tooth, or the fann'd snow that's bolted
> By the northern blasts twice o'er.   (IV. iv. 373)

It had been habitual for the Elizabethan lovers in Shake-speare's early plays to compare their beloved's eyes, skin, hair or hands to various beautiful things, and the device of piling up, on such occasions, several comparisons, is an old one. "As soft as dove's down and as white as it" is quite in this style. But the next two lines surprise us by the strangeness and novelty of the images, the simile becoming, moreover, as Mr. Bethell has pointed out, more complex by the introduction of the metaphor of "bolting".[1] All this is no longer typical Elizabethan style, but an anticipation of Donne.

It may be objected that by merely noting down all these small details and tiny touches we do not get much further in understanding the real meaning of the play, in penetrating to the core of the matter. There certainly is some truth in this warning. For we are apt to get too much absorbed by the examination of the minutiae and may lose hold of the full and rounded view of a Shakespearian drama. But a study of this kind can never be more than one of several approaches which we must in the end coordinate in order to arrive at a more comprehensive appreciation of the play. And then we discover that there is more in the details of imagery than we at first sight anticipated. This holds good of *The Winter's Tale*, too. The contrasting and blending of the ideal romance-world with the realistically and drastically represented village life[2] is more than a mere collocation of different atmospheres, and contains a deeper meaning which in fact leads us a little nearer to the play's central problem. Shakespeare evidently wanted to show that the renewal and regeneration of a decaying world as symbolized by the Perdita-Florizel episode in the fourth act must have

[1] Bethell, *op. cit.* p. 23. "Bolted" introduces a metaphor into the simile and supplies the further image of "wheaten flour the snow is made purer by being twice sifted as wheaten flour is sifted of its impurities".

[2] A German critic has well compared the fourth act to a combination of Romanticism with a Dutch painting by Teniers, representing a peasants' fair (Gustav Landauer, *Shakespeare*, 1923, p. 257).

roots in the firm reality and simplicity of the country-life
as well as in the more refined court-world.[1] "Country and
court are necessary to each other, Shakespeare seems to
imply, the sober virtues of the one and the graces of the
other compounding a perfect whole", as Mr. Bethell has
put it. And this necessary union is again indicated by the
imagery which at the same time possesses dramatic irony,[2]
for the speaker Polixenes, by his subsequent action against
his son, himself deviates from the procedure which he
recommends here as an organic law:

> You see, sweet maid, we marry
> A gentler scion to the wildest stock,
> And make conceive a bark of baser kind
> By bud of nobler race: this is an art
> Which does mend nature, change it rather, but
> The art itself is nature.   (iv. iii. 92)

We have above noted the gay display of all the trifling,
trivial knick-knacks, so much coveted by the peasants.
This, again, does more than merely to create atmosphere
if we look at the import of the whole scene. For it is to form
a significant contrast to the love-making between Florizel
and Perdita which goes on in the midst of this merry
bustle and is on such an entirely different plane. It is
Florizel himself who avows

> Old sir, I know
> She prizes not such trifles as these are:
> The gifts she looks from me are pack'd and lock'd
> Up in my heart; which I have given already,
> But not deliver'd.   (iv. iii. 367)

Thus Shakespeare subsequently utilizes Autolycus' trifles
in order to suggest his favourite theme of appearance and
reality that, in some way, also runs through *The Winter's
Tale*.

[1] For this cf. Chapters III and IV of the second part of Mr. Bethell's study. For the idea
of rebirth see also Dr. Tillyard, *op. cit.* p. 42.
[2] See S. L. Bethell, *op. cit.* p. 27.

CYMBELINE

A N examination of the structural significance of the
imagery in *Cymbeline*, particularly its distribution all
over the play and its allotment to the various characters,
will also throw some light on a few characteristic features
of this play. Almost all critics seem to agree that there are
weaknesses in the play, clumsy and imperfect passages as
well as structural deficiencies and inconsistencies in the
plot which it is difficult to account for. There is, in some
passages, not only in the "archaic" soliloquies, an obvious
falling back into early habits, into a style that, in the great
tragedies, had long been superseded by a more perfect
and subtle manner.[1] Of some of these passages it has been
said that they do not seem to have been sufficiently assimil-
ated to the fabric of the whole. Other passages, however,
seem to have been written *deliberately* in that artificial
style, Shakespeare making the formal and rhetorical
language do dramatic service. We must refrain here from
going more fully into this matter which has been so
well set forth by Mr. Granville-Barker.[2]

In looking at some of the passages which from other
points of view have also been criticized we become aware
that the type of imagery occurring in them would not
have been possible in any of the great tragedies. Take, for
instance, Belarius' speeches. He has an obvious tendency
to embroider his speeches with elaborate comparisons,
wise sayings, beautiful images. After having explained to
Guiderius and Arviragus his former position at Cymbeline's
court he ends:

[1] Some critics have tried to explain the different style in these last plays by Shakespeare's
adapting himself to the new conditions of the Blackfriars theatre and the different audience
he would find here. For a warning against these altogether too one-sided explanations see
U. Ellis-Fermor, *The Study of Shakespeare*, 1947, p. 9.
[2] See H. Granville-Barker, *Prefaces to Shakespeare, Second Series*, 1930.

> then was I as a tree
> Whose boughs did bend with fruit: but in one night,
> A storm or robbery, call it what you will,
> Shook down my mellow hangings, nay, my leaves,
> And left me bare to weather.   (III. iii. 60)

The passage is in keeping with the tree-imagery running through the whole play, as Professor Spurgeon has already shown. But this manner of indulging in elaboration is certainly more germane to the early plays than to the tragedies. How this tree-image can be turned into "dramatic imagery" may be seen from the last scene when Posthumus, this time forgetting his usual rhetoric habits of speech, answers to Imogen's

> and now
> Throw me again.

with the magnificent line[1]

> Hang there like fruit, my soul,
> Till the tree die!   (v. v. 264)

Another case in point is the beautiful passage in the fourth act where Belarius compares the two princely boys to the winds:

> They are as gentle
> As zephyrs blowing below the violet,
> Not wagging his sweet head; and yet as rough,
> Their royal blood enchafed, as the rudest wind,
> That by the top doth take the mountain pine,
> And make him stoop to the vale.   (IV. ii. 171)

Again, the subject matter of these images corresponds to the leading motives in the imagery of the whole play and, moreover, subtly reveals the princely nature of the two brothers.[2] But the wording is not in the dramatic style of the tragedies. On the other hand, it is characteristic of Belarius to take his time to reflect upon everything, to couch what he wants to say in beautiful, decorative, slow-moving language. This is brought out by many of

---

[1] Professor Spurgeon is right in calling this line "ten words which do more than anything else in the whole play to bring him in weight and value a little nearer to Imogen" (*Shakespeare's Imagery*, p. 293).

[2] See G. Wilson Knight, *The Crown of Life*, p. 200.

his speeches. But he is not the only character in the play
to use this kind of language. Mr. Granville-Barker justly
speaks of a "decorative bias" running through the whole
play, of a "new Euphuism of imagination", of a consciously
artificial and sophisticated style. There is in *Cymbeline* a
tendency, similar to that in the early plays, to "insert"
maxims, rhetorical exclamations, images and comparisons.
Imogen, breaking the seals of Posthumus' letter, makes
this pretty rhetorical excursion, extemporizing on the bees:[1]

> Good wax, thy leave. Blest be
> You bees that make these locks of counsel! Lovers
> And men in dangerous bonds pray not alike: (III. ii. 35)

Still worse is the artificial "aside" in which she apostrophizes
Experience:

> Experience, O, thou disprovest report!
> The imperious seas breed monsters, for the dish
> Poor tributary rivers as sweet fish. (IV. ii. 35)

and, after having caught sight of Cloten's headless body,
she even thinks fit to utter a pretty comparison:

> These flowers are like the pleasures of the world;
> This bloody man, the care on't. (IV. ii. 296)

In a similar vein Posthumus, when finding the book after
the dream-vision exclaims:

> A book? O rare one!
> Be not, as is our fangled world, a garment
> Nobler than that it covers: let thy effects
> So follow, to be most unlike our courtiers,
> As good as promise. (V. iv. 134)

Pisanio, in order to vent his indignation over slander,
invents no less than three images to describe the effect of
slander (III. iv. 35). Arviragus, in his famous flower-imagery
passage, when arriving at the ruddock's bill (which is to
carry to Imogen all the flowers) ingeniously inserts an
apostrophe to the bill

> O bill, sore-shaming
> Those rich-left heirs that let their fathers lie
> Without a monument! (IV. ii. 225)

[1] Cf. Granville-Barker, *op. cit.* p. 288.

Iachimo, in that highly dramatic and magnificent scene in which he tries to seduce Imogen, exerting all his powers of eloquence, in similar fashion inserts two additional definitions for the "cloyed will":

> The cloyed will,
> That satiate yet unsatisfied desire, that tub
> Both fill'd and running, ravening first the lamb
> Longs after for the garbage.   (I. vi. 46)

The frequency of parentheses in *Cymbeline*, striking the reader even if he only superficially peruses the pages, may illustrate this habit of rhetorical insertion, although sometimes these parentheses indicate the easy, colloquial, natural style which is also to be found in *Cymbeline*. Rhetorical, too, are the frequent apostrophes which usually contain imagery. Iachimo, when seeing Imogen asleep in her bed exclaims:

> Cytheria,
> How bravely thou becomest thy bed, fresh lily,
> And whiter than the sheets!   (II. ii. 14)

The other rhetorical devices, as antithesis, parallelism, conceit, also occur frequently, adding to the formal, decorated style of the play. Some of these passages (to the above-quoted examples more could be added) are in such bad taste that critics have hesitated to credit Shakespeare with them. The whole problem is too intricate and complex to be discussed here. Shakespeare's use of imagery could, at any rate, provide a valuable criterion in this connection. It would, however, not do to reject as un-Shakespearian all passages which in diction, imagery and dramatic fitness show a style inferior to that of the tragedies, typical rather of the early plays. *Cymbeline*, being the first of the romances, shows Shakespeare's search after a new style which may fit that strange blend of subject matter, of supernatural and realistic elements, of contradicting moods which are inherent in the complicated plot. In this experimental vein, he also takes up again earlier habits of style, but these formal, decorative, artificial patterns of style are only *partly* to be called clumsy and unmotivated insertions. Partly, as

Granville-Barker has admirably demonstrated, they have been adapted by Shakespeare to the dramatic situation and "turned to strict dramatic account".[1] The method of picking out isolated passages and analysing them as to their style and diction is therefore often misleading, and should only be used with due caution. The example of *Cymbeline* also warns us not to think of "the development of Shakespeare's imagery" as of a steady upward movement, a ladder, so to speak, of which each scale shows a higher degree of perfection. This development involves a return to earlier habits of style and certainly retrogressive movements as much as it does a perceptible advance towards subtlety, complexity and closer interweaving of imagery into the texture of the play.

If we now proceed to examine the distribution of imagery in *Cymbeline* we find that in the first act there are only two scenes containing any considerable number of images. In i. iv., it is the romantic situation of Imogen trying (according to Pisanio's report) to visualize Posthumus' departure at sea, which prompts imagery. These passages, in keeping with the "romance-situation", at the same time reveal Imogen's tender and delicate nature, her predilection for minute and tiny things.[2] i. vii. is the next scene to display an ample and peculiar use of imagery. Iachimo, in trying to persuade and seduce Imogen, employs highly coloured, glaring imagery which is to intensify his stormy eloquence. It not only (like his whole manner of speech) reflects his character, but also possesses dramatic irony. For the recurrent motives in his imagery are repulsive, contemptible and negative things put often in contrast to Imogen's purity.[3] While Iachimo, by these comparisons, wants to accuse Posthumus falsely, he actually describes his own mean character, his own attitude. And, unconsciously,

---

[1] Dr. Tillyard, too, dwells on this problem. See *op. cit.* p. 68 and *passim*. For critical remarks on Granville-Barker see pp. 70–71.

[2] See G. Wilson Knight, *The Crown of Life*, pp. 153–154. For comment on the scene see Granville-Barker, *loc. cit.* p. 291.

[3] "Sluttery, to such neat excellence opposed/Should make desire vomit emptiness, Not so allured to feed" (i. vi. 44); "the cloyed will . . . ravening first the lamb longs after for the garbage" (46); " . . . solace I' the dungeon by a snuff" (86); " . . . by-peeping in an eye/Base and unlustrous as the smoky light/That's fed with stinking tallow" (108); " . . . to be partner'd/With tomboys . . . " (121); " . . . diseased ventures" (122); "such boil'd stuff/As well might poison poison!" (125).

the audience, knowing of Posthumus' complete innocence, will relate these images[1] to Iachimo.

It is remarkable that the important scene, where Iachimo proves to Posthumus Imogen's apparent faithlessness, contains very little imagery indeed (if we except Iachimo's description of Imogen's bedchamber). Posthumus appears throughout the whole play as a rather colourless character, possessing little imagination; and this is reflected by his language.[2]

We then enter an entirely different atmosphere in the scene which first introduces Belarius and the two princes into the action, showing them in their mountainous retreat. The significance of this "new world", its contrast to the "old world" and the rôle it plays in the composition of the drama have been emphasized by Dr. Tillyard.[3] In comparing these mountain-scenes with the other scenes at court we become aware of several differences involving the use of imagery, which is richer and more exclusively drawn from nature in these scenes. The pace of the speech is slowing down, the diction is more musical, the atmosphere more remote; there are more passages where the dramatic action seems to be suspended so that reflective and decorative imagery can be developed, there is also an increase of melodramatic passages. It has already been pointed out how typical it is of one character appearing in these scenes, Belarius, to indulge in elaborated and reflective imagery so that his speeches, being, on the one hand, an expression of his temperament, at the same time serve Shakespeare's purpose of creating a strong nature-atmosphere in these scenes. But, besides Belarius, there is also Arviragus who has a strong bent towards imagery. Whereas Guiderius uses very little imagery, being the more realistic and soberly minded of the two brothers, Arviragus is of a far more imaginative and poetic disposition and resorts to images, comparisons and conceits whenever he is to speak. This

[1] The sensuous and florid imagery in Iachimo's soliloquy in ii. ii. may be compared to the imagery in i. vi.

[2] The images he uses are mostly conventional and presented in the form of simple comparisons, e.g. "As chaste as unsunn'd snow" (ii. v. 13), "will give you that like beasts" (v. iii. 37), "to grin like lions" (v. iii. 38).

[3] See E. M. W. Tillyard, *op. cit.* p. 27.

difference appears even in the first two speeches we hear from the two brothers. Arviragus says:

> what should we speak of
> When we are old as you? when we shall hear
> The rain and wind beat dark December, how,
> In this our pinching cave, shall we discourse
> The freezing hours away? We have seen nothing;
> We are beastly, subtle as the fox for prey,
> Like warlike as the wolf for what we eat;
> Our valour is to chase what flies; our cage
> We make a quire, as doth the prison'd bird,
> And sing our bondage freely.   (III. iii. 36)

Guiderius, to be sure, had also used the prison-metaphor, applied by him to their life: "A prison for a debtor, that not dares/To stride a limit" (34). But Arviragus beautifies and poeticizes this realistic metaphor into the image of the imprisoned bird's cage.

When, in the sixth scene of the same act, the brothers meet Imogen, who offers money for the meat she has taken, Guiderius only asks laconically, "Money, youth?" But Arviragus exclaims:

> All gold and silver rather turn to dirt!   (III. vi. 54)

Or compare the brothers' comments on their impression of Imogen—Arviragus enthusiastically praises Imogen's singing and calls her angel-like ("How angel-like he sings!") while the more realistic Guiderius praises Imogen's cookery:

> But his neat cookery! He cut our roots
> In characters,
> And sauced our broths, as Juno had been sick
> And he her dieter.   (IV. ii. 49)

Arviragus, however, is more concerned with the more immaterial side of Imogen and even now employs a sophisticated and artificial conceit:

> Nobly he yokes
> A smiling with a sigh, as if the sigh
> Was what it was, for not being such a smile;
> The smile mocking the sigh, that it would fly
> From so divine a temple, to commix
> With winds that sailors rail at.   (IV. ii. 51)

This, to be sure, is a conceit in the manner of the early plays. But its *function* is different; it has not merely a surface-value and is not only "an exercise of wit for its own sake",[1] but it corresponds to Arviragus' imaginative bent, and, at the same time, finely reflects the unique impression Imogen has made during her preceding appearance. The difference between the two brothers is carried on. Guiderius makes the acute observation:

> I do note
> That grief and patience, rooted in him both,
> Mingle their spurs together.   (III. ii. 56)

whereupon Arviragus ejaculates, using that intricate type of abstract imagery:

> Grow, patience!
> And let the stinking elder, grief, untwine
> His perishing root with the increasing vine!
>   (III. ii. 58)

Later in this scene, it is, of course, Arviragus who, in melodramatic fashion, gives us that famous and beautiful enumeration of flowers which so considerably contributes to the scene's colour and atmosphere. Guiderius, however, shows his very different attitude in cutting Arviragus short, impatiently objecting to his brother's "wench-like words":

> Prithee, have done;
> And do not play in wench-like words with that
> Which is so serious.[2]   (IV. ii. 229)

The use of imagery is thus a subtle means of bringing out the difference in temper and character in the two brothers.

If, lastly, we inquire into how the dramatis personae in *Cymbeline* are characterized through other persons by means of images or comparisons, we find that Imogen gets by far the largest share of them. Her dominant and peculiar position in the play thus becomes expressed as well as the fact that she is the best-wrought character in *Cymbeline*, although there is something vague and impalpable

---

[1] See S. L. Bethell, *op. cit.* pp. 21–22.

[2] This ironic criticism of Arviragus' style proves that Shakespeare did not simply fall back here into rhetorical style, not knowing how to write better, but that he quite consciously did so.

even about her. Perusing the names applied to her, we feel,
however, that there is more conventionalism in them than
in the images characterizing a heroine of the great tragedies
(e.g. Cleopatra). The fact that Imogen is compared with
or set in relation to bright and shining things (diamond,
jewel, radiant sun, lightning), to a lily, a bird, a temple, to
snow, tender air and a heavenly angel does not go far
beyond the conventionalism of the Elizabethan sonnets.[1]
The imagery, seen from this point of view, thus again
confirms the general impression which we receive when
reading the play.

[1] G. Wilson Knight, *op. cit.* p. 156: "She receives the glistering idealization usual in
Pericles and *The Winter's Tale*, here denied to Posthumus and reserved for her and the royal
boys themselves."

Part IV

SUMMARY AND CONCLUSION

SUMMARY AND CONCLUSION

THE aim of this study has been to trace the development of Shakespeare's imagery throughout his work and to consider it as an integral part of the more complex evolution of his dramatic art. With regard to the use of imagery in Shakespeare's tragedies and in the plays of his mature period, the term "development" will, however, need some modification. Whereas it had been possible, in Shakespeare's early plays and in the dramas of his so-called "middle period", to observe a steady advance in the various ways of employing imagery and of adapting it to several dramatic ends, which allowed us to speak of a gradual "development" in the true sense of the word, this kind of approach was less exclusively applicable with regard to Shakespeare's great tragedies of which, in this study, only six have been dealt with. Here, the term "variation" would be equally justified to describe the use of imagery. After Shakespeare had reached that complete mastery over the various elements of style and diction which we find in plays like *Othello* or *Macbeth*, the question becomes irrelevant whether the use of imagery in e.g. *King Lear* is superior to that in *Macbeth* or vice versa. It is, rather, a *different* way of using imagery but not a worse or better manner that we could put down as "progress" or "advance". For the imagery, in these plays, obeys the varying requirements of expression, atmosphere and characterization, its functions and uses being ruled by the inherent structural law of the particular respective tragedy in question. A study of Shakespeare's style and diction, viewed in all their aspects, would also show that we cannot explain the striking difference between *King Lear* and *Macbeth* by any such simple formula as "advance", but must also take into consideration that in *King Lear* Shakespeare wanted to represent something that was quite different from *Macbeth* and that, consequently, other and new means of expression had to be found.

These qualifications were thought necessary in order to avoid misunderstandings which might easily arise by applying the term "development" too rigorously to the evolution of Shakespeare's art. Of course, there is "evolution" in Shakespeare's great tragedies in so far as each tragedy presents a new problem which, on the part of Shakespeare the dramatist, requires a new mode of presentation, sometimes even a new dramatic technique, and, consequently, new resources of diction, style and imagery. But, studying these masterpieces, we do better to speak of an extraordinary widening of Shakespeare's creative ways and designs, of an accretion of unforeseen new possibilities, instead of allotting markings and speaking of "improvement". The development of Shakespeare's art must not be thought of as a ladder consisting of equal steps, each step being nearer to "perfection" than the last one.

Not even with regard to Shakespeare's development in his early period (where this picture could be applied with greater aptitude) is this comparison of a ladder wholly satisfactory. For we are only too easily tempted to judge Shakespeare's early plays by standards which ultimately derive from our knowledge and appreciation of his masterpieces. We take, for instance, the gradual abandoning of rhetorical devices as an indication for Shakespeare's growing dramatic skill, as a proof that he gave up artifice because he had learned how to write "more naturally". And from the abundance of ornament and rhetorical elements in his early dramas we generally infer that Shakespeare wrote in this style because he did not know how to write better, and because he had inherited this fashion from his predecessors. We are apt to say "Shakespeare had to overcome this style in order to find his own way". Against these statements, each of them containing some truth, a warning must be uttered. In Shakespeare's own time, the rhetorical style was held in high esteem and the idea "of overcoming this style because it was something inferior and unnatural" would certainly have sounded very strange to Elizabethan ears. Recent studies have thrown more light on Shakespeare's use of rhetoric and on the rôle played by rhetoric in the sixteenth century. These investigations have also shown to what astonishing degree rhetorical devices are used, and deliberately and consciously used, both by the early *and* by the mature Shakespeare. Criticizing the use of imagery in the early plays, we should therefore also take into consideration the fact that Shakespeare had here in mind a different ideal of style. This style possessed its own merits and found expression, not only in diction and imagery, but in all other elements of dramatic art as well. Thus the artificial and formal quality of the imagery has its equivalent in the artificial and symmetrical grouping of the characters (e.g. in the *Comedy of Errors*). And the imagery's tendency to typify and conventionalize rather than to individualize, to express commonplace truisms instead of unique experiences also corresponds to the whole manner and atmosphere of these early plays. The following summary should be understood as implying these qualifications.

Our study set out by investigating the relation of imagery to its context, the term "context" being understood not only as the texture of the language, but also as implying the respective dramatic situation. In the early histories and in *Titus Andronicus* this relation could be described, in most cases, as unorganic and loose, the images being "inserted" into the text as something that could easily be cut out again without impairing the structure of the scene. The way in which these images (very frequently occurring in the form of comparisons) were linked up with the context by *as* or *like*, or were added and piled upon each other, revealed this unorganic character of the imagery from the more formal point of view, while the disproportion and inappropriateness existing between the dramatic situation, the image used at that particular moment, and the character using the image, manifested this inadequate connection on other levels. The occurrence of genuine epic similes, which by virtue are not germane to drama, and of elaborate conceits in the manner of the sonnets showed that Shakespeare the poet and Shakespeare the dramatist were still at conflict with each other. There was a certain showiness and obtrusiveness in the imagery of the early plays. We could feel the naïve pleasure of the dramatist who, by inventing and inserting these images on any conceivable occasion, wished to show off his skill and knowledge and to embellish his language. Elizabethan exuberance, well known to us as a stylistic feature of Elizabethan poetry and prose, was also manifest in the abundant and exaggerated use of imagery in Shakespeare's early plays. "Imagery for imagery's sake" could therefore be said of many passages in the early dramas. Much of the imagery could be described as digression and we could watch a tendency to spin out, expand and elaborate images. In the early histories a connection could be seen between this feature and the rhetorical habit of "amplification".

In Shakespeare's early comedies the predilection for witty and ingenious comparisons was suited to the world depicted in these plays, and thus the imagery here, though in the main still ornament, embroidery or arabesque, possesses a certain appropriateness. Moreover, Shakespeare, while bringing, in *Love's Labour's Lost*, the art of quibbling and punning, the play upon words and images to a high degree of technical perfection, at the same time distances himself from this fashion, by mocking at its misuse and exaggerating it sometimes to such a degree that its absurdity strikes us.

In the three parts of *Henry VI* it was observed how certain types of speech and situation gave rise to certain recurring types of imagery. Thus the persuading, argumentative and protesting speeches—so frequent in these early histories—fostered the insertion of proverb-images, whereas in the monologues other types of imagery—more organically related to the context—could be traced. The imagery in the monologues showed a higher degree of directness, possessed more expressive power, and seemed altogether more necessary and organic than the "padding" or ornamental images in the formal speeches. We also inquired whether certain events or situations were particularly favourable for the breeding of imagery, and found that, of all events, death was most certain to produce images. Considering the important part played by the imagery in the mature plays in producing a nature-atmosphere, it was illuminating to trace Shakespeare's first tentative steps in this technique, which show a definite lack of skill and subtlety.

The discussion of the imagery in *Richard III* started

from an estimate of some distinctive features characterizing plot and structure, style and language of this play. The greater speed of the action, the concentration of the plot, the all-pervading presence of the figure of Richard III, the firm grasp of incident and character, all this also affected the use of imagery. On the whole, the images have become shorter, more concise, less "independent", but also less general and digressive. Shakespeare's growing faculty to give expression to a greater intensity and directness of feeling was reflected by the more direct and spontaneous use of imagery as well as by the form of the images themselves. There were, moreover, instances of a closer relation of the images to their context, the images being prepared for, as it were, by metaphorical language as well as by certain devices of style. We could also trace Shakespeare's creative power in coining new compound metaphors. And, lastly, we had a clear example of a consistent dramatic use of imagery in the manner by which recurrent animal symbols were used to characterize Richard and to create a pervading atmosphere of brutality, danger and repulsiveness.

Richard II, on the other hand, showed a new *raison d'être* for imagery in so far as it was the poetical and reflective nature of the king himself that again and again led quite naturally to an abundance of images. A new stage of organic relation between images and play became manifest in the abdication scene, where Shakespeare makes the poetical image grow out of the outward situation and conveys to us—through the image—the symbolical significance of what we were watching on the stage. In this play, compared with *Richard III*, Shakespeare's art of characterizing leading figures had become more complex and more revealing.

The imagery in *Romeo and Juliet* shows a wider range and variety than in any foregoing play, particularly as far as type and form of imagery are concerned. Shakespeare now consciously discriminates and distinguishes between the different styles at his disposal, and his art of adapting images to character, situation and mood begins to develop. It has often been emphasized that Shakespeare experiments in this play, trying various styles and modes of presentation. But, while thus experimenting, he realized the intrinsic stylistic value and significance of these different levels of diction and assigned to them a proper place in the structure of his play. The inherited conventional style becomes restricted to actually conventional situations and characters, whereas, in the scenes and characters which are beyond this conventional level, we see a new manner and language developing that sometimes reaches an astonishing degree of intensity and perfection. There were, in *Romeo and Juliet*, several indications that Shakespeare has become aware of the dramatic uses inherent in imagery. Images appear at dramatically significant moments, they help to intensify and heighten the inward experience, at the same time transforming into poetical vision the outward elements of the situation (as could be shown in the balcony and garden scene). This Shakespearian faculty of fully realizing and interpreting through imagery the potential meaning of a scene acted on the stage also marks a new stage of organic relationship between image and drama. Moreover, Shakespeare's art of fusing, again through imagery, the expression of personal mood with the creation of atmospheric background as well as with the representation of the play's leading motif constitutes a new way of lending more weight and complexity to the single image. Shakespeare thus makes his imagery serve several ends at one time.

The study then proceeded to examine, more briefly and summarily, a few aspects of the development of Shakespeare's imagery in the plays of his so-called middle period. The amalgamation of the images with their context was studied, and various examples were given of how images could be evoked through association, of how they were prepared for in advance and of how they lingered in the poet's memory, every now and then arising from the subterranean stream of imagination and creeping into the language. The single metaphor, sometimes of rare and strange kind, gained in importance and suggestiveness, making us grasp the hidden processes and combinations of the dramatist's thought and imagination. The way in which Shakespeare, notably in this "middle period", develops a peculiar manner of expressing abstract notions through figurative language, mingling the abstract with the concrete world, offered material for an interesting investigation, here only hinted at as another instance of Shakespeare's growing mastery over the resources of metaphorical language.

Lastly, in a chapter on the function of imagery in the dramatic structure the dramatic function of imagery to prepare and forbode events was illustrated by examples from *The Merchant of Venice* and *King John*.

In an introductory chapter on the development of Shakespeare's imagery in the tragedies, the manifold dramatic relevance of the imagery, its structural significance and its inner consistency were emphasized. The imagery, especially in the first few acts, often implants certain expectations in the minds of the audience, it puts riddles, as it were, and hence arises a dramatic tension which is not without influence on the imagination and attitude of the audience. For the dramatist the imagery becomes a subtle way of influencing and leading the audience through the play without their knowing it. The various trends, chains and patterns of imagery combine to form, as it were, a second network of action running below the actual plot, and interconnecting with it in several ways. It was pointed out that the more veiled, unobtrusive and indirect manner of expression offered by imagery corresponded to the characteristic art which Shakespeare used on many levels in the tragedies, whereas, in the early plays, it had been his aim to make everything as clear as possible. In this connection, ambiguity and dramatic irony had to be mentioned as lending more depth and complexity to the images. This also involved the phenomenon of a *double entendre* in the interpretation of a given situation, on the part of the audience, on the one hand, and on that of the actors, on the other.

In another paragraph it was shown how, in the tragedies, it is through the imagery that the cosmic and superhuman powers enter into the drama, and how imagery is the chief means of bringing to light the close relationship between man and these elemental and cosmic forces. But the world of nature also—animals, plants and flowers—creeps into the play through the imagery, not merely to provide background or atmosphere but to take part in the action and to express symbolically correspondences and interrelations which underlie the real action and often contain the essential meaning of the play. We then turned towards an examination of Shakespeare's novel methods of personification and his striking manner of visualizing abstract qualities, these features being compared to Shakespeare's technique in his earlier dramas. The comparative method was also applied with regard to certain stylistic patterns typical of Shakespeare's early plays, but now recurring, though in quite different application and function.

The line of approach pursued in the last chapter but one was then taken up, and the form in which images now appear, the suggestive and evocative force of the single metaphor and its appropriateness to the thought expressed, were illustrated by various examples. It was pointed out how the speed of the action as well as the rapidity of thought and the vehemence of passion combined to produce imagery of extraordinary compression and of a surprising blend of elements. By this type of truly dramatic imagery which has no parallel in contemporary drama or poetry, Shakespeare has created, all for himself, a unique instrument of dramatic expression equally adapted to the general style and tone of the tragedies as to the manifold other usages to which he turns it. Lastly, it was explained how, in the tragedies, the imagery, through its recurring themes, serves to bind the scenes and acts closer together, to make the dramatic texture more coherent and intricate. The impression we have in reading the tragedies, that almost every passage is in diverse ways related and interconnected with other passages before or after, derives, in a high degree, from the rôle played by the imagery. Thus the imagery, in lending a unifying colour and "key" to the tragedies, helps to create an organic unity which makes us forget the lack of the classical unities of time and action.

Several of these problems broached in the introductory chapter were then traced more fully in the following paragraphs on six single tragedies. Each of these chapters focused attention on a few specific functions of imagery or aspects of the relation existing between image and structure, image and character, image and dramatic theme. This selective method was chosen in order to avoid an undue increase in the size and compass of this study; for a full discussion of the imagery even of one single tragedy in all its aspects would have required a volume in itself. The obvious disadvantage of this method, that many important points could not be made and that much had to be left unsaid, had to be put up with in order to ensure, on the other hand, the possibility of a comprehensive survey of the development of Shakespeare's imagery in all its variety; for to grasp and view this simultaneously would have been impossible in any full-length study of an individual play.

In the chapter on *Hamlet* the difference existing between Hamlet's and the other characters' use of imagery was examined, and the value of Hamlet's imagery in revealing his mind and attitude was studied. We saw that Hamlet employed images as a mask or disguise in his rôle of feigned madness as well as a way of telling the truth to other people without their noticing it. In order to show how, in Shakespeare's tragedies, the image has become an integral part of the thought and how a reduction of metaphorical language into plain speech makes us lose that very element which is of greatest importance for the understanding, not only of a single passage but sometimes of the whole play, Hamlet's famous phrase of the "native hue of resolution" being "sicklied o'er with the pale cast of thought" was commented upon. Further study was made of the relation between the subject matter of the imagery and the actual events happening or being described in the play. Lastly, the function of imagery to suggest the play's central theme and to forbode coming events was examined.

In *Othello*, out of the many lines of approach open to the student of this play's imagery, one only was selected— the contrasting use of imagery by Othello and Iago, which offers a particularly striking example of Shakespeare's art of adapting language to character. Light could be thrown on this relation not only by the subject matter but also by the form and style of images as well as by the way in which the images reflected the inner development and crucial experience of the characters.

The study of the imagery in *King Lear* had to face more far-reaching problems. The unique and unprecedented rôle played by the imagery in *King Lear* demanded a consideration of Lear's character and of the "inner drama" that takes place in him. The growing importance and abundance of the images in Lear's speech could be explained by his becoming more and more isolated in the human world which meant that he was thrown back upon himself. As he lost the faculty of communication, of reasonable dialogue with his human partners, so he gained imaginative insight, and created, through his images, new partners, a second world, as it were, within the human world, with which he could communicate and to which he felt himself related. To speak predominantly in images becomes for Lear the most appropriate form of utterance and self-expression, equally fitting to bring to light his visionary power, to reveal the secret and incoherent workings of his distracted and raving brain, and to manifest his extraordinary faculty of speaking to the elemental world beyond our human reach. The sequence of images in Lear's speech contains the full story of his spiritual transmutation. In no other play of Shakespeare's is so much of the hero's inner development conveyed to us solely by images; in no other tragedy, too, does the imagery tell us so much of what Shakespeare himself thought of his characters and of the problems presented by the outward action of the play. The preponderance of imagery, notably in the second, third and fourth acts, could be further accounted for by a characteristic feature of this tragedy: the widening of the human drama into something more universal, more comprehensive, so that, in Bradley's well-known phrase, we are witnessing "a conflict not so much of particular persons as of the powers of good and evil in the world". These cosmic powers, the world of nature and of the elements, are made to enter into the play and to take part in its action through the imagery. It was also shown how, in the first acts, the images possessed that "prophetic significance", often combined with dramatic irony, which helped to prepare future events and made the audience darkly expect and anticipate the course of the action. The images in *King Lear*, compared to other plays, appear to be more closely interconnected with each other, falling into clearly distinguishable patterns. Moreover, they have more relevance as to the "inner drama" and the hidden sense of the play so that a detailed and complete analysis of the imagery in this tragedy would yield particularly fruitful results.[1] A special paragraph was reserved for the images, comparisons and proverbs employed by the Fool which provided an altogether new and original manner of utilizing imagery. Lastly, the rôle played by the nature-imagery and particularly the animal-imagery in *King Lear*, was discussed.

The colourful and rich atmosphere of *Antony and Cleopatra* will have struck every reader of this tragedy. The chapter on this play therefore drew attention to the subtle and varied ways by which the imagery gradually builds up this atmosphere. Again Shakespeare makes his images serve several ends at the same time. Images simultaneously heighten the atmosphere, characterize the dramatis personae and provide an adequate expression of mood for the speaker just at the right moment. This adaptation of an image to the particular exigencies of the dramatic situation has reached, in *Antony and Cleopatra*, an especially high degree of perfection. The function of certain sequences of symbolic imagery in accompanying Antony's rise and fall and in giving expression to his relationship to the cosmic powers was dealt with; and lastly, the attempt was made to point out how Cleopatra's "infinite variety" finds its equivalent in the varied and even contradictory images that describe her.

In the chapter on *Coriolanus* the question was raised to what degree we are justified in drawing from the imagery conclusions as to Shakespeare's own views and his personal likes and dislikes. While it was in general thought right to approach this problem, with the utmost reserve and caution,

[1] This has in the meantime, after completion of this book, been carried out by Robert B. Heilmann, in his study, *This Great Stage, Image and Structure in King Lear*, Louisiana State University Press, 1948.

Coriolanus seemed to provide an exception to the rule. The lavish and outspoken use of images and the depreciatory names for the "rabble" seemed to indicate a strong antipathy on the part of Shakespeare to this class of people, especially as this was brought out by other plays as well. In contrast to this category of images, attention was drawn to the numerous images characterizing Coriolanus and Shakespeare's use of this imagery to ensure that striking "omnipresence" of the hero, which is one of the play's most typical features.

The study of the imagery in *Timon of Athens* offered several interesting problems. We could see how a significant connection existed between the strikingly uneven distribution of the images over the acts and scenes, and the abnormal development of Timon. The causes calling forth the abundance and frequency of images in the last acts were examined, and several new functions which the imagery had here to fulfil, could be pointed out. The strange phenomenon that an image could, at a later stage, be turned into reality was illustrated by several examples, as well as the reverse process of a real event in the drama being utilized for images and comparisons. Lastly, it was shown how Timon's inner experience and his attitude towards the world were mirrored through a sequence of characteristic images, and here again the question arose whether we are entitled to draw any conclusions from this preponderance of metaphors of disease and decay as to Shakespeare's own attitude.

Taken as a whole, the tragedies thus showed Shakespeare's art of adapting imagery to dramatic purposes at its height. The functions fulfilled by the imagery are here, as we have seen, of a specially complex and varied nature and the dramatic relevancy of the images is extraordinary. For, speaking of Shakespeare's dramatic art in the tragedies, it would be quite impossible to leave out the rôle played by the imagery; it has, indeed, become an important and most refined instrument in the hands of the dramatist. This, then, seems to be Shakespeare's unique achievement. He has contrived to transform a means of expression, which by nature and virtue originated in the poetical sphere, into a purely and specifically *dramatic* instrument of unforeseen effectiveness and complexity.[1]

The imagery in the "romances" showed on the whole no further development on the directions which we could trace in the tragedies, but rather betrayed a return to the more poetical and descriptive imagery of some of the comedies of Shakespeare's middle period. The slower speed of the action being characteristic of the romances fostered a type of imagery that was less condensed, allowing for subtle and refined elaboration. The happy balance between thought and expression that had been often upset in the tragedies was again achieved in the romances and consequently affected the form and style of imagery.

Whereas, in the tragedies, the imagery often anticipated events, its function was, in *The Tempest*, to the contrary effect: it was "afterthought", recalling the sea-storm of the first scene by frequent allusion and reference. This sea- and tempest-imagery was subtly adapted to the various characters and marked their different spheres of being. By an examination of the varied and complex nature-imagery we could gain more insight into Shakespeare's technique of creating that strong earthy atmosphere pervading the whole play and so forcibly appealing to our senses. The relation between man and nature—an important aspect of the magic island—was also subtly mirrored by the play's imagery. Lastly, the distribution of imagery to the characters in the play as well as its relation to the structure of the drama was examined.

The imagery in *The Winter's Tale* was chiefly examined from the viewpoint of the contrast between the different spheres around which the action revolves. It was shown how considerably the imagery helps to emphasize and bring out this contrast, adding colour, background and life

---

[1] In the last part of his German book on the subject of Shakespeare's imagery the author has attempted to show how, in Elizabethan literature, imagery was at home primarily in poetry and prose, and retained, when transferred into drama, in most cases the marks of this poetical or prosaic usage. An investigation of the Elizabethan critical essays could also show how, in the main, the critical remarks on the use of imagery were confined to the rôle it played in poetry and prose. The *dramatic* functions and qualities which can be taken over by imagery seem never to have been discussed in Elizabethan criticism. It was Shakespeare alone who fully explored these possibilities. Marlowe seems to be the only other dramatist before Shakespeare who can be said to have used imagery in a specifically dramatic way.

to Shakespeare's dramatic conception. For this kind of study the juxtaposition of drastic and realistic peasant-life with the poetic delicacy of romantic lovers in the fourth act offered a particularly illuminating example. The symbolism of this imagery was discussed as well as its function in the dramatic structure.

With *Cymbeline* the question arose in how far the imagery could serve as a test for the critical opinions held about this play. The lack of uniformity of style in *Cymbeline*, the falling back into earlier habits of style, could be well illustrated by the inconsistent use and form of imagery, it being turned again to melodramatic and rhetorical purposes. On the other hand, *Cymbeline* offered some fine examples of Shakespeare's art of adapting imagery to character and showed how Shakespeare used it as a means to individualize the speech.

The author is aware that in this study a compromise had to be struck between the need for a detailed analysis of single plays and a more summarizing survey. Such a compromise will always remain unsatisfactory in some way, and, consequently, many readers are likely to feel that something is missing. Some will regret that such important plays as *Macbeth* or *Troilus and Cressida*, have not been dealt with in special chapters, others will complain that of *Twelfth Night*, *All's Well that Ends Well*, *Much Ado About Nothing*, and also of *Henry IV* altogether too little has been said. Others, again, will contend that it would have been better to follow systematically one line of approach from the beginning to the end (e.g. the relation of the images to their context, or Shakespeare's technique of characterizing his dramatis personae through imagery) instead of trying so many aspects and broaching many problems which were not exhaustively discussed. Any such systematic and complete investigation would, however, have resulted in an exclusion of a number of relevant and modifying aspects, and would also have isolated too much the particular phenomenon under consideration. It appears that the study of Shakespeare's plays is in danger of being split up into several highly specialized avenues of approach which have become separated from each other instead of being coordinated and combined. Those who study Shakespeare's dramatic art are primarily concerned with plot and character and are apt to neglect style and diction. And the students of his language, of his imagery, do not, as a rule, trouble much about plot and character, or about other aspects involved in an all-round study of a play, viz. the sources, the themes and problems presented, the task of the actor, etc., etc. As, however, all these aspects are closely connected with, and are dependent on, one another, any too specialized investigation, concentrating all the attention and all available resources of research on one element only, is likely to view this element as something isolated and to forget about its continual dependence upon many other factors in the drama. The singling out of imagery for a too specialized study seems to have led to an undue emphasis on Shakespeare's "philosophic patterns", and to a curious temptation to read a symbolic meaning into every other image occurring in the text. The present study, while attempting to avoid this danger and therefore approaching the subject of Shakespeare's imagery from various angles in order to show its bearing on the manifold aspects of his dramatic art, has, on the other hand, incurred the risk of a somewhat unsystematic and perhaps disorderly presentation for which the author begs indulgence. It appears, however, that a proper estimate of the evolution of Shakespeare's art could only be reached, if *still far more* were to be done to correlate the separate methods of investigation and to show the interdependence of style, diction, imagery, plot, technique of characterization and all the other constituent elements of drama. The present study is to be understood as a first tentative endeavour to indicate some directions in which the examination of the development of Shakespeare's imagery as seen against the background of the growth of his dramatic art may be pursued, but it does not claim to have exhausted the subject in any systematic or comprehensive way.

BOOK LIST

I. Books on Imagery in General

Stephen J. Brown, *The World of Imagery* (*Metaphor and Kindred Imagery*), London, 1927.

H. Pongs, *Das Bild in der Dichtung*, Marburg, 1927.

Owen Barfield, *Poetic Diction*, London, 1928.

John Middleton Murry, "Metaphor" (1927), in *Countries of the Mind*, 2nd series, London, 1931.

Lillian Hornstein, "Analysis of Imagery: A Critique of Literary Method", *PMLA, LVII* (1942).

Una Ellis-Fermor, "Imagery in Drama" in *The Frontiers of Drama*, London, 1945.

C. Day Lewis, *The Poetic Image*, London, 1947.

Cleanth Brooks, *The Well-Wrought Urn*, New York, 1947.

Kenneth Severs, "Imagery and Drama", *Durham University Journal, X* (December 1948).

II. Books Dealing with Elizabethan Imagery

Henry W. Wells, *Poetic Imagery, Illustrated from Elizabethan Literature*, New York, 1924.

Elizabeth Holmes, *Aspects of Elizabethan Imagery*, Oxford, 1929.

Wolfgang Clemen, "Bild und Gleichnis im elisabethanischen Zeitalter" in *Shakespeares Bilder*, Bonn, 1936.

Mario Praz, *Studies in Seventeenth Century Imagery* (partly relating to Elizabethan Imagery), London, 1937.

Moody E. Prior, "The Elizabethan Tradition" in *The Language of Tragedy*, New York, 1947.

Rosemond Tuve, *Elizabethan and Metaphysical Imagery, Renaissance Poetic and Twentieth Century Critics*, Chicago, 1947.

III. Books and Articles Dealing with Shakespeare's Imagery

[The more important books up to 1936 are discussed by Una Ellis-Fermor, *Some Recent Research in Shakespeare's Imagery*, Shakespeare Association, London, 1937. More recent studies in Shakespeare's Imagery are dealt with in the same author's article "Shakespeare and his world: The Poet's Imagery", *Listener, XLII*, July (1949).]

G. Wilson Knight, *Myth and Miracle: An Essay on the Mystic Symbolism of Shakespeare*, London, 1929.

Msgr. F. C. Kolbe, *Shakespeare's Way*, London, 1930.

C. F. E. Spurgeon, *Leading Motives in the Imagery of Shakespeare's Tragedies*, London, 1930.

G. Wilson Knight, *The Wheel of Fire*, Oxford, 1930.

George Rylands, *Words and Poetry*, London, 1930.

C. F. E. Spurgeon, *Shakespeare's Iterative Imagery* (Annual Shakespeare Lecture of the British Academy, 1931).

G. Wilson Knight, *The Imperial Theme*, Oxford, 1931.

G. Wilson Knight, *The Shakespearian Tempest*, Oxford, 1932.

C. F. E. Spurgeon, *Shakespeare's Imagery and What It Tells Us*, Cambridge, 1936.

John Middleton Murry, "Imagery and Imagination", Chapter XII, in *Shakespeare*, London, 1936.

D. A. Traversi, "Coriolanus" in *Scrutiny*, June, 1937.

Hereward T. Price, "Function of Imagery in Venus and Adonis", *Papers of the Michigan Academy of Science, Arts and Letters*, XXXI (1945).

Edward A. Armstrong, *Shakespeare's Imagination, A Study of the Psychology of Association and Inspiration*, London, 1946.

Cleanth Brooks, "The Naked Babe and the Cloak of Manliness" in *The Well-Wrought Urn*, 1947.

G. Wilson Knight, *The Crown of Life, Essays in Interpretation of Shakespeare's Final Plays*, London, 1947.

Sister Miriam Joseph, *Shakespeare's Use of the Arts of Language*, New York, 1947.

J. C. Maxwell, "Animal Imagery in *Coriolanus*", *Modern Language Review*, XLII (October 1947).

R. D. Altick, "Symphonic Imagery in *Richard II*", *PMLA*, LXII (June, 1947).

E. R. Curtius, "Das Buch als Symbol (Shakespeare)" in *Europäische Literatur und lateinisches Mittelalter*, Bern, 1948.

Francis R. Johnson, "Shakespearian Imagery and Senecan Imitation" in *Joseph Quincy Adams Memorial Studies*, Washington, 1948.

Audrey Yoder, *Animal Analogy* in *Shakespeare's Character Portrayal*, New York, 1948.

Robert B. Heilmann, *This Great Stage, Image and Structure in King Lear*, Lousiana State, University Press, 1948.

Mikhail M. Morozov, "The Individualization of Shakespeare's Characters through Imagery", *Shakespeare Survey*, II, 1949.

T. W. Baldwin, "On the Literary Genetics of Shakespeare's Poems and Sonnets", *Urbana*, 1950.

E. C. Pettet, "The Imagery of *Romeo and Juliet*" in *English*, VIII, 121–126 (1950).

Alice S. Venezky, "Shakespeare's Pageant Imagery" in *Pageantry on the Shakespearean Stage*, New York, 1951.

The fullest comments on single images, comparisons, etc., are to be found in the volumes of the *New Shakespeare* (Cambridge University Press), edited by Professor John Dover Wilson.

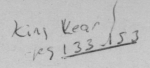

King Kear
res 133-153

INDEX